MINDFUL MATRIMONY

MINDFUL MATRIMONY

Enriching Your Marriage for the Rest of Your Lives

Raymond and Furugh Switzer

GEORGE RONALD PUBLISHER
OXFORD

George Ronald, *Publisher*
Oxford
www.grbooks.com

ISBN 978–0–85398–571–6

A catalogue record for this book is available from the British Library

Cover design: Steiner Graphics

Contents

APPENDIXES

Acknowledgements

We would like to express our deepest appreciation to our
dear parents, whose marriages were the matrix of our
upbringing, and whose unresolved struggles we inherited. We
can now say, with wakeful hearts, that these have provided us with
grist for the mill of our own marriage and that, in transmuting
these into greater understanding and an ever-deepening love for
each other, we feel an abiding joy and sense of fulfilment. A deep
appreciation also goes to those precious gifts entrusted to us –
our beloved children – who are inheriting all that we are leaving
unresolved and who, we are confident, will also come to embrace
the challenges and occasions for growth this will inevitably bring
into their own marriages. From our parents and our children we
have learned marvellous lessons about life, its fascinating depths
and possibilities, and about the greatness of our Creator.

To the growing rank of psychologists, social researchers,
therapists and educators who have come to realize the
crucial importance of the marital relationship in the ongoing
development of the human psyche and human society, and
whose theoretical and practical findings have helped us in our
own marriage and in our work, we are profoundly thankful. Our

appreciation also goes to the many couples who have turned to us for counsel, therapy and education, and whose courage and devotion in doing the work of marriage has inspired us to move forward on the mission we have taken on .

In helping to hone the text of this present endeavour we would like to thank our editor, May Hofman and, in particular, Annabel Knight, who kindly reviewed the whole work and provided many helpful suggestions before we sent it off to the publisher.

Finally, and most importantly, we acknowledge our souls' deepest gratitude to Bahá'u'lláh, whose Revelation has revolutionized all of our relationships.

Prologue

Sitting opposite each other at a table in the corner of a quiet restaurant, May and Jonathon, oblivious of people around them, gaze into each other's eyes. He has made up his mind that THIS IS THE NIGHT he will ask her to marry him. A waitress is standing nearby, looking bored, she has clearly been waiting for some time for the couple to order from their menus.

Jonathon: It's so good to be with you again. I missed you so much. I had to stop myself from catching the bus home last night, I just couldn't wait one more day . . .

May: I know! It's only been two days but it seems like two weeks. I've missed you so much.

Jonathon: Two weeks! It felt like two years! I couldn't stop thinking about you. You were on my mind day and night. I tell you, I need to be with you ALL the time.

May: Me too! I just couldn't concentrate on anything, knowing that you were so far away, it's like part of me was missing.

Everyone was getting so annoyed with me at work, but I didn't care.

Jonathon: Me too! And my colleagues were really making fun of me, not that I care either. Everything without you is so dull. They always complained before – that I was a man of few words, and now they say I've lost my ability to listen. But it's because I'm just thinking of you constantly. (*suddenly serious – concerned he may seem irresponsible*) But I do try my best to keep half alert when the boss enters the room!

May: (*laughing*) I bet you are great at your job. When I first met you I thought you would never talk – you were definitely the 'strong silent type'.

Jonathan: Well, heating engineers are not known to be great conversationalists . . .

May: (*laughing again*) You were so mysterious.

Jonathon: Well, I can't shut up now! You see, it's all your fault, you are so easy to talk to. Everyone says that about you, you are so sweet and charming, everyone loves you.

May: (*with a sweet smile*) YOU are the sweet one! You know, I'm saying your name to myself so much that I kept calling John – you know, the sandwich guy – 'Jonathon'. It was quite embarrassing!!

Jonathon: (*laughing out loud*) I LOVE hearing you say my name. Such a boring name, 'Jonathon'. But the way you say it, it makes me feel like a movie star or something. Last night I woke up calling your name in my dream. May, it's so magical . . . like a light summer breeze . . . May . . .

The waitress comes for the second time. 'Are you ready yet?' They laughingly apologize and ask for yet more time since they have not had any chance to look at the menu. They are oblivious to the waitress's bad mood.

Jonathon: What would you like to eat, my love?

May: I'm not sure. What about you?

Jonathon: I like the sound of the baked salmon.

Waitress: Let me guess – you'll have that too?

May: Yes!! I was just thinking about the salmon. We'll both go for that.

They finally order and get back into their own world.

Jonathon: (*gazing into his beloved's eyes*) You look *beautiful*. This colour brings out the deep blue in your eyes. I missed those eyes so much . . .

May: (*smiling, with a shine in her eyes*) You don't look bad yourself. Is that a new shirt? And have you been going to the gym?

Jonathon: Yeah, got it yesterday . . . for our date today. And yes, thank you for noticing, I HAVE been working out. I just have so much energy I need to burn it off – I feel like I'm going to explode . . .

May: (*looking at the flower he has just given her*) This is so beautiful.

Jonathon: Not as beautiful as you are (*holding her hand*).

May: (*slightly tearful*) How did you know this is my favourite flower?

Jonathon: When I saw it at the flower stand, I knew this was for you (*feeling proud he got it right*).

May: This has been my favourite flower since I was a child and I have always liked this shade of pink (*delighted to see how well he has come to know her*).

Jonathon: (*bringing up her hand to kiss and hold*) I have so much to tell you.

May: I can't wait to hear it all.

Jonathon: The day before yesterday, after we said goodbye . . .

* * *

Two years later, around 8 p.m., Jonathon arrives at home, throws his briefcase on the couch and sinks into it . . .

Jonathon: What a day! I'm exhausted.

May: (*trying to stay calm*) Didn't you say you would be home by six?!

Jonathon: Sorry, got carried away with this new proposal. (*Silence. May stares at him. He senses her mood and tentatively asks*) Is there anything to eat around here? I'm starving.

May: (*sarcastic*) Is there anything to eat? Well – since I thought we were going out tonight the answer would be – no – there isn't anything to eat!

Jonathon: (*irritated with her lack of ability to understand*) I told you I had to finish this proposal. You know how important it is.

May: (*raising her voice*) You could have at least called. I've just been sitting here on my own for two hours watching TV like some loser housewife . . .

Jonathon: I got carried away writing and lost count of hours. I said sorry, didn't I?

May: (*shouting louder with frustration*) But you said that last time too. I thought, we are finally going to have a night out, just you and me, and I got all dressed up for it too. You haven't even noticed, have you?

Jonathon: (*looks at her for the first time since arriving*) What did you do to your hair?

May: So you finally noticed my hair. Well, thanks a LOT.

Jonathon: But your hair was short already.

May: I had it COLOURED – O my God – I spent a fortune at the hairdressers on that special organic colouring for pregnant women. Forget it! You're hopeless . . .

Jonathon: (*worried*) A fortune? How much did you spend? (*seeing May's furious expression he hastily changes the subject and tries to speak reasonably*) Listen, I have been working all day writing this proposal, all so that I can get a better position to ensure a good future for you and our baby.

(*May is silent*) After all, it was you who wanted a baby, wasn't it?

May: (*exploding*) What???? ME ?? who wanted a baby? YOU'RE the one who wanted kids, and anyway, how about working hard to ensure a good *present* for your WIFE.

Jonathon: (*silent, fuming*)

May: (*becoming more crazed with frustration*) . . . we both agreed to have a baby, but it's me who is exhausted and feeling sick all day. When are you going to grow up and take responsibility for your decisions?

Jonathon: (*trying to keep a cool head, attempts to bring more logic to the situation*) Have I become the devil now for working two extra hours for my family's well-being? Is this my punishment for working hard?

May: Family? What about me? We don't even have a family yet and I've been waiting here for you after a full tiring day, not knowing what to do or expect. Your mobile was off. (*starting to cry*) How was I to know where you were?

Jonathon: I hadn't noticed it was out of juice. (*restless and confused as to what to say*) These days I feel I have to report to you every minute of my life and about my every move. What is your problem, anyway? Don't you trust me? Don't you believe that I was working in my office?

May: (*amazed at how out of touch he is*) This is not a question of trust.

Jonathon: (*baffled*) What is it then?

May: It's about caring.

Jonathon: You mean I don't care about you?!

May: If you cared you would have thought of me instead of the proposal. At least you would have called. You don't think of me at all.

Jonathon: (*with a helpless tone*) This is so unfair. I've been working like hell because I care.

May: If you cared you would notice how I feel these days. You would have noticed my new dress and the fact that I went to so much trouble with my hair.

Jonathon: (*confused as ever with her moods*) You have become so demanding. Is this something to do with pregnancy hormones?

May: Oh, that's so typical – blame it on hormones. A woman wanting to be noticed by her husband is demanding? Is it demanding to you to be concerned about how your wife feels?

Jonathon: (*losing it*) How about you being concerned about *my* feelings? I am completely worn out and this is what I come home to!!

May: Sometimes I don't think I know you any more. In fact I think I never really got to know the real you.

Jonathon: What about you? Where did all this moodiness come from? You're crazy. You have become such a drama queen.

May's tears give way to racking sobs. Feeling helpless and incapable of consoling May, Jonathon leaves the room and goes to the kitchen, thinking that no matter what he does or says, nothing is good enough. He leaves her to cry by herself.

Feeling abandoned, May's sobs intensify further, seeing this as proof that he doesn't care. All kinds of thoughts race through her mind.

After a few minutes he comes back, feeling desperate to do or say something.

Jonathan: Come on, let's order a pizza. Let's relax and watch TV. (*Holds her and tries to kiss her. Feeling disrespected, she frees herself from his arms.*)

May: You've obviously forgotten and couldn't care less that pizza makes me throw up?! You can have your pizza and watch your beloved TV by yourself! (*She storms out of the room and slams the door behind her, leaving him bewildered.*)

*** *** ***

What happened?!

· · · · · · · · · ·

For Sale
Wedding dress, size 12
Worn once by mistake

· · · · · · · · · ·

It might be hard to believe that this is the same couple who only two years earlier seemed born for each other. One is naturally befuddled. What happened to the two soulmates who could hardly bear to be apart? Why do married couples find themselves, within the span of a few weeks, months or years, totally mis-understood and frustrated? When do they lose sensitivity and attunement to each others' feelings along the way? Why can't he understand her feelings and pay attention to them? Why is it so

8

difficult to satisfy her – and what more does she want anyway? Do people really change after getting married, or were they blind to the real self of the other? What was it in the first place that blinded him in his choice? What was it that lured her into this relationship? Should they have spent more time getting to know each other before getting married? Does this mean that love and passion never last? Does marriage always feel like a trap after a while? Does this happen to all couples? Can conflict be prevented? Should they stick it out and live the rest of their life with the resentment growing between them, at least for the sake of their children? Should they divorce and find more suitable partners while there is still time? Taking part in the often bewildering scenes of marriage, one may come to boil it down to the ultimate question: Did I make a mistake in my choice of partner?

These questions are among the many that are repeatedly raised in our seminars, workshops and therapy sessions, wherever we have been. They are the concerns of many singles and couples that we encounter around us. In the chapters that follow, we are going to bring in spiritual and psychological perspectives to answer these and many other questions about marriage and its purpose for us today.

If you are of the belief that relationships are made in heaven and a good marriage should occur naturally, you may find it difficult to last beyond Chapter 1 or 2. If, however, you are in pursuit of a fulfilling, continuously enriching relationship with your spouse and have an inkling that good marriages – like beautiful gardens, awe-inspiring buildings, or children who exhibit a panoply of virtues – take work, energy and conscious attention and that marriage has a spiritual purpose beyond our own personal interests, then this book should have something to offer you.

Our approach

What we will share with you are the insights we have gained over the years from different major sources. Our foundational source, our underlying beliefs and conceptions come from the prophetic vision of 'unity in diversity' in the Bahá'í Revelation. The principles and writings of the Bahá'í Faith point the way forward for establishing unity while recognizing and honouring the differences and diversity found in the human race. We find the differences between husband and wife to be akin to the kind of differences encountered between peoples of the world.

The second source influencing our approach is the social sciences, especially psychological and social theories and findings related to marriage. These findings have gone through a revolution in the last couple of decades and are shedding new light on human behaviour and the workings of the human mind. The theories and practice of psychology, especially in the field of couples therapy, have been moving radically away from the previous reductionist, individualistic orientation towards a more relationship-based approach. This revolution which is taking place in the psychological understanding of marriage is significant in helping couples to make sense of the dynamics of this most intimate of relationships. Besides being informed of most of these new developments, we have had the opportunity of being trained in Imago Relationship Therapy, which we find particularly relevant as it sees couplehood as a spiritual path.

We have also been in the privileged position of working closely with couples, sharing in their struggles and learning from their experiences over many years and this has greatly enriched our perspective. Additionally, we hope to offer in this book some of the insights and the experience of our own journey of couplehood, now over 22 years. The work on this journey has brought incalculable blessings and joy to us and to our family life.

Far from positing 'the way', we sincerely hope that you will choose from what we offer whatever you feel will be of benefit to you and your specific kind of relationship. We believe that everyone deserves a rich and fulfilling marriage and that we are all capable of achieving this. In this process we will also pave the way and make it easier for our children to have healthy fulfilling marriages of their own.

Mindfulness

As the title of our present endeavour is *Mindful Matrimony*, a few words about mindfulness is in order. Mindfulness is something that has a strong tradition in Buddhism and Hinduism. It has also often been cultivated in the monasteries and religious schools of other faiths. Significantly, it is also being adopted more and more into Western psychology and medical science. The word 'mindfulness' connotes presence, being awake and alive to what is. Reference to mindfulness can be found increasingly in psychological literature. But what does mindfulness have to do with marriage?

In order to see ourselves and our partners accurately, we need to search for the unconscious patterns and habits of thought that seem to come out of the woodwork and derail our best efforts to create unity. In this process, we need to be present for each other, open and awake to the differing (and often complementary) version of reality our partner frequently presents to us. The process of being mindful and present to our partner in difficult times is an intrinsic challenge to our ego, which strives, when entering into conflict, to make the other conform to its expectations or, on the other hand, resentfully cave in. Our minds, especially in the intimate context of the marital relationship, tend to get triggered automatically, pulling us into regressive behaviours which cause ruptures in our feelings of connectedness.

Jonathon in the example above felt he had a good reason for forgetting a planned night out. May felt she had an equally valid reason for being hurt and angry at his lapse. While each is talking, the other is in another world, triggered by what is being said. Neither is mindful or present for the other. It may be that both Jonathon and May are very spiritually oriented people, very religious. But whatever spiritual orientation they may have has been usurped by primitive, animal-like patterns of attack and defence.

Ruptures occur in marriage more readily than in other relationships for reasons that will be covered in the next few chapters. What we will try to offer is a possible way to the kind of mindfulness that would not only make repairs possible and natural, leading to growth and deeper connection, but would help prevent most conflicts and their causing any serious damage to our souls as we share the journey of life together.

· · · · · · · · · ·

In every marriage more than a week old, there are grounds for divorce. The trick is to find, and continue to find, grounds for marriage.

Robert Anderson

· · · · · · · · · ·

Cultivating the virtues that are required in order to remain mindful in relationships is always challenging. Ironically, we often tend to think we can relax our standards when we are at home, but the opposite is true. It is our belief that bringing mindfulness into the most central of our relationships – marriage – will bring us the greatest dividends. We will heal, grow spiritually, become a healthy model to our children, and provide them with a safer and more authentically nurturing environment to grow up in. We will become better community members, more compassionate with people different from us, more able to heal rifts in relationships and to help others to do the same. The world is desperate for people like this, and marriage is the perfect factory for the mass production of this – so far – rare and highly prized good. This, we understand, is the spiritual purpose of marriage.

Where do we start this journey?

• • • • • • • • • •

In the opinion of the world, marriage ends all, as it does in a comedy. The truth is precisely the opposite: it begins all.

Attributed to Anne-Sophie Swetchine

• • • • • • • • • •

In order to understand, in human terms, the befuddling dynamics of this intense and intimate union called marriage, we have to go back to that other intense and intimate union which exists between infant and parent, and understand how this evolves through the child's formative years. It is the forgotten or repressed aspects of these relationships which we bring into our marriages that present challenges for us in maintaining love and intimacy. Looking mindfully into past experiences helps us move from mindless reaction into caring presence. Marriage will become, as we shall see, the best suited vehicle to help us heal the wounds from our childhood and finally bring our growing-up process as individuals – and ultimately, collectively, as humanity – to a safe and much more aware conclusion. We hope, ultimately, to convey that when we learn to bring mindfulness into matrimony, we will make these connections, heal the wounds, and learn to move on and participate in the healing of the wider wounds that exist between us as peoples to achieve the long-awaited coming of age of humanity. For us, marriage is full of hope and potential waiting to be tapped.

Those of you who have little taste for psychological theory, or aren't interested in exploring the emotional ground to our adult problems, may find the next three chapters a bit daunting. If the going gets too laboured, you may want to move on to Chapter 4 which starts the marital journey in earnest. However, we recommend that you at least get a taste of the background to the whole story. So let's start at the beginning.

PART I

THE PATH TO MINDFULNESS

1

Long Before We Meet

Each one of us is the fruit of a union between a father and a mother. This is the beginning of the story for each of us, and when we marry, our story in the making with all its ins and outs will mingle, interact and merge with that of our partner's. So let's begin by looking at this emotional, physical, psychological and, ultimately, spiritual developmental tale. The spiritual undercurrent of this tale is gleaned from our understanding of the Bahá'í teachings.

Beginnings

At the moment of our conception through the attraction of male and female elements, our body starts its journey of growth. At the same moment our soul comes into being and develops, in intimate association, with the emergent elements of our physical self. The Bahá'í writings tell us that our coming into being is an expression of the love of God: 'O Son of Man! I loved thy creation, hence I created thee.'

And love, in its various manifestations, will continue to feed our being and propel our growth on the journey. When we are born into this world our soul is pure and unadulterated, but not developed. This soul basks, figuratively speaking, in the light of God, but must live and develop through the instrumentality of the physical body with which it remains associated throughout its life on this planet. Our parents are, so to speak, God's agency for our coming into this world which is the venue for the first stage of our spiritual journey. The primary purpose of our life in this world is the development of our human and spiritual potential, a process which brings us closer to God. What our soul naturally yearns for is connection with its Creative Source, and it is also primed to recognize this.

Our first home

• • • • • • • • • •

We're all citizens of the womb
before we subdivide
into sexes and shades
– this side, that side

Ani Difranco

• • • • • • • • • •

The physical world, including the womb and the wide world we are eventually born into, is also an expression of the love of God. In the world of the womb we do not yet have a sense of self. It is believed that the nature of our consciousness in the womb world is one of undifferentiated being. We develop ears, for example, while in the womb, including the capacity to hear, but the sounds we hear – the beating of our mother's heart and the muted accents of her voice – are not heard as something different from our self, because there is no self. There is just being; listening is going on. It is imagined that this state of the developing embryo is much like the state of Nirvana described by the Buddha or, figuratively, the Garden of Eden before we were expelled from it.

The womb world becomes the home of momentous physical developments. A single fertilized egg develops into a marvellously complex little creature in a mere nine months. Incredibly, this development recapitulates about three billion years of evolution. No wonder nature provides such a protected environment for this process. We appear to play no active role in the matrix. We float in body temperature brine. We are fed through the placenta connected by an umbilical cord to our mother's circulatory system. We get our needed oxygen from the same source.

Connection to our mother is crucial to us. While we are void of a sense of self in this womb world, our mother can make a difference to us by the choices that she makes. She can eat food which is healthy so that our nourishment is better. She can maintain a healthy lifestyle so that toxins which might get passed on to us do not build up in her blood system. She can maintain composure, and that peacefulness will be passed on to us because we are living in the environment of her body. Of course, even these factors which can make a difference to our development are not entirely in her hands because she is living in connection with the outside world, which will have an effect on her. The quality of the air she breathes, the nature of her relationships, especially the closest ones – most significantly the relationship with her partner – will have an effect. Marriage, even at this first stage of life in the womb, is already having an impact on our development, as do other factors of the outside world with which, through our mother, we are vicariously in contact.

We arrive

We eventually come to grow so large that we start to push the walls of the womb to their maximum, thus triggering the significant revolution that propels us from this comfortable, cosy nook into a world of light and clamour, vast beyond our as yet undeveloped imagination. The mother who has given birth, and anyone who has been present at a birth, senses the momentousness of this occasion.

• • • • • • • • •

A baby is God's opinion that the world should go on.
Carl Sandburg

• • • • • • • • •

For us, a massive change and disruption has occurred. Now, all of a sudden, we need to get oxygen by breathing air through our own lungs. We need to get nourishment through our own mouth and digest it with our own organs. Our skin feels temperatures at variance with our own body's temperature, to which we need to make adjustments. Our eyes open to this world of light. Our ears hear sounds unmuted by amniotic fluid and the walls of the womb. Our nostrils breathe in smells unlike those of our mother. With all these changes and vagaries and all the potential dangers in this world, we are most fortunately taken into the caring arms of – in most cases – our parents.

The following passage from the Writings of Bahá'u'lláh explains the essence and purpose of this transition:

O Son of Bounty! Out of the wastes of nothingness, with the clay of My command I made thee to appear, and have ordained for thy training every atom in existence and the essence of all created things. Thus, ere thou didst issue from thy mother's womb, I destined for thee two founts of gleaming milk, eyes to watch over thee, and hearts to love thee. Out of My loving-kindness, 'neath the shade of My mercy I nurtured thee, and guarded thee by the essence of My grace and favour. And My purpose in all this was that thou mightest attain My everlasting dominion and become worthy of My invisible bestowals.

The new world

In the years following our birth, the love of God is manifested most directly through the love of our parents. Parents become the first signs of God to the newborn baby. The connection to our mother remains crucial. Although this connection can now be replaced by others, we remain in a position of complete dependency. We need to be held, fed, changed, kept warm and loved. The first person, the one most exquisitely primed, to give this care is our mother. As the one who carried us on the nine-month journey in the womb, she is the one most naturally attuned to our needs for nurturing and can now provide for these in a more conscious, visible way. Her familiar smell, voice, heartbeat and ability to nourish us with breast milk, bring familiar aspects of the womb world into this one. This helps to comfort us.

In the beginning, in the best-case scenario we are padded from all possible danger. We are the centre of attention. Most of our needs are attended to almost magically and, if not, are looked after as soon as our wailing brings them to our caregivers' notice. When we open our eyes to this world, they are met with the eyes of our caregivers, most lovingly and welcomingly. We are hugged, kissed and generally entertained to distraction. We are cuddled and coddled, fed, kept warm, kept dry and generally paid close attention to at all times. Life is a banquet from which we may escape into peaceful sleep any time we desire. A king or queen could wish no more.

Beyond symbiosis

· · · · · · · · · ·

The precursor of the mirror is the mother's face.

D.W. Winnicott

· · · · · · · · · ·

When the infant first looks into the eyes of its mother, or others who come to gaze in awe at the miracle of new life, does it see an 'other'? We may think so, and indeed the baby quite quickly develops the capacity to recognize the faces of the different others who care for it. But developmental psychologists believe that at this early stage the infant's consciousness is still largely global and undifferentiated. The things the infant needs come its way. Those providing for its needs are experienced by the infant as being there only to care for it, a kind of extension of its own world. Its desires are the axis of the world's being.

· · · · · · · · · ·

A baby is an angel whose wings decrease as his legs increase.
Anonymous

· · · · · · · · · ·

A dramatic shift in this perception eventually takes place. As the baby grows under the nurturance of its caregivers, it develops new capacities. It starts to become mobile and can move out in pursuit of new experiences. It strives to make sense of more and more of the sights and sounds around it. It starts to be a little less than completely reliant on the self of others to get what it wants and needs. Of course, all this time, the complete dependency of the baby on others for its needs is to some degree a burden on these others, taking time, energy and other resources which are impor- tant to those adults who are involved, directly or indirectly, in its care. The baby is quite unaware of this. As this little being starts to move into the adult world, it also starts to become a source of greater concern, of potential harm to itself and to things of importance to adults. Aspects of its caregivers start to emerge that are impatient for the little one to learn the ways of the world and to look after itself.

· · · · · · · · · ·

. . . the desolation and terror of, for the first time,
realizing that the mother can lose you, or you her,
and your own abysmal loneliness and helplessness without her.
Francis Thompson

· · · · · · · · · ·

A collision starts to take place between our will as a child to have our needs and desires taken care of, and the will of our caregivers to have us conform to certain desired behaviours in this world of theirs. There emerges, gradually, a shift in perception. Where we had been experiencing ourselves as the centre of creation, we come to see that our whims and desires are not the stuff of the universe. In fact, others – upon whom we are completely dependent – have a will of their own, and growing expectations of us. We refer to this radical shift, from the toddler's point of view, as 'dethronement'. There are now demands upon us, some of them very hard to understand, some very unnatural (toilet training is an early example), some difficult to manage because we really haven't developed that much yet. Our caregivers, previously viewed as an extension of our desires, now start to become 'other' to us. And as this new sense takes shape, so also does the sense that we are a self who is unique and distinguished from others. This emergence of self-awareness is hugely significant and entirely human. This self is eventually going to be instrumental in our marital relationship. Let us, then, pause a moment to explore its nature and its development further, for it is precisely the elements of our self which will come into collision with the elements of our partner's self when we grow up and marry.

Self

Self has really two meanings, or is used in two senses, in the Bahá'í writings; one is self, the identity of the individual created by God. . . . The other self is the ego, the dark, animalistic heritage each one of us has, the lower nature . . . It is this self we must struggle against . . . in order to strengthen and free the spirit within us . . .

With the emergence of self, a process of differentiation is occurring: symbiosis is being transformed into the awareness of self and the concomitant awakening to otherness. Before this development there was just a body craving for its needs to be met, together with a soul yearning for connection. Simply put, the emerging human can now be seen as having a three-fold existence: a physical or lower nature related to our body, a human nature emerging from the awareness of self with its capacity of free will, and a divine nature related to our soul. This emergent self, as it matures, can lead this being on its spiritual path of development, closeness to God and connection to others. Paradoxically, this sense of self, developed as ego, will often become the greatest barrier to that soul's connection to its Creator and a source of alienation from others.

· · · · · · · · · ·

Life is just a chance to grow a soul.
Arthur Powell Davies

· · · · · · · · · ·

The self is destined to have a huge impact on all our relationships – to God, to nature, to other humans. In a fascinating manner, our spiritual development will take place in the context of all these relationships; they become our crucible. Standing between the animal and the divine, our sense of self is an admixture of the ego and our true identity as a spiritual being. The ego element of our self is strongly prone to our lower, self-centred nature. It is for this very reason that humans stand in need of guidance to direct their self towards its higher purpose. Religions have traditionally provided us with a two-fold process, whereby we may consciously battle subtle ego elements to bring our true self to the fore and develop our soul. The first is spiritual discipline: basically prayer, study of holy texts, fasting and meditation. The second consists of principles: laws and teachings which help us transform our relationships in the world. These two processes, of course, are not entirely distinct; they blend and meld, interact, feed and nurture each other.

The process of developing our spirituality in the context of our human relationships pertains especially to our focus on marriage. Marriage is one of the conditions created by God for humans. Animals mate; only humans wed. Marriage is a union formed from the conscious coming together of a man and a woman in the closest possible way. It is a physical, emotional, intellectual and spiritual bond. All the teachings and exhortations about human relationships apply to the marital relationship, but marriage has some significant additional requirements and freedoms. Given the unique intensity and depth of this relationship, the human ego is destined to surface all the more insistently, creating huge challenges to the connection and unity of a couple. Let us, then, explore some of the psychological dynamics of the ego's development.

· · · · · · · · · ·

My husband and I divorced over religious differences.
He thought he was God, and I didn't.

Anonymous

· · · · · · · · · ·

Psychological perspectives

Psychology has advanced our understanding of the development of our human nature and the impact of childhood, especially the early years, on gaining our identity and functioning in the world. In our early years, our parents stand at the forefront of our world. While they are sheltering us from the overwhelming complexities and demands of this world, they emotionally also bring into our relatively simple world many of the complexities they are struggling with themselves. They may not talk to us about these complexities and trials but they are nevertheless an unconscious conduit for these. We are so connected to our parents, so in need of them, that we become sensitively attuned to their psychic reality. We may not have words for what we intuit, but we feel deeply their hurts and confusion. We are on constant alert and we will make any adjustment we feel we have to in order to keep this crucial relationship functioning for our survival. At early stages of our development, the adjustments we make are preconscious – we don't even have a sense of self yet. But even after we start developing a sense of self, we will often respond unconsciously to the felt reality of our parents.

· · · · · · · · · ·

You don't really understand human nature unless you know why a child on a merry-go-round will wave at his parents every time around
– and why his parents will always wave back.
Attributed to William D. Tammeus

· · · · · · · · · ·

With our arrival, our caregiver's world has also been revolutionized. For most of them, we are a dream come true. Even to those for whom our conception was a surprise or a problem, the sight of our vulnerable lovability usually brings them around to as perfect a service as they can manage. But our constant need of attention comes to be taxing at some point, if not from the very beginning. The world of our caregivers is demanding, and all the more so with our arrival. Some mothers face depression, struggle with breastfeeding, sleeplessness, interfering parents, irresponsible partners and a variety of other problems which may be related or unrelated to our arrival on the scene.

• • • • • • • • • •

One of the most obvious results of having a baby around the
house is to turn two good people into complete idiots who
probably wouldn't have been much worse than mere
imbeciles without it.

Georges Courteline

• • • • • • • • • •

Our first relationship

The infant–parent relationship starts as extremely intimate: lots
of body contact, skin-to-skin contact, deep and sustained eye
contact, unabashed smooching and game playing. At this stage,
what the infant needs is reliable warmth, care, attention and
nurturing. Babies need this care; without it they will die, while
deficits in this care will cause wounds to the psyche. If the parents
are able to adequately provide this care, the infant becomes what
psychologists call securely attached. A secure attachment provides
the feeling of safety and equanimity which enables a child to meet
the challenges of development and other stresses it is bound to
face in this life. This attachment – which will be challenged with
additional demands as the child moves through different stages
of development – is the foundation for the ongoing relationship between the parents and the child, and for the psychological
well-being of the child. This secure attachment also becomes the
foundation for all subsequent human relationships, the most crucial being its eventual marital relationship.

• • • • • • • • • •

Most of us become parents long before we have stopped
being children.

Mignon McLaughlin

• • • • • • • • • •

As described earlier, in growing up we face the inevitable trial of dethronement, but this can be exacerbated by the probable insufficiencies of our parents or other caregivers. We may bear the brunt of our caregivers' frustration, or of outright anger and rage. We may be left too much to our own devices, or our parents may inconsistently vacillate between paying attention to us and being unavailable, leaving us in doubt about our value to them and about our own lovability. Given the backdrop of our complete dependency, these scenarios are felt as deeply threatening.

· · · · · · · · · ·

Don't worry that children never listen to you;
worry that they are always watching you.
Robert Fulghum

Children are natural mimics who act like their parents
despite every effort to teach them good manners.
Anonymous

· · · · · · · · · ·

Not only is our relationship with our caregivers instrumental to our development, but as we grow up, what we see in the relationships of those around us – including siblings, extended family and other significant figures – impacts the way we learn to relate to others. Amongst these, the most significant is the relationship between our mother and father. If this relationship is open and loving, secure attachment most naturally accrues. If not, a sense of insecurity will prevail, undercurrents of fear will dominate, and many unhealthy dynamics will result.

In short, what our parents and our caregivers (which may include siblings) are for us, and what they are not, have a huge impact on our being. As we shall see, the experience of our early significant relationships, which is mainly out of our control, will be 'remembered' implicitly and explicitly – and will manifest itself when we grow up, search for, and get into a relationship with a loving partner.

Personality development: Ego boundaries

The more we are looked after properly, the more our natural joyfulness and energy stays with us. When we don't feel safe and secure in connection with our caregivers we will react, trying to make it 'better' or to reduce the fear and hurt. We will also move into anticipating problems and reacting before they happen. For humans, what constitutes a threat can be something that is not really a threat at all but, in our undeveloped child's mind, it is perceived as a threat. Many things that parents do out of love can be perceived by a child as being threatening. However, we use our huge human potential to manage our way through as best we can. This includes a wide array of responses to the various stimuli, or anticipated stimuli, our world challenges us with. Some of our patterns of reacting come from our natal strengths; some strength is developed out of need. With repetition, we will come to identify with these reactive modes of behaviour as aspects of our personality. This is an acquired sense of self which in fact serves, in many ways, to keep us a safe distance from others and conspires against true intimacy.

· · · · · · · · · ·

The walls we build around us to keep sadness out
also keep out the joy.

Jim Rohn

· · · · · · · · · ·

Remember, we are primarily a soul, yearning for connection to our Creator. As social creatures, however, we are primed to connect to others in our collective journey towards God. Wanting intimate engagement and making contact with other souls in their diverse make up becomes a way of finding completion and thus an aspect of fulfilling our soul's yearning. Psychologically, however, our woundedness from our childhood – or even trauma from our adolescent or adult experience – calls forth modes of protection which tend to keep us disconnected. But deep down inside we harbour a yearning for the bliss of those times of deep, unconditional loving connection. Although there was no greater joy than the bliss of abandoned, unselfconscious closeness to our caregivers, the instability in these and other relationships come to be experienced as potential sources of hurt and thus threats to our survival.

· · · · · · · · · ·

Your children vividly remember every unkind thing you ever did to them, plus a few you really didn't.
Mignon McLaughlin

· · · · · · · · · ·

How we use our energies to protect ourselves

In response to danger, animals instinctively call forth one of four general reactions: flee, getting out of the situation as fast as possible; freeze, keeping still in hope that the threat will not notice you and go away; submit, giving in to the inevitable; or attack, aggressively moving in to try to dominate the situation. Humans will fall back on these same primitive responses, but they will be called forth in much more diverse kinds of situations. Psychologically, we can feel threatened by many kinds of different stimuli. Also, the manner of using these responses takes on many subtle and diverse appearances.

Generally, the first three reactive modes described above can be characterized as being a minimizing or a constricting of energy, while the fourth is maximizing or an expanding of energy. As humans, we elaborate on the minimizing or maximizing modes in various ways. We all develop, to varying degrees, our capacities in both these primary forms of expressing our energy, but each individual tends to favour one over the other. Often, if a child experiences his or her parents as being controlling and too intrusive, it will tend to withdraw or avoid contact as a defence. Conversely, if a child experiences his or her parents as being under-involved and uninterested, it will tend to go after the parent, cling or do things to get attention. Minimizing and maximizing are the yin and yang of ego defence and they start very early. Retreating or pursuing are both ways of protecting ourselves from what is felt as potential hurt. These are the ways we build walls, judge and separate our 'self' from the 'self' of others. Our ego is at the centre of these mechanisms; it is obsessed with serving its own interests. These reactive modes, expressions of the acquired self, keep us out of touch with the higher and true self – our own and that of others. In this way we avoid authentic connection. In later chapters we will see how we take these minimizing and maximizing responses into our marital relationship.

· · · · · · · · · ·

As any action or posture long continued will distort and disfigure the limbs;
so the mind likewise is crippled and contracted by perpetual application to the same set of ideas.

Dr Samuel Johnson

· · · · · · · · · ·

Over and above parents – society

Society influences us much more than most of us suspect. Even in our earliest years of development when we have little direct contact with outside society, its ways are being passed on to us through our parents. As we grow older we encounter society more directly and are consequently more directly influenced by it. In this process, we come to the conclusion that certain aspects of our functioning are not right, not good, not productive, not mature, not adequate. In response to these negative messages, we tend to close down in those areas of functioning and rely more on other areas which seem to get us through with less notice or criticism, or which may be appreciated and praised. Some of these functions may be gender-related, both in their nascent strengths and their social reception. The four general functions which come to be affected by social contact and societal impositions are feeling, thinking, sensing and acting.

• • • • • • • • • •

The life history of the individual is first and foremost an accommodation to the patterns and standards traditionally handed down in his community.

Ruth Benedict

• • • • • • • • • •

Feeling
• • • • • • • • • •

Feelings are not supposed to be logical.
Dangerous is the man who has rationalized his emotions.

Attributed to David Borenstein

• • • • • • • • • •

Feelings are an important aspect of our being. We are born fully alive to our feelings but socialization can have an oppressive influence on our ability to be conscious of them and to express them. Moreover, male brains tend to operate differently from female brains. Males are generally less able to recognize feelings and to discuss how they feel. While this weakness in males is by no means universal, the tendency has come, in most societies, to define 'maleness' in certain significant ways. Society takes this propensity, sanctions it as principle, and then uses it as a bludgeon for the expression of feelings in men. Many boys learn from their parents that 'men don't cry'. In this way many males, already weak in the area of accessing feelings, get the message that having feelings is not good, or at least not for men. In male-dominated societies, being 'emotional' is equated both with weakness and with women. This not only discourages in men any motivation to explore their feelings; it brings them to judge women negatively when they 'get emotional'. In this way, too, women get a negative message about feelings: while they are 'doomed' to have them, they are viewed as inferior whenever they bring feelings up, especially to men. In any case, anyone living in a social context where feelings are not valued may well be inclined to suppress this aspect of their functioning regardless of gender.

Thinking

· · · · · · · · · ·

Did you ever stop to think, and forget to start again?
A. A. Milne

· · · · · · · · · ·

We all have the capacity to think, but a gender bias has built up around this capacity as well. Because of this, women sometimes hide or veil their intelligence, and men often feel intimidated by women who show their intelligence. For example, it has long been believed that girls tend to be weaker in mathematics than boys. Present-day studies are challenging this conception and, while the outcome is still not entirely clear, it may be that mathematical abilities in girls tend to develop later than in boys. School systems may be geared to pupils whose maths skills develop earlier, giving those whose abilities develop later an early negative experience that tends to derail their sense of accomplishment. With a gender bias in the system, many females get the message that being good at maths is not feminine, so that even many girls who are good at it may feel shamed into repressing it. There is research that shows that girls do better in single-sex schools because as soon as they hit adolescence they start hiding their abilities so as not to compete with the boys and therefore be 'undatable'! Beyond this issue of social acceptability, any child who is anxious concerning the expectations of his or her significant caregivers can get its thinking ability tied in knots and close down certain aspects of its intellectual functioning. As with feeling, the function of thinking in general may become hindered in its development if a child receives chronic negative messages about his or her mental abilities.

Sensing

••••••••••

Our own physical body possesses a wisdom which we who inhabit the body lack.
We give it orders which make no sense.
Attributed to Henry Miller

••••••••••

A baby is fully alive in all parts of its body, and is very flexible. Some of this is lost through psychological wounding as we grow up and which we have described earlier. Psychological wounding has a physical component. The ego barriers we build up results in a kind of body armouring as well. Further to this, the function of relating to our bodies and sensing may also become arrested or repressed in response to social messages we receive from those around us. If we do not seem to develop apace with others, or if our body becomes a source of shame for us, we shut down certain of its capacities. We may get the message that we are clumsy, weak, ugly, too sensual, too active, too tall or too short, too fat or too thin, for example, and internalize these messages to such a degree that we close ourselves off to our body or develop rigid patterns in relation to it. One result of modern society, for many of us, is that we are obsessed with how we appear to others and become alienated from our internal sensing of our own body.

Acting

· · · · · · · · · ·

When it comes to getting things done,
we need fewer architects and more bricklayers.

Attributed to Colleen C. Barrett

· · · · · · · · · ·

Babies act and move instinctively. As long as they have developed the physical capability, if they want something or want to do something, they go for it. They just do it. Socialization throws a wrench in this for many of us. The function of acting, getting things done, moving on our ideas, can get repressed in ways similar to the repression of the other three general functions. We may get shamed for taking initiative, told repeatedly not to do this or that. Later we may be told not to step out of line or to 'think' before we do something. Even later we may get blanket messages such as, 'you can't do anything' or 'you will never succeed'. With this kind of input we may, in time, step back from taking initiative and retreat into other forms of functioning which have less risk involved or which don't draw attention.

· · · · · · · · · ·

Kids: they dance before they learn there is anything that isn't
music.

William Stafford

· · · · · · · · · ·

Messages we receive from our social milieu have a varying impact on us. Some of us shut down in one or two areas, but do well or even overcompensate in one or two others. The reasons for repressing our primary functions of thinking, feeling, doing or sensing become lost to us. Rather, we come to define ourselves in terms of our ability or lack of ability in these areas. When running into certain difficulties because of our limited development in certain areas we say things like 'I'm not good at maths,' 'I'm not the sentimental type,' 'I'm a procrastinator;' 'I'm not into sports/dancing,' – each of these to a large extent in accordance with which of the primary functions we have repressed.

By the time we reach puberty, our original wholeness and sense of aliveness has left us with unconscious wounds and curtailed capacities, whether through deficits in nurturing, over-involved parents, or messages internalized through socialization. With puberty, our bodies move into becoming adult but psychologically there is usually a lot of healing that we yearn for, and a lot of developing and retrieving of our basic functions.

Adolescence – the search begins

· · · · · · · · · ·

Adolescence is a new birth, for the higher and more completely human traits are now born . . . Adolescence is the time when an individual 'recapitulates' the savage stage of the race's past.

G. Stanley Hall

· · · · · · · · · ·

During adolescence some of our anger and frustration over our upbringing and socialization may come to the surface in the form of rebellion, a focus on peer acceptance, a distrust of authority, a retreat into social isolation, brooding, coolness, wild experimentation with new behaviour, apathy, extreme idealism or other forms of behaviour which have come to be known as adolescent syndromes. But the yearning for close connection, caring nurturance, unconditional acceptance, which we have come to cover up, also comes to the surface as we contemplate relationships with the opposite sex. Our sex drive is developed and this helps propel our desire for contact, and the more powerful drive for love becomes hungry for fulfilment. Both these drives are further stimulated by modern-day society through its various media. We start scanning the horizon for a partner, fuelled by higher hormone levels, intoxicated by dreams of romance, excited by the prevalent images which bombard us from ubiquitous media.

· · · · · · · · · ·

Don't hold your parents up to contempt.
After all, you are their son,
and it is just possible that you may take after them.
Attributed to Evelyn Waugh

· · · · · · · · · ·

Adolescence, however, brings our consciousness – including our awareness of our free will – to a higher level. This consciousness may be veiled by our woundedness, but insofar as it breaks through we may come to recognize more clearly our spiritual nature and seek out our spiritual Source. On this level, we become attracted to high ideals. We look for the good, search out connections that feed this spiritual awareness. We want to work for others, for the world, and to raise children who will have this high aim as well. We look for a partner who will want to work with us in this great enterprise.

Despite the more conscious awakenings of our higher self as we check out different possibilities for mating, we are uncannily, and unconsciously, influenced by much of our childhood experience. We have emerged from childhood with certain basic needs left unfulfilled. We have developed adaptive styles in response to deficits in nurturing and hurts – perceived or real – at the hands of significant others during our developmental years. Some areas of our functioning we have repressed or left underdeveloped. We have an internalized memory of our significant others in relation to both their nurturing and wounding contact. While we may develop certain conscious and spiritual conceptions of what we are looking for, our quest is most often primarily directed by a powerful unconscious drive for completion and healing. Let us proceed to have a look at where this quest leads us and how, if properly understood, it can lead to a convergence of our highest spiritual yearning and psychic healing.

2

The Quest for Completion

• • • • • • • • • •

Relationships are all there is.
Everything in the universe only exists because it is in
relationship to everything else. Nothing exists in isolation.
We have to stop pretending we are individuals that can go it
alone.

Attributed to Margaret J. Wheatley

• • • • • • • • • •

In the last chapter, we looked at elements of our childhood
that most of us do not pay much attention to. Part of what
we *do* pay attention to is developing our survival mechanisms,
the strengths that carry us through the minefield of life. We
come out of childhood with all kinds of baggage, patterns of
behaviour and unconscious reflexes. We have survived, and
what we developed in order to survive has become extremely
important to us. These abilities were developed with a backdrop
of utter dependence; thus, at some level, we hold on to them as
a matter of life and death. These survival mechanisms become
our identity and elements of our ego.

But at the same time we have a deep yearning for the feeling of oneness and wholeness with which we started the journey of life. In the beginning, we felt no sense of separateness; we were living in full connection. Thus, part of our yearning is for connection, a connection which is nurturing and caring, authentic, without pretence, unconditional, everlasting. Unconsciously, we are also looking for healing, the reclaiming of lost and repressed parts of our selves. We are not alone in this and we cannot do it on our own. Our ultimate yearning is for connection to God, but the human journey always involves other humans. A natural and intrinsic longing, one which also guarantees the propagation of our species, is for a helpmate on this challenging but enriching journey. Our inner longing is complemented by physical, psychological and social factors, often including a sense of loneliness, social pressure, peer pressure, and nature, with the strong hormonal impulse of the sex drive. All these propel us to look for a partner.

· · · · · · · · · ·

When a girl marries
she exchanges the attentions of many men
for the inattention of one.
Attributed to Helen Rowland

My advice to you is to get married. If you find a good wife,
you'll be happy;
if not, you'll become a philosopher.
Attributed to Socrates

· · · · · · · · · ·

Moving into adulthood, therefore, we carry two competing propensities: our ego's survival mechanisms – which serve as a kind of protection but which tend to keep others at a safe distance or engulfed – and a deep longing for wholeness which seeks authentic, intimate connection. The unconscious longing to find completion and resolution of childhood hurts urges us on to find a match which will provide the perfect love and connection we have been missing since infancy. Let us have a closer look at the factors that seem to attract us to a person, factors that often resonate with our unconscious forces in a mystical way.

Forces of attraction

Just what is it that eventually draws us to certain individuals in our search for a mate? Is it opposites that attract, or similarities? There has been a lot of research in recent years into factors that lead to attraction, that bring people together. Some of these factors are physical, some psychological, some social. Research has not yet highlighted spiritual elements, but explanations of psychological factors are bringing us closer to this, revealing fascinating facets of God's design for marriage. And since not much has been written about spiritual attraction in itself, let us start with this. We need to keep in mind, however, that all of these are parts of a whole, aspects of our complete self, and there are no clear demarcations between them. Each has an effect on the other.

Attractions of our higher self

• • • • • • • • • •

Everything that rises must converge.

Teilhard de Chardin

• • • • • • • • • •

One of the premises of this book is that marriage, properly understood and practised, leads to spiritual growth. This growth can be partly understood as a process where our survival mechanisms – elements of our ego – are held in abeyance, allowing our higher self to exert its influence and develop. This brings spiritual closeness, a feeling of connectedness which transports us beyond our lower functioning. But there are those who have already done a lot of spiritual work on themselves before looking for a partner, and all of us have, to varying degrees, inherited a spiritual legacy from our forebears. We all have a spiritual nature and deep (sometimes deeply buried) spiritual yearnings. When we see spirit manifested in another, the spiritual side of our self is naturally attracted. This can be quite conscious, but perhaps less so in the case of spiritual inheritance where we have not actually done the work ourselves. There is a beauty in a soul that has advanced in the consciousness of its yearning for connection to God. On some level everyone is attracted to this beauty but, at the same time, we may feel unequal to the challenges that living with someone like that may present; our ego may feel threatened by spiritual attractions. Our higher selves are open to connection and are especially attracted to all manifestations of spirit in others. These spiritual attractions can be very strong and beautiful and a good start for the inevitable work of couplehood.

Physical attraction

. . . .

People see you as an object, not as a person,
and they project a set of expectations onto you.
People who don't have it think beauty is a blessing,
but actually it sets you apart.

Candice Bergen

. . . .

Aspects of an individual's physical appearance often capture our attention. How a person looks, holds their self, moves, grooms their self, all this holds a fascination for us, giving us clues as to a person's emotional, sexual, even intellectual and spiritual mien. Culture often plays a major role in highlighting areas of physical attraction. In some cultures, being fat is attractive, in others it is viewed negatively. All parts of the body, from the back of the neck to the feet, can become the focus of erotic attraction, depending on the culture.

Many of these factors are primitive. For example, men are still attracted to subconscious indications that a woman is well fit to bear children. Women are attracted, on the same level, to men who exude an aura of strength and security. All of us tend to be more attracted to individuals who look after themselves and this, as Helen Fisher – an anthropologist and a leading expert on the biology of love and attraction – has pointed out, also exists for primates and even other mammals.

Interestingly, another primitive, subconscious factor is smell. The body smell of some potential partners attracts us much more than others; smell can cause us to be drawn to a person or to be repelled. We are not talking about perfume here, but down-to-earth body odour. Of great fascination is the fact that researchers have found that those whose smell attracts us have a genetic makeup significantly remote from our own. This difference in genes is complementary in such a way that the matches formed as a result of this attraction would greatly reduce the likelihood of birth defects or constitutional weakness. These are not factors of similarity but of genetic distance and difference. The more remote our genetic connection, the more this augers well for our offspring's health. This is what our olfactory lobe is able to subtly pick up!

• • • • • • • • • •

God's wisdom hath decreed that partners to a marriage should be of distant origins. That is, the further removed the relationship between husband and wife is, the stronger, the more beautiful and the healthier will their offspring be.

'Abdu'l-Bahá

• • • • • • • • • •

Psychological attraction

Psychological elements involved in our attractions, as has been mentioned, have a lot to do with our childhood experiences. One of these psychological elements has to do with similarity. All the love that was given to us as children we hold in a kind of unconscious embrace; all that we longed for and didn't get, the hurts and disappointments, were also registered and are carried with us. These act as a largely unconscious guide: we search for someone who will match and meet these criteria. While it doesn't make much conscious sense to us that negative parental traits found in a potential partner can serve as factors of attraction, the tendency to this is very strong. The familiarity of even negative experiences brings a kind of comfort. This is why, for example, children who are brought up with parents with addictions often find themselves in similar situations with their partners when they grow up – this, despite conscious resolution not to go down this path.

The psychologist Harville Hendrix calls this map of unconscious elements 'imago'. Our imago contains both the best and worst aspects of our experience with our early caregivers. These might be seemingly small details about the way the caregivers speak or hold themselves, the tone of voice, the manner of touch, personal expressions. However small these details may seem, they resonate powerfully when we find someone in our adult life who is similar in these particular ways.

• • • • • • • • • •

*Marriage is an alliance entered into by a man who can't
sleep with the window shut, and a woman who can't sleep
with the window open.*
Attributed to George Bernard Shaw

• • • • • • • • • •

Another source of psychological attraction emanating from our childhood has to do with difference. We have earlier described the four functions of feeling, thinking, sensing and acting which become affected by our socialization. Here opposites tend to attract. Someone whose *feeling* capacities are repressed may be impressed by someone who expresses feelings fluidly and with ease. Someone whose *thinking* function has become repressed may be attracted to someone who thinks clearly. In a similar way, those who tend to minimize in certain kinds of encounters are often attracted to someone who maximizes in those same cases. Interestingly, this attraction to difference seems to be greatly augmented when we fall in love.

Jonathon and May

These psychological dynamics were at play in the case of Jonathon and May in our original scenario from the prologue. In their early encounters, Jonathan was mesmerized by the ease with which May could express herself and converse. This was an area he had largely shut down in his childhood. He had learnt to withdraw in relation to people, in order to protect himself from possible hurt. When he saw how well May was able to relate to others, it became an unconscious point of attraction. In fact, he was attracted to the part in himself that had remained dormant. On May's side, the opposite was taking place. She was fascinated by this mysterious-looking quiet man who seemed to be functioning quite independently of others, something she had not learnt to develop in her upbringing. She had learnt to go for attention and cling in order to get the love and affection she wanted.

Before falling in love, we may consciously deride people who function in areas we feel weak in, but if critical aspects of our imagos match, the attraction takes over and we open our hearts to this wonderful new reality. Interestingly, with the demise of romance, as we will discuss later, we will probably retreat back into our earlier orientation and see our partner's energies in these areas as a big part of their 'problem' and a challenge to us. As their marriage wore on, May came to resent that Jonathon was so distant and independent. He, on the other hand, became very impatient with May's energy and need for attention and conversation.

Falling in love

. . . .

On an unconscious level, they feel connected once again with
their caretakers, only this time
they believe their deepest, most fundamental,
most infantile yearnings are going to be satisfied.
Someone is going to take care of them;
they are no longer going to be alone.

Harville Hendrix

. . . .

When critical aspects of these various conscious and unconscious elements are triggered in the presence of a potential partner, we get very excited. We use our great powers of imagination to fill in the blanks and start picturing an ideal life with this partner. If this person is not similarly triggered we are thrown into the ferment of unrequited love and find ourselves in a pit of deep despair. But if the potential partner is also attracted to us, we are propelled into a new reality. When we fall in love with a partner who reciprocates the love we have for them, we feel that our quest for completion has finally come to an end. Once love has struck, the defences of the ego concerning closeness crumble to dust and the obsession of needing to be with the other, almost at any cost, takes over. We haven't had this closeness and feeling of oneness since the womb world and early infancy. Coming to be in such a special and intimate connection with another human being brings us exhilaration. Our soul's yearning is being met.

The magic of romance

· · · · · · · · · ·

Nobody is perfect until you fall in love with them.

Anonymous

· · · · · · · · · ·

There is a beauty in romance that is attested to by poets, writers, composers and artists across the board. Falling in love is akin to spiritual experience and when it happens it seems that new spiritual energies become available to us. When in love, a sceptic may suddenly become full of hope and optimism. For some, it is as though they have always dreamed of this but never dared to articulate it, then they are struck with it and 'hallelujah!' Where we had repressed our desires, now we want it all. Lovers often stay together late into the night, sleepless, gazing into the heavens, feeling connected to each other and all that is. Moonstruck.

· · · · · · · · · ·

You know you're in love
when you don't wanna go to sleep at night
because your life is better than a dream.

Anonymous

· · · · · · · · · ·

Whether for good or for ill, most of us want to fall in love. We are often entranced by it even when it is portrayed in movies or literature. Commercial interests manipulate us with this fascination. Most agree, except the lovers, that love is blind. In psychological terminology, the dynamics of romance are unconscious. Moreover, love becomes unmanageable when the lover is not around or available. While Helen Fisher calls it a drive, some psychologists call it a disease. Harville Hendrix has said that the intensity with which a couple experiences romantic love is in direct proportion to the woundedness of their childhood. Whether intense or mild, mutual attraction is not a bad thing. Rather, this could be nature's way of matching psyches, so that in the long-term relationship the largely unconscious wounded aspects of our psyches can be brought to the surface and possibly healed. Since it is romantic love that nowadays has become the primary impulse for bringing couples into marriage, and also because a yearning for romantic feelings often persists even after the initial romantic stage has receded, it is good to have a look at its nature. Perhaps we can uncover the mystery of keeping romance alive throughout our marriage.

Chemistry and brain science

The moon has become a symbol of romance. When mortal man landed on the moon it seemed to some as though science had invaded a sacrosanct place of lovers. More recently, science really has invaded this seemingly mystical wonder of romance, and what has been uncovered can help us to grow into a higher level of understanding love and the challenges of long-term relationships. We have long said that when two people hit it off there is a certain chemistry. Let's look at what some of this chemistry is.

PEA, or phenylethylamine, is one of the neurochemicals that start to flow when two people are strongly drawn to each other. PEA speeds up the flow of information between nerve cells. It elicits a feeling of excitement. Another chemical involved is norepinephrine, a kind of amphetamine which stimulates adrenaline production, causing our heart to race. Dopamine is also released. This is an overall 'feel good' amphetamine. Put all this together and you have a chemical feast which produces the euphoric feelings of love and bliss. These are the chemicals that help us break through our ego barriers, producing all kinds of energy and new hope. In this state, even men can stay up and talk all night. Author and therapist Patricia Love has noted that when monkeys are injected with PEA they become 'hypersexual' and appear to be 'romantic', but only when another monkey is present. For humans it seems to be much the same: in order to feel the high of romance we need our partner. When we are separated from our beloved our spirits plummet and we fall into a withdrawal we call 'lovesickness'.

• • • • • • • • • •

After a quarrel, a husband said to his wife,
'You know, I was a fool when I married you.'
She replied, 'Yes, dear, but I was in love and didn't notice.'
Anonymous

• • • • • • • • • •

At the same time, very interesting things are happening in our brain when we are in love. MRI scans of people in love show some concentrated blood flow into the ventral tegmental area in the brain stem, particularly in a group of cells which produce the dopamine referred to above. This is the very same area associated with the rush one gets from cocaine use! Because of this connection of romance to this primitive part of the brain, Helen Fisher, who carried out this research, has come to see romantic love as a basic drive, one that is much more powerful than the sex drive.

Fisher has researched romantic love for much of her professional life and has observed the following characteristics in people who are in love: intense energy, focused attention, euphoria and mood swings, 'sweaty palm syndrome' (something like stage fright), and emotional dependence on contact with one's beloved, coupled with separation anxiety. People in love are very sexually possessive of each other; they crave emotional union and obsessively think about each other. All this is involuntary, independent of our will! When one lover has been dumped by the other, MRI scans show that the same areas as those for being in love stay lighted, but other areas that have been identified with addiction, craving and deep attachment also light up. This has led Fisher to conclude that romance is also an addiction, with a very strong tendency for relapse when trying to wean oneself of the powerfully intruding memories associated with one's past lover.

Three love circuits in the brain

Romance, then, has its own circuitry in the brain and, according to Fisher, this is one of the three brain circuits related to mating. The other two are the sex drive and attachment. She believes that the sex drive evolved early so that as many offspring as possible could be conceived. The sex drive does not focus on one individual but can be drawn to a range of different partners. The romantic drive apparently evolved to enable a more intensive one-on-one connection at the period when, according to Fisher, our human ancestors had come down from living in the trees and started walking on two legs. The female, at this time, needed the protection of a male because she had to carry her baby with her and could not alone fend off attacks effectively. The male, in turn, would not have been able to protect a group or harem of such 'handicapped' mates.

As humans evolved further, the needs of human offspring increased. Children needed to be taught more and looked after much longer. The intense but relatively short-lived romantic drive was not enough to hold the male by his mate's side for the years their children needed to be nurtured. For this purpose, the attachment circuit was brought into play. Attachment is a softer, less intense but in some ways deeper form of connection which lasts and helps keep a couple together for a much longer period, enabling the pair to continue serving the developmental needs of their children.

Not surprisingly, the three brain circuits which involve mating are to some degree connected. A sexual orgasm releases testosterone which triggers dopamine, one of the chemicals associated with romance. Similarly, dopamine triggers testosterone, the main hormone involved in the sex drive, for both males and females. Orgasms also produce oxytocin which is associated with attachment. Similar connections exist between the romance and attachment circuits. One of the lessons to learn here is not to have a sexual relationship with someone you don't want to fall in love with or form an attachment to. And hold yourself back from falling in love with someone you don't want to have a long-term relationship with. (This theme was developed in Raymond's book *Conscious Courtship*.)

As it stands, it may look like nature has wired us nicely for the long-term monogamous relationship which serves the human infant's need for very long-term nurturing. Why then all the troubles with infidelity and broken marriages? Fisher points out that, biologically speaking, the degree to which we *are* faithful companions is actually quite remarkable. Only 3 per cent of mammals stay together as mates to rear their young, and the human need for this is much more long term and complex than in other cases. But the human brain, as marvellous as it is, seems not to be complete enough in its design to adequately promote long-term fidelity. The three brain systems which have evolved for mating can work quite independently and often do. It remains possible for an individual to be deeply attached to one person, romantically involved with another, and sexually engaged with a range of others.

Returning to our theme of the now grown-up human seeking completion after the challenges of childhood, it may seem that our biological evolution has not prepared us well enough for an integrated love that lasts long term. Whether Fisher's model is adequate or not, it is at least clear that our physiological makeup is not sufficient to guarantee an integration of circuitry that we can comfortably say will protect us from engaging in affairs that will imperil the couple's relationship. It appears that our hormonal drives could easily propel us into a large number of relationships. At different times and with different people some of these could become intensely romantic, while with others we could form deep attachments. These and other factors have led some social scientists to conclude that humans are wired for serial or sequential monogamy, that we aren't biologically prepared for the very long-term commitment which best suits the needs of our children. But not only do children thrive and develop best when brought up in an environment fuelled by the mother and father's love for each other; each parent also longs for dependable love and intimacy from his or her partner as part of his or her quest for completion. It is during infancy that the attachment circuits develop and it is this attachment that we yearn for most deeply as an adult. It is only in the context of enduring and caring attachment that our wounds from childhood can be healed. How, then, can we integrate these possibly disparate functions and drives into a completed circle?

Human evolution

What God has not provided through evolution, He has granted through providing us with the teachers and guidance that we need to complete the circle of partially competitive mating drives. He has not programmed the outcome, as seems the case with other creatures. The human being came to possess self-awareness, higher intelligence, and with this, volition. In the case of love and the need for it to be long term, he has given us the necessary ingredients and the willpower to carry it through. In this, we humans play a vital role. Our volition is required, and the more this has developed through human history the more our institutions have evolved. In this area, religion – defined in the Bahá'í writings as the 'essential connection which proceeds from the reality of things' – has historically played the dominant role. Somehow the paradigmatic thinkers, or Prophets, understand this essential connection and become the channel of knowing what we humans need at the interface of biological evolution and human nature.

Historically, religions gave us the institution of marriage and provided us with laws relating to it. This institution has evolved as humanity has developed. At earlier stages, for example, polygamy was permitted and divorce quite easily granted. Eventually, the importance of commitment to one's betrothed became, in one way or another, more emphasized. A model of marriage with clearly defined roles and hierarchy was instituted with Christianity and continued with Islam. (Interestingly, polygamy, which was not explicitly discarded by Jesus, eventually fell out of grace, apparently because it contravened the laws of the Roman Empire. Muhammad permitted a greatly limited number of wives on condition of treating them all with justice, a condition to which close attention is apparently rarely paid). With all these developments, humanity has gradually grown in capacity. Now, however, there has been a massive new development.

Although some form of romance apparently came into play for early man, it may have become problematic for us when we started to become civilized and required longer-term mating relationships. For much of human history the institution of marriage could do without romance. Mates came to be chosen by parents or elders. Romance could occur after the couple married, but they may not have even met each other until the wedding. Much more crucial to marriage was the attachment circuit to keep the couple together, and the sex drive so that they could procreate. Momentously, in more recent times choosing one's own partner has more and more become the standard and thus the role of romance has come to the fore. In the United States, for instance, 90 per cent of young people insist that they will not marry without falling in love with their future partner, even if they were to meet someone who otherwise fulfilled all their criteria. It is as though this is the real declaration of independence: 'I will choose my own partner and my confirmation in this choice will be our passionate love for each other.'

Before this development, when roles were more structured, a greater degree of safety was provided. The structure of marriage and the relationship of society to this institution provided for a very stable environment for the children to grow up in. Boundaries were clearly set, people were brought up to know what was expected of them, and strong social sanctions existed to support the framework. Husband and wife had their own clear places set for them and, in society as whole, similar structures existed and people found their place according to their social status. However, there was relatively little room for movement within these structures and the potential of the human spirit was greatly constricted. Gradually, freedom of choice, the principle of gender equality, a push for universal justice and universal education, and other factors eventually stretched the capacities of these social and matrimonial structures beyond their limit.

But the human psyche requires structure for its growth. As sociologist Peter Berger has clarified, we humans need a 'nomos', a socially constructed ordering of experience, without which we face the terror and anarchy of anomie. This is true of the powerful drive of romance and the less powerful drive of sex. Society's older structures, under the influence of religious teachings, provided rigid boundaries to prevent the sex drive from distracting humans from focusing on the need to marry and form families. Now that the even more powerful drive of romance has been released, some are beginning to see the need for this drive to be roped in as well. In fact, when viewed in the wider context of the developing human spirit, it can be seen that while awareness of certain protective boundaries are needed, neither of these drives are evil or in need of being repressed. Rather, what we need to do is learn how to attend to our relationship in such a way that these possibly competing drives become integrated and the bond of marriage becomes strong enough to provide the assurance our psyches, and our children, long for. We are now in a position to become conscious of realizing the nature and the role of these drives, moving us from our relatively unconscious, fragmented processes of childhood to the completion of our maturation as adults. However, our initial surges towards greater freedom and experimentation in these domains have not been without injury.

Commitment

* * * * * * * * * *

. . . any romance that does not end in marriage fails.

John Updike

* * * * * * * * * *

Romantic love, in its full-blown initial phase, is temporary. Scientists believe that the chemicals associated with it wear out or that our receptors become dull to them. This is not to say that couples who have been together for a long time cannot be romantically attached. Helen Fisher has interviewed couples who are in love after twenty years of marriage, but their MRI scans, while similar in most respects to those of young lovers, have parts of the brain lit up which are identified with bringing serenity and calm. When lovers pass the neurotic or compulsive romantic stage, even when romantic feelings are kept alive they take on a somewhat transformed calmness.

* * * * * * * * * *

It would be impossible to fall in love with someone that you really saw.

Attributed to Fran Lebowitz

* * * * * * * * * *

One of the beauties of romance is that it can help us break through the conundrum of almost unlimited possibilities. In our present age, now that the choice of a partner is up to us, we find ourselves bewildered at the range of our options. Added to this, if we are conscious of the huge requirements of family life, the most essential being the enduring love of husband and wife for each other, we become further hamstrung. Who can be good enough for us? Who can be good enough as a parent for our future children? Maybe if I wait, the flaws I see in this person won't exist in another. Maybe I am not ready myself. These thoughts and others stymie our ability to make a decision, to take the step of committing ourselves. Romance can cut through this red tape with a vengeance.

· · · · · · · · · ·

Getting married is very much like
going to a restaurant with friends.
You order what you want,
then when you see what the other person has,
you wish you had ordered that.

Anonymous

· · · · · · · · · ·

Given the temporary nature of intense romance and the process by which it can break down, we need something more to carry us through the tough times which follow. Romantic feelings, which dominate the romantic stage of love, reveal themselves to be tender and fallible when the forces of this period come to a close. Romance reveals, albeit temporarily, some of the strengths available to us when we learn to be a good lover. But our survival mechanisms tend to conspire against our ability to be a loving partner. Once the chemicals of romance have lost their potency, we need consciously to overcome many ingrained behaviours in order to answer the yearnings of our partner. In this process there are many tests and trying times. When in love, we *feel* forever committed to our beloved. Marriage is a way of formalizing that commitment so that when the feelings temporarily wane, the relationship survives for the good of all. But, of course, the good of all is not guaranteed by marriage without it being a mature commitment, one that brings us to take care of the love we have and bring about a fuller integration of all three of the mating circuits referred to above. How to do this is most of what the rest of this book is about.

3

Have I Made a Mistake?

· · · · · · · · · ·

Marriage, n.
The state or condition of a community consisting of
a master, a mistress and two slaves, making in all, two.
Ambrose Bierce

· · · · · · · · · ·

Our developmental process through childhood and our yearning for completion can finally get us to the magic of romance, which can catapult us into commitment. As long as our romantic feelings are still alive, we feel complete; we feel that we have finally arrived at our long-dreamt-of destination. But the temporary effects of our brain chemistry are up against the entrenched patterns of our egos. These patterns are what have kept us going with a relative lack of intimacy. Our egos have learned to be wary of, and sceptical about, the operations of 'the other' in its various manifestations. While still entranced by romance, our partner is not experienced as other. 'We are one,' is the mantra of lovers. But otherness is destined to rear its foreboding head.

While romance, with all its sparks and fireworks, may be the most exciting stage of an intimate relationship, what follows operates in stark contrast. Because the image of our beloved during romance takes on almost god-like proportions, it hurts all the more when he or she starts to become the source of pain to us. When we open to the hope that romantic love engenders, the dashed hope becomes that much more painful. Pain and woundedness seem to be woven into the design of the human creature. We have pointed out that falling in love is perhaps the first and fullest release from what seems to be the woundedness of life, and that this release and opening up hearkens back to that much earlier time in the womb and early infant stages when we were looked after almost magically. The fall from romance probably echoes the primal pain associated with the dethronement described in Chapter 1.

• • • • • • • • • •

'If you'll make the toast and pour the juice, sweetheart,'
said the newlywed bride, 'breakfast will be ready.'
'Good, what are we having for breakfast?'
asked the new husband.
'Toast and juice,' she replied.

Anonymous

• • • • • • • • • •

When the first chinks in the armour of romance start to appear, our egos immediately start to kick in. Psychologically, this often occurs as soon as we make a commitment. For example, research in the United States has revealed that a majority of couples do not have a good experience on their honeymoons. When we consciously commit to something, our egos automatically become wary. We want to read the small print. What may have been flowing naturally along now needs to be examined. Our egos don't want to commit to anything without close examination. This is when the questions start to come. What's going on? What have I gotten myself into? Do I really know this person?

Once the ego clicks in, our behaviour also changes. We become more careful, reticent about giving and risking. This, in turn, triggers 'the other'. What's going on here? What happened to my hero or my queen? Questions easily lead to conflict. Feelings can easily be deeply hurt because we have opened ourselves to this other as never before. We can be wounded by seemingly small things which echo hurts from childhood when we felt similarly vulnerable. The intense desire of the lovers to get back the magic can, in the early phases of romantic trials, succeed in bringing back loving feelings. In time, however, the chinks in love's armour become gaping holes and other unconscious forces take over, forces that have long-practised tactical sophistication to fall back on. Harville Hendrix explains that, when we fall in love, what we do is project all that was good and tender in our early caregivers onto our beloved. In other words, when we fall in love we are not seeing before us the real human we love, but rather an idealized projection of our soul's longing of being cared for perfectly. When we do start to see the faults in our beloved we are not only let down, we are devastated. All our old-world resentment comes to the surface, this time focused on the person we have married. This is our fall from grace – or, psychologically speaking, our second fall from grace; and as far as our ego – which has now reawakened with a vengeance – is concerned, the one we married is to blame. Psychologically, we start to tell ourselves in some manner: 'Now I see who this person really is, I have been duped, and I am angry as hell!'

• • • • • • • • • •

I grew up to have my father's looks,
my father's speech patterns, my father's posture,
my father's opinions,
and my mother's contempt for my father.
Attributed to Jules Feiffer

• • • • • • • • • •

This starts a dynamic in the relationship which can end in divorce or can go on interminably as a kind of power struggle where couples get wrapped up in blaming each other in some way – subtly or overtly – for the unfair position they have been put in. A common version of this is called the 'parallel marriage', where battles may not be apparent but a safe distance is kept so each can more or less get on with their business without waking the dragon within. Most marriages either break up or stay locked in some version of this conflict stage.

When these kinds of cases come into our office, we hear all sorts of variations of the refrain: 'This is not the person I married' or 'Now I know who my spouse really is and I don't like him (or her).' We have to agree with them that they are probably right in saying that they didn't really know their spouse when they first fell in love, but we also have to gently break the news to them that they don't know them yet. Here is the explanation.

What it is that comes to the surface when our beloved starts to appear like a dragon out of hell is not who they really are but, rather, a projection of all that was difficult and painful in the behaviour of our caregivers, in conjunction with our partner's ego trying to survive in reaction to our own survival mechanisms. In other words, the fall from grace is simply the other side of the coin of the fall into grace: we were blinded when we fell into the romantic haze; we remain blind when we fall out of it. If we really want to know who our partner is – and in the process who we ourselves really are – we need to pass through both these phases and move into a relatedness which is not tainted by unconscious projection. Until we clean our lenses from the taint of projection, we will tend to fall back on well-rehearsed survival mechanisms which drive our relationships into deeper trouble. Psychological projection is one of the most enduring of Freud's legacies; having come to the understanding that the first two stages of marriage are fraught with it, it might serve us well to have a closer look at what it is and how it works.

Projection

. . . .

*How strange that we should ordinarily feel compelled to hide
our wounds
when we are all wounded!*

Scott Peck

. . . .

An ego does not see itself well and, in truth, does not like to see itself at all. This is our understanding of the 'persistent self' described in the Bahá'í writings. In fact, since Bahá'ís do not believe in an independent force of evil in the universe which works in opposition to the force of good, it becomes clear that all references to 'Satan' in the Bahá'í writings are references to our persistent self, as 'Abdu'l-Bahá explains: there is nothing else in the universe that casts a shadow from the light of God.

> . . . the evil spirit, Satan or whatever is interpreted as evil, refers to the lower nature in man . . . God has never created an evil spirit; all such ideas and nomenclature are symbols expressing the mere human or earthly nature of man. It is an essential condition of the soil of earth that thorns, weeds and fruitless trees may grow from it. Relatively speaking, this is evil; it is simply the lower state and baser product of nature.

The ego does not like to look at itself because the self is flawed and our ego does not like to see flaws in itself. This quite simple mechanism is denial. The means by which the ego operates in denial are varied and intricate. Being smart and successful in this world, far from exemplifying freedom from denial, leads often to more sophistication in covering up. Gaining power in this world is often just another survival mechanism, a way of denial which makes our self look good and those 'under us' less so. In a dog-eat-dog world denial can take us far, but in close relationships it fails utterly.

Denying what we don't like to see in ourselves, what we unconsciously do is project what we don't like or can't accept in ourselves onto others. Imagine a film projector. The film is analogous to the unacceptable aspects of our own self. These are things which we disowned as we were growing up because we were told they were bad and were responded to with criticism or disdain. For this reason we disowned them or denied them, but they are still there within us, in our 'film'. When we come across a person who treats us in a way that evokes unconscious painful memories of early hurts, the projector turns on and those images on the film are projected outwards on to the other, analogous to a screen. Viewing them on this screen, we get angry and self-righteous. We point to the flaws on the screen without realizing that our disdain may say a lot more about us than the other. This doesn't mean to say that others don't have faults, but it does mean that our emotional reaction to the other usually says a lot more about us than our egos, lost in denial, like to acknowledge. Projection is one of the psychological mechanisms which propel us further into contention or gridlock.

· · · · · · · · · ·

Adam and Eve had an ideal marriage.
He didn't have to hear about all the men she could have
married . . .
and she didn't have to hear about how well his mother cooked.
Anonymous

· · · · · · · · · ·

Symbiosis

We come into the world with complete energy, but this gets cut off as we grow up. We tend to be attracted to a partner whose energy profile complements ours. If we have repressed our physical or sensory energy we are attracted to someone who is still alive to his or her body. But this person is likely to have repressed energy expression in an area where we are relatively strong. This complementarity fuels the power we feel in romance. There is a feeling of completeness that comes not just because we have let down our ego barriers, but because in letting them down we open ourselves to our partner's energy 'offering'. This gives a kind of illusion of completeness, but it feels real. The illusion refers to the fact that it is only in the romantic connection that we access this wholeness. With this comes an unconscious contract that we have to 'keep this': you have to stay with me in this way or we 'lose it'. This is a kind of collusion which feeds the symbiosis explored by Harville Hendrix. Of course, we do 'lose it', but the subsequent rage we feel does not end the collusion. In making the other person wrong for causing the loss, we stay enmeshed.

Projection skews perception. In the romantic phase, we don't want to see imperfections in the other, so we project all that is good onto our partner. In the power struggle phase, we project negativity onto our partner. This tendency to project in both phases is rooted in the fusion of relationships, which characterize both these phases. This is a kind of symbiosis that does not allow differentiation or diversity. The feeling of oneness in romance is not a unity which allows otherness. In truth, it goes something like this: 'We are one. (And I am the one!)' Moving out of romance into conflict is a continuation of this symbiosis, but now with a negative face. When our partner presents a face that doesn't conform to our sense of oneness, we take it as betrayal and work to move him or her back into line. Of course, our partner falls into a similar internal dynamic with us, and this is the essential foundation of the power struggle. We are struggling, but we are still essentially stuck together, albeit reluctantly or resentfully.

The fall

The fall out of romance brings us squarely into the arena of power struggle. Instead of living in a dream, we may at times find ourselves in a nightmare, and there seems no easy way out. When psychologists refer to the second stage of marriage as conflict, they don't necessarily mean there is a lot of fighting or arguing going on. The conflict may be going on inside the minds of the combatants without coming out into the open. There can be open conflict or there can be smouldering silence or there can be retreat into our own spaces with little significant contact or communication. Some relationships move into a kind of niceness where the husband and wife unconsciously draw up a kind of contract with each other that says, in effect, 'I won't get into anything heavy if you don't'. The conflict stage has all kinds of variations. What they have in common is a dynamic that prevents couples from breaking through denial and achieving resolution. Most couples continue in power struggle or divorce; few move on to pick the true fruits that marriage has to offer, which is to move out of symbiosis into conscious connection and individuation.

In the stage of romance our partner appeared larger than life, as a god or goddess, a knight in shining armour or a princess in line for the throne. In the stage of conflict our partner remains something larger than life but in a negative way. He or she has a kind of power over us akin to the stage of romance, but in this stage it is coercive and hurtful. In both cases – the romantic and the conflicted – our partner's effect on us seems larger than life because in both cases they bring to the surface feelings our parents evoked when we were children, and at that time our parents appeared larger than life. They knew the world that we didn't; they had the power of life and death over us. With this backdrop, they also had the power to comfort us and care for us, reassure us and make us feel safe under their protection.

Our intimate relationships, especially the ones to which

we are committed, inevitably take us back to our childhood. If we could watch ourselves from the outside as our egos get bruised in our marriage, we would see how childlike we become. Actually, on some level we realize this and for this reason hide this kind of behaviour, as much as we can, from the gaze of the outside world. But we do not pause to imagine how we really look from the outside because our egos are fully engaged, usually in making the other look as wrong as possible. Again, making the other look wrong can be overt and tyrannical, or it can be done passively and quietly, martyr-like or manipulatively. The motivation of the ego is to win and this is what the stage of conflict seems to be about. Even the victim of the more powerful tyrant is seeking the moral victory of the self-righteous wronged one. What we saw in the case of Jonathon and May was a more overtly conflicted expression of the power struggle. Let's have a closer look at what was going on below the surface.

Jonathon and May

When first married, Jonathon assumed that everything was in order. He was a responsible husband working hard to provide for his family, which he loved. One aspect of self he had learnt in his childhood experience was that by working hard and achieving results he could win the favour and approval of his caregivers. To him, getting on with his projects and achieving results equalled feelings of satisfaction in others. He was unable to relate to May's feelings of hurt and anger in response to his instinct for hard work. Rather, what he anticipated and really looked for – in fact, what he expected from the one who he believed loved him most in the world – was appreciation and approval of his successful attempts at achieving results. Not receiving this brought on feelings of insecurity, an unpleasant, long-forgotten territory to him. Further, Jonathan's mother had been over-protective of him, and as he grew into his adolescence he had developed a minimizing reflex of withdrawal to protect his sense of self from outside and unwanted intrusions. If he was not criticized or cross-examined in his behaviour, he could get along well and stay in connection. However, if May criticized him and got at him about things he did or didn't do, this echoed the fears he had felt as a child of being smothered by his mother, and he would fall back on his good old technique of retreating.

May, on the other hand, had developed a maximizing reflex to struggle and cling for closeness and love with a mother who was over-engaged with housework and the demands of looking after four children. Having to compete and struggle for the attention of her parents, she developed ways and means of pursuing them and drawing attention to herself. To her, full attention to her existence and her needs equalled feelings of security and being loved and became, in fact, a measure of her own lovability. When she first met Jonathon, she thought she had finally found someone who saw her as special and would take the kind of notice of her which filled an ancient longing. During their courtship he was engrossed in her and she basked in the attention she received, feeling loved and secure. But as he became more occupied by his work and goals she once again found herself scraping for love and attention. Now this familiar feeling of uncertainty was even more painful than before, because she had thought that she had finally found someone she could rely on for love and, to her, his lack of attention meant lack of love. Furthermore, his retreating at the moment of her desperate bid for attention and her absolute vulnerability was an added blow to her feelings of security and being loved.

Tradition

Because this stage is not very rewarding, or downright painful, separation and divorce have become a common way out. But what did the earlier generations do that enabled them to stay together? Divorce rates around the world were very low up to the 1950s. Was there something working then that we should learn about?

We are all, much more than we suspect, influenced by our society. Divorce has become much more acceptable and this opens the door for those who, in the past, may have stayed in marriage because society looked upon such a move in a very critical way. Western societies have, in addition, become much more individualistic. We want more for ourselves – and our selves don't often want the kind of pain or pretence that marriage in the stage of conflict offers. But beyond this, there was the tradition of male dominance and a stricter separation of roles in marriage which 'held things together'. Many still think that, with the higher rate of divorce and the problems which accompany it, we should go back to the more traditional model. But if we look more closely at the dynamics of the traditional model, we see that something important was missing. Keeping to rigid roles is a way of denial, a way of keeping us from becoming more of what we can be. Equality, we shall see, brings us into a new realm, while keeping to traditional roles locks us in and holds us back from moving into a more mature, more fulfilling way of being and relating. Men, quite understandably, are much more comfortable with traditional roles. In the first place, these were the roles of fathers and that is what sons picked up on. Beyond this, having the power associated with the man being head of the household often enabled men to avoid looking within, exploring their vulnerabilities, admitting their frailties.

Under the guise of being in control, much that is true and valuable is kept below the surface. This is basically an immature, fear-driven posture. Society is breaking away from this posture and although we are experiencing all kinds of confusion and break-up because we haven't yet found our way through, there is no real way to go back. The troubles we are experiencing with the new world standard of equality is growth trying to happen.

The traditional, more authoritarian, conception of marriage was a less mature structure. We did not fully grow up with it even when it seemed to work quite well. That is why we fall into childlike power struggles when we come face to face with our partner in marriage. With the new standard of equality our immaturity is brought into stark relief, pointing out to us shortcomings that previously we could afford to ignore, as 'Abdu'l-Bahá explains:

> The world in the past has been ruled by force, and man has dominated over woman by reason of his more forceful and aggressive qualities both of body and mind. But the balance is already shifting; force is losing its dominance, and mental alertness, intuition, and the spiritual qualities of love and service, in which woman is strong, are gaining ascendancy. Hence the new age will be an age less masculine and more permeated with the feminine ideals, or, to speak more exactly, will be an age in which the masculine and feminine elements of civilization will be more evenly balanced.

Interestingly, up to the 1960s when the traditional model was still held to by most couples, divorces (a relatively low number) were almost always instigated by husbands. In the transition years of the 70s and 80s this shifted, until by the 90s divorce rates had grown to their present level and most were being instigated by women. This paints a picture of marriage where the rules have changed. Equality requires relating, something women have long been strong in but which men tend to avoid. It may be that men are often reluctant or slower to make the shift to a culture where masculine and feminine traits are in better balance, leaving women feeling frustrated and confused. It may also be that women lack the patience and care needed to bring males more gently and inclusively into this new reality, leaving men feeling weak, shut out or incapable.

This may seem like a very negative picture, one where we seem doomed to go around in circles, repeating a cycle of experiencing pain from unconscious sources and acting out in childish ways or, like the proverbial ostrich, sticking our head in the sand as though nothing were wrong – also a very childish stance.

• • • • • • • • • •

Almost no one is foolish enough to imagine that he automatically deserves great success in any field of activity; yet almost everyone believes that he automatically deserves success in marriage.

Attributed to Sydney J. Harris

• • • • • • • • • •

But what we are experiencing in our marriages is actually an unprecedented opportunity to grow up. Since this is happening on a world-wide scale, we can see that if we collectively start to learn the lessons that marriage has to teach us, we can move into the long-awaited stage of maturity of which, according to the Bahá'í writings, we are on the verge. Beyond this, we can start to bring up our children with fewer wounds and a more mature outlook as well. This may be a fundamental step towards rearing the 'new race of men' also referred to in the Bahá'í writings. This might be part of what Shoghi Effendi meant when he said to Bahá'ís that, in this period of transition, we are the 'generation of the half-light'.

• • • • • • • • • •

After all these years, I see that I was mistaken about Eve in the beginning;
it is better to live outside the Garden with her than inside it without her.

Mark Twain

• • • • • • • • • •

Establishing a new pattern

· · · · · · · · · ·

Marriage is our last, best chance to grow up.
Attributed to Joseph Barth

· · · · · · · · · ·

As we look at the momentous role that marriage is to play in the establishment of a new world order, we need to take a serious look at how to get marriage off to a solid start. Being now awake to the transitory nature of the romantic phase of love, let us proceed mindfully to take the first steps in protecting the sacred bond of marriage so that the promise of growth which is inherent to the marital relationship can be realized. This calls for coming together consciously and, in a sense, drawing a circle around ourselves which demarks the sanctity of couplehood. This first step is discussed in the next chapter.

PART II

ESTABLISHING CONSCIOUS PARTNERSHIP

4

Boundaries

When a couple marries a new entity comes into being – the marriage itself. This is the 'we' of couplehood. The marriage ceremony, usually in the presence of family, relatives and friends – and most significantly, God – is the signal event making it clear to all that this is a couple now, around which a sacred circle has been drawn or, to use Bahá'u'lláh's image: 'a fortress for well-being and salvation' has been built.

The ceremony and all it signifies is, however, just the beginning. The nature of the circle drawn around the couple is not yet clarified. The lives of the husband and the wife have, up to this point, been all about the emergence and expression of the individual self. These individuals may have had dreams about marriage and who their partner would be, but until the point of finding that partner the world was a field of possibilities, of potential partners. Since reaching adulthood each of them has been, in the eyes of the world, an available single, probably in search of the most suitable other who was also available. Getting married is a massive shift from being available to being unavailable, at least in terms of being a possible mate to anyone other than the one to whom we are married.

How do the two individuals involved make this shift from being single to being married, one of a pair? In the past, much of what constituted the boundary around a married couple was outlined by society itself. Sometimes the boundary of marriage was more akin to an impenetrable barrier, open only to close family members or other members of one's sex. In some cultures those who are married wear special clothes, ornaments or colours, or the husband grows his beard, to signify that they are no longer single and available. The wearing of a special ring serves the same purpose in many cultures. Language is used with special forms of pronouns or terms to honour this difference.

As countries around the world are in varying degrees of making the shift to including females as equal participants in the workings of society, these signs of the marital boundaries have often become diffuse. Most societies have let go of many of the traditions, practices and laws which surrounded the married couple in their relationship to others in society. Men and women interact closely in society, both before marriage and after. In time, as our societies move out of their present adolescent and experimental stage, it is likely that society will do more to clarify the nature of the marital boundary in a world which honours the equality of the sexes. At present, it devolves mostly on the pair themselves to determine the nature of the boundary and the practice of maintaining it.

• • • • • • • • • •

*The current of the world has its boundaries, otherwise it could have no existence,
but its purpose is not shown in the boundaries which restrain it,
but in its movement, which is towards perfection.*
Rabindranath Tagore

• • • • • • • • • •

The shift from being single to being one of a pair – except during the romantic phase – is neither automatic nor easy. What is required is the conscious creation of a new boundary around the two, along with a reexamination of the ego barriers of each partner. But it can help to remember that boundaries are not a new invention and that life itself would not exist without them. Biologists tell us that life began with the formation of the first cells. The earth had long had all the elements needed for life to begin, but their existence was too diffuse and scattered for the complex chemical reactions that make up life to take place. Not until the needed molecules were able to contain themselves in a small sac – a boundary – could life begin. How this happened is still something of a mystery to evolutionary biologists. They believe that it occurred on the shores of the primordial ocean, that is, on another boundary: the place where land and sea meet. Nature provides us with the profound metaphor that developmental leaps occur at boundaries and that growth takes place within them.

Once cell walls were developed, life began. The amazing complexity of single-cell activity is still being uncovered. It has long been known that cell walls are permeable, meaning that molecules can get in and out, but the circumstances for these exchanges are not at all simple. In fact, these workings of the cell membrane are so complex that some biologists are now asserting that the 'brain' of the cell, long thought to be its nucleus, is actually the cell wall.

Marriage is analogous to the coming together of a sperm and an egg cell to form the fertilized zygote. Two single entities come together to form a third, more complex, entity, ripe with new potential for differentiation and reproduction. In marriage, as in the cell, all kinds of new activities and interactions take place which are crucial for its potential to become realized. Both the cell and a healthy marriage have a permeable boundary, in contact with the environment around it but careful about the nature of the contact, of what comes in and out, and when. A significant difference in marriage is that the decision regarding the boundaries needs to be made consciously, and the first principle in this development of consciousness is that the relationship between the husband and the wife is now the primary one. All other relationships are viewed from the perspective of the marital relationship. Let us look at this further to see how it works in practice.

The centrality and primacy of the couple

· · · · · · · · · ·

I draw circles and sacred boundaries about me;
fewer and fewer climb with me
up higher and higher mountains –
I am building a mountain chain
out of ever-holier mountains.

Friedrich Nietzsche

· · · · · · · · · ·

The Bahá'í writings state that marriage is sacred. We have pointed out that in this transitional, adolescent stage of collective human development the marital boundary no longer has a clear social definition. This means that certain forces and elements from without are ready to 'invade' the parameters of this sacred institution. These forces can be very subtle and compelling; sometimes conscious, sometimes unconscious; sometimes external, sometimes internalized. Let us have a look at some of the more crucial relationships that, if not handled in a way that is conducive to the growth of family life, can compete with the primacy of the marital relationship. These are: other relationships with the opposite sex; relationships with children, parents and extended family; relationship to work; relationship to self and God. Ultimately, the nature of all of these relationships will have to be discussed and decided upon by the couple themselves. Let us take them one by one.

The primacy of the couple in relations with the opposite sex

What kind of intercourse is acceptable between a married person and people of the opposite sex? What kinds of specific behaviour, body language, words, invitations, intimations, situations and attitudes constitute the marital boundary? In what ways is the marital boundary open to the world? What are the ways, in relationship to the outside world, that the sanctity of marriage can be protected and preserved? In a healthy marriage, these questions come to be answered through consultation with one's partner. Early on, as the pair venture out into various social occasions, it is likely, given the as yet untamed reflex of being single, that lines will be crossed or perceived to have been crossed. These events will occasion feelings – sometimes powerful feelings – of anxiety, fear, jealousy and danger. These feelings need to be expressed respectfully and received openly and graciously, a process we will explore in greater detail in the next chapter. Without a respectful approach, conflict or distancing is the inevitable result.

Jonathon and May

May and Jonathon had been married for less than a year and small frustrations had been building up here and there. They were invited to a New Year's Eve party at the home of one of her friends. He wasn't excited about going because he thought he wouldn't know many people there, and being a shy and quiet person often created problems for him. After a few rounds of argument he gave in and they both set off to the party. Half-way through the evening a young man, apparently an old friend of May's, came up to their table and with much excitement about seeing her after some time, started bantering with her, and she back with him, each showing signs of fond familiarity. Putting his hand on her back and at times on her shoulder, he continued to talk to her in a flirtatious manner. Jonathon, sitting across from her, felt more and more uncomfortable; simmering quietly in his anger he retreated into his own world. Eventually filling with resentment, Jonathon started to make a move, catching May's attention to signal that he wanted to go home. Much to her disappointment about leaving before midnight and all the anticipated excitement, May grudgingly consented and, amidst the complaints of others, they finally took their leave. It didn't take long before they were deep in a fight. She felt deeply distressed, accusing him of having ruined a wonderful evening where she could have finally enjoyed seeing her old friends, and doubting that she would ever be able to have a good time with her husband at social events. He, on the other hand, was over-reacting about her behaviour with this young man and asking all kinds of questions about their past history and other particulars concerning their relationship. The blow of this incident, as insignificant as it might seem, took its toll on their relationship and set a pattern of chronic conflict around socializing outside the home.

Most jealousy issues can be prevented by creating healthy boundaries, something that Jonathon and May had not yet accomplished. Let's play back this scenario and see how consciousness of boundary issues could have prevented the unfortunate outcome. In this case, the 'intruder', who had evidently continued his interest in May and was excited to see her again, didn't know much about Jonathon and didn't know that May had got married since their earlier encounter. Instead of falling into the exchange of banter with him, May could have actively interrupted and introduced Jonathon, sharing the news of their wedding. She could have also cut this old suitor short by deflecting his physical intrusions. Jonathon, his identity as May's husband having been made clear, would more likely have made an effort to be part of the conversation or, if the newcomer was so clued out that he continued to pick up where he had been heading with May, the door would have clearly now been open for Jonathon to assert himself in the exchange. In this way, a boundary would have been created and Jonathon could have felt that he and May were safely perceived as a married couple. Handled in this way, they would have felt even closer and more secure as a couple and Jonathon would have been much more willing to stretch himself into this social occasion and to be open to going out more often.

When a couple is married and the boundary of marriage is securely maintained, they give off an aura of being married even when they are apart. The aura of couplehood comes from a consciousness of being married, and this can be kept in place even on occasions when there are as yet unrepaired ruptures in the relationship. It is, of course, important to deal with such ruptures as soon as possible, but even if we are carrying a lot of resentment or anger towards our spouse, we can still remember our responsibility towards the marriage. Maintaining the aura of couplehood can prevent most intrusions.

Good fences make good neighbours

As suggested earlier, the boundary of marriage is not a barrier. Securely attached couples do not close themselves off from the world. Rather, the trust they have in each other and the security of the boundary serve to enable them to be ever more open and loving to other people. In fact, it is very important for couples to open their home to guests and engage in social occasions, associating with a variety of people. It is also important to foster individual friendships, which can be very close ones. How this is achieved starts by honouring the primacy of the marital relationship over all other relationships. Our spouse is probably the best judge of how accomplished we are at this. When this is earnestly taken care of, one can safely venture further with other relationships, always returning to this most important one for feedback on how our outward relating is going or is perceived. This doesn't mean that one spouse lords it over the other. Rather, loving, open, receptive dialogue, where the feelings of each are honoured and brought forward, eventuate in new and greater understandings on how to be in the world as a married person in relationship to others.

· · · · · · · · · ·

I broke up with my husband.
He moved in with another woman.
I draw the line at that.

Anonymous

· · · · · · · · · ·

It needs to be stressed, however, that in these dialogues each partner needs to become aware of his or her true sensitivities and to bring them forward candidly. We are emphasizing this because, in these times, most people have learned that they should be liberal and tolerant about who their partner relates to and how they do it. Thus, even though something may be telling them that they are not comfortable with their partner's flirting, for example, they silence that voice with the largely widespread view that flirting is okay and we shouldn't interfere with our partner or be domineering. Rather, the voice that we should be silencing is the voice of society, as it is largely misguided or without any clear vision about the importance of marriage and the principle of chastity. While we should not be domineering or interfering, our sensitivities need to be voiced in honest and safe consultation, just as we should earnestly listen to the voice of our partner and do our best to enter into his or her reality. Our partner's point of view can help us to step out of a hardened sense of self and entitlement which often arises out of past habits or behaviour. These processes bring forward new understandings which become the property, in a sense, of the marriage. Holding back on either expressing oneself or listening deprives the relationship of crucially important insights. Being open and respectful in this way, we constantly refresh or update our socializing map.

· · · · · · · · · ·

It's a slippery slope, Carrie.
Without boundaries you never know what might happen.
Sex and the City

· · · · · · · · · ·

Through this ongoing process, we grow in our understanding of what constitutes chastity in the context of being married, or any steps that might contravene the marital boundary and thus lead to unchaste behaviour or thoughts.

Case study

Michael and Sara met 10 years ago and fell in love. It was love at first sight. They were both very responsible, committed and regular churchgoers. It didn't take them long to decide to get married. Even though they had differences and conflicts at times, their marriage on average was a happy one. In the first five years they both worked full time and enjoyed the benefits of couplehood and their relative freedom. In the sixth year of their marriage they had their first child, followed by the second one in the following year. Sara gave up her job and stayed home to look after the children. Understandably, their life went through a revolution with the coming of the two little ones. The overwhelming work of looking after the children and other chores at home and working extra hours to make more money for the family had made them both exhausted and short-tempered. The time they could have for each other became almost non-existent. Even though Michael loved his wife and the children, at times he found himself preferring to stay longer at work than to come home to chaos and an exhausted wife who was quick to bring up his failings. As Michael became more absent and uninvolved, Sara felt unloved and uncared for, and was therefore not so loving and welcoming as she used to be in the early times. She immersed herself in the care of her little ones who needed her and truly loved and depended on her.

Around this time, one day at work while having a coffee break, Michael was joined by his co-worker Susan. In the past they had occasionally had coffee together, but recently it seemed that their paths were crossing more often. As she sat opposite him, looking into his face she commented that he looked tired and asked if he had had a bad night. Michael told her about the children and how they keep waking up in the middle of night and so on. She showed a lot of sympathy and compassion for him as a father. The next day during coffee, while praising him for his expertise at work she inquired more about his private life, saying that his wife must be happy to have him as a husband. He smiled and paused, but couldn't resist sharing a bit about the difficulties he was having getting any attention from or time with his wife. It felt good to have a beautiful woman like Susan interested in his problems and listening to him. It felt like she understood him completely. The following day they decided to go for lunch instead and he ended up, with her encouragement, sharing more about his frustrations at home, all along receiving undivided attention and sympathy from Susan and internally noting the difference between her and Sara. They could also laugh together, something he had been missing at home and with Sara for a long time. Even though he felt guilty at having these pleasurable encounters, Michael convinced himself that it was just a friendship and that deep in his heart he knew he really loved his wife.

Michael and Susan started to meet regularly and frequently, since they were enjoying each other's company and these talks were a pleasant relief from the many stresses in his life. If she was not around he would feel her absence and look out for her, either on email or by text messaging. But he didn't have to worry too much, because she too had become quite attached and fond of him and sought his company often. One thing led to another; it wasn't long before their relationship had turned into a full-blown affair, all too unbelievable to himself.

It was after a few months into this that Sara found a message on his mobile by accident and was naturally beside herself. She was inconsolable; she couldn't believe that someone as responsible and religious as Michael could do such a thing, especially with her being left at home caring full-time for two challenging toddlers.

Much can be said about this all-too-common type of scenario. For our purposes, let us focus on the boundary contraventions. Michael was understandably unhappy with his marital situation but the first person he should have spoken to about it was Sara. The last person would be a female who was attractive and showing interest. The more troubled a marriage and the more vulnerable or starving we are for affection – or even just kind conversation – the more careful we need to be not to involve ourselves in other relationships that may fulfil our unmet emotional needs. Discussing frustrations we have within our marriage with someone outside the marriage usually constitutes a boundary contravention. If the person is a member of the opposite sex, the exposed weakness of our marital relationship can become a door through which even more intimate conversations may take place, leading into very dangerous territory indeed. This makes people much more vulnerable to the liberal and increasingly unchaste attitudes found in our societies. Even innocent internet connections with someone of the opposite sex that we find interesting (or interested!) in troubled times in marriage can result in devastating consequences.

The vulnerability dimension is, of course, big in this case, but sometimes the marriage can be working better than Michael's and Sara's and still fall prey to infidelity when boundaries are not consciously managed. We should not ignore, however, that in cases such as the above, not addressing the problems they were having as a couple and not making the time and effort to keep the relationship healthy was a huge oversight. It is one thing to protect marital boundaries; it is quite another to do the necessary work within the boundary to keep the relationship healthy. Both are crucial. Thus, having in place clear channels of conversation around these issues is perhaps the greatest aid to warding off affairs – an increasing menace which behaves as an infectious disease running rampant. This important subject is discussed more fully in Chapter 9.

Social media

• • • • • • • • • •

Let there be no secrets one from another.
Attributed to 'Abdu'l-Bahá

• • • • • • • • • •

In present-day society we have at our fingertips a myriad ways of connecting with other people. Also, perhaps born out of the extreme individualism of western society, we have developed a sense of privacy which should not be invaded, even by our spouse. 'Abdu'l-Bahá, however, is reported to have said that married partners should not keep secrets from each other. By implication, doesn't this mean that our communications with others should be open to our partners? This may be surprising to some, but we believe that there should be transparency within the marriage in all areas of our relationships with others. We do not believe that reading our spouse's email messages, text messages, or list of mobile calls need constitute a boundary violation of the individual. A couple can decide to keep all these channels open as a convenient way of keeping up to date with each other in a world where there can be a mind-numbing number of interactions in one day. Openness, and the willingness to share everything possible, strengthens the bond that unites. Except for things that we want to surprise our spouse with, or perhaps state secrets if, for example, we are working in an institution with strict controls on information, what is it that we would want to hide or withhold from our spouse?

Privacy in a marital setting does not mean secrecy. If we are wary about our spouse reading certain of our messages received or sent, it is probably a sign that we have crossed or are about to cross our marital boundary. When we are married, everything we say or do should be something that we would not want to hide from our spouse. When our spouse is not with us, we should still be carrying them with us spiritually, and when we reconnect physically we can be open about what we have been occupied with. The technological record of messages and communications is just a useful extension of this and can be seen as a helpful way of updating details which may have been forgotten. This doesn't mean that there is not an important place for trust in a relationship or that this is about prying into our spouse's activities. In fact, this kind of transparancy can help create a background of comfort and safety which can bring about a level of trust that is impossible to create otherwise.

Old friends and the singles scene

Another thing that we may feel somehow entitled to is our old circle of single friends, male or female. It is quite natural that our relationships with former singles take an abrupt turn once we have married. As stated before, with marriage a new entity is being created. The 'we-ness' of a couple is, in many ways, a new world under construction and quite naturally becomes our focus, just as having a baby does. The task of developing the entity of couplehood more naturally brings us to yearn for contact with other couples with whom we share this new kind of reality, just as having a baby makes it natural to want to share the company of other mothers and fathers. This necessarily tends, to a degree, to a marginalizing of those relationships which may have been very important to us before we crossed into this new territory. It might be hard for some of our single friends to realize this, but other married couples will readily understand it. Because our single friends may not have the awareness of what couplehood involves, we may need to find gentle, educative ways of informing them that things have changed. They need not be offended that we naturally have less time to spend with them. This should not be expressed to them as something required by our spouse. Rather, it is a naturally occurring shift, very much a new stage of life.

Keeping contact with previous single friends can be precious and those friendships are to be valued and maintained. However, there needs to be a shift in setting priorities in spending time and energy. Once again, the degree to which we succeed in making this shift from being single to being one of a pair is often something we can learn from our partner. Couples can often fill in gaps of consciousness for each other if they are really open to it. For these reasons, when our partner has something to say about feeling neglected or being put on the back burner, we should welcome what he or she is saying and take it to heart rather than feeling it as an imposition.

Some examples of boundary violations with the opposite sex include:

- body language signals that show openness, availability, and interest

- talking to members of the opposite sex about difficulties or disappointments in your marriage, or other personal matters

- repeated one-on-one intimate meetings (such as going for coffee or lunch) with a co-worker or friend of the opposite sex

- continued conversations or chats on Facebook, Twitter, MySpace, etc., without the knowledge and approval of our spouse

- jokes or comments with sexual connotations

- feeling and feeding an attraction to someone other than our spouse

- easy familiarity in our bodily interactions with friends of the opposite sex

The primacy of the couple in relation to children

Some would say that the parent–child relationship is more important than the husband–wife relationship. There is no denying the importance of the parent–child relationship and the weighty responsibility of raising children. Modern science weighs in heavily regarding the needs of children to securely attach to parents from infancy and to be affectionately nurtured and educated into young adulthood. The Bahá'í writings also underline the importance of the parent–child relationship.

Let us take the most obvious needs of the human infant to be nurtured and cared for. Without certain minimal care, a human infant will die. Without secure attachment and minimum tutelage, they will not grow up to be emotionally healthy.

Doesn't this mean that the needs of the infant, especially for maternal nurturing, take precedence over all other relationships, marriage included?

Our answer to this is that the birth of an infant does indeed tend to shift the focus away from a married couple's attention to each other. The mother, especially, has strong instinctive compulsions to nurse and nurture her baby. Most significantly, she needs the support and protection of her husband to be able to contentedly manage this huge new responsibility. In many ways, the infant takes centre stage; even in societies where extended family bonds are not strong, grandparents are sometimes invited into the family circle to share their experience and even to share the load of child-rearing. But in all this, the healthy functioning of the husband–wife relationship remains paramount, even though it is likely to be severely tested.

With the birth of a baby, the roles of husband and wife usually tend to revert somewhat back to the more traditional model. This shift makes it even more important to consider certain crucial factors of the husband and wife bond. Husband and wife are still equal, so that while the mother, as first educator, plays a more significant role as nurturer at the beginning, their functioning as equal partners still requires plenty of decision-making without outside interference or blanket presumptions of who does what. Furthermore, because one of the central purposes of marriage – that of procreation – comes into clearer focus with a baby's birth, so does the importance of harmony between husband and wife. If this relationship ceases to function well, the foundation of the whole edifice of support for the children starts to shake and all the family relationships are adversely affected.

If the wife feels a lack of support or responsibility from her husband, her unhappiness can affect the flow of her milk from her breasts. This is how directly the husband–wife relationship affects the infant. If the husband has not come to terms with the shift of his wife's focus to the infant, his feelings will sour and this will again affect his wife, and the reverberations will flow to the infant. Breaches in the husband–wife relationship will call forth help from others, often from relatives. This can degenerate into interference which will eventually exacerbate the whole touchy scene.

As the child grows, the tendency to sacrifice the spousal relationship for the parent–child relationship may become more subtle. First of all, this kind of sacrificing is, to some degree, almost inevitably necessary. The demands of raising children are huge, and they go on for years. Children take a lot of care and attention and the spousal relationship has to make shift for this to be done. Having said this, the primacy of the marital bond still holds. The needed shift for the sake of the children should be made consciously and in consultation with each other, and the feelings of both partners should be reexamined regularly.

The bond of attachment between husband and wife is in some ways very similar to the bond between parent and child. We have a primal yearning for this kind of attachment which includes giving and receiving love and affection. When struggles in the marital relationship arise – and these struggles can be set off by the attentions required by children – there is the already discussed tendency to create distance or move into conflict. When this kind of rupture in the marital relationship occurs, there is a strong tendency to move into closer relationship with the children to get our attachment needs met. Looked at from the outside, this is a subtle shift which is hard to argue against. Children need attention, we may tell ourselves. In fact, what the children need more is to feel secure in mother's and father's love for each other. The extra attention a child receives because of the attachment needs of a parent can be experienced as a burden rather than a boon.

Examples of boundary violations with children include:

- making major decisions concerning the children without prior consultation with our spouse

- talking about our partner in front of the children in any way which is not respectful, whether he/she is present or not

- giving in to demands of a child without consulting with our spouse

- deciding to spend family money on children without consultation with our spouse

- listening (and perhaps, empathizing) with a child about grievances concerning the other parent, belittling or speaking disrespectfully of them

- disagreeing on a disciplinary issue with our spouse in front of the children

- unilaterally spending extra time and energy with children which would otherwise be time for the couple together

The primacy of the couple in relation to parents

Clarifying the marital boundary with respect to extended families can be more challenging and delicate than establishing it in relation to members of the opposite sex. Culture and religious beliefs can be confounding factors here. Some societies still have extended families living together with established hierarchies that don't put the married couple in the centre. Here again, there may be some who think that the parent–child relationship is more important than that between a husband and wife. Let's have a look.

The parent–child bond is our original source of attachment. It is special and enduring: even if our relationship with a parent turns acrimonious or distant, the parent still lives within us. Even in cases where one or both parents are completely absent from a child's upbringing, their very absence lives, in some form, within the child's narrative and psyche. A parent's importance to us is ongoing, it goes deep, and it needs to be honoured. The husband and wife each have a mother and father, and all the major religions underline the importance of honouring these relationships. It is, in fact, one of the responsibilities of marriage, to take care of these most significant of extended family ties.

• • • • • • • • • •

One of my greatest lessons from Mom was the time I told her, as a boy in my mid-teens, that even after I got married one day, she'd always be my favorite girl. Immediately – in a kind but definitely serious manner – she said, 'No, I won't be. When you get married your wife will be the most important person in your life, and that includes Daddy and me.' The biggest lesson about love and marriage that my mom and dad taught us kids was on how to talk 'about' your spouse. Have you ever heard husbands and wives, when speaking to others, make unkind remarks about their spouses? It's one of those things people just seem to do. Sure, they're 'only kidding', or maybe they are not. But words matter. And words teach, whether positively and negatively.

Bob Burg

• • • • • • • • • •

But to repeat, when we get married a new entity is born – the marital bond. This doesn't end other relationships, but the bond between husband and wife becomes central. Keeping contact with parents and caring for them, extending hospitality to other family members, visiting relatives – all these forms of relating emanate from the relationship between husband and wife, who discuss all they need to about how to attend to these other relationships and their relative priorities. This is the reason the husband–wife connection is primary and needs to be attended to above all other relationships. When love and understanding exist between the married couple, other relationships benefit from the very best wisdom that two intimately bonded souls can bring to bear.

We all come into a marriage with some kind of relationship to our parents. Often these relationships are at the front of our minds. Sometimes they weigh on our minds. Often there is a lack of resolution in these relationships, or a lack of awareness about unhealthy aspects they may have. Marriage can become a healthy means of resolving these issues. The point of view of a newcomer on the scene can provide us with the perspective we need to make changes in our relationships and behaviours with our parents. The inputs of a spouse about an unhealthy pattern of relationship or overriding influence of a parent is something to be listened to, but once again this needs to be talked through in a respectful, caring way. If this is done, we stand to gain greater clarity on what changes we need to make regarding how we think about our parents or how we behave towards them. This is delicate work, and while doing it we need to remain open to our partner's feedback through empathetic listening, awake to our partner's sensitivities when expressing ourselves.

An added element involving parents involves their satisfaction – or lack of it – with the choice of spouse their son or daughter has made. It is often hard for parents to see their own child with clear sight and, added to this, there is a tendency to regard other people's parenting as somehow faulty. The Bahá'í requirement that the parents' consent to the marriage be obtained prior to the wedding helps to bring a conscious closure to this kind of prejudiced attachment, but even with consent being given there is no guarantee that this common tendency will come to an end.

The whole idea of consent is filled with wisdom. This is

the last step in the parents letting go. They are not to interfere with the choice of partner, but their consent is needed for the marriage to go ahead. This is a great responsibility for parents, perhaps their last major official role in 'looking after' their child. Once consent is given, it is time to whole-heartedly support and encourage this most significant union by giving it full trust and the loving space to grow. But just as newly-weds are challenged with their new role in life of being no longer single and available, so parents are often challenged with having to let go of the power they have wielded as parents. They may be inclined to judge their child's partner and interfere in the affairs of the new couple. They may also not feel confident in their own child and continue to treat him or her as a child. In face of all these kinds of unfinished business, it becomes part of the married couple's duty to clarify the boundary.

Case study

Alexio and Roseanne found each other, fell in love and started thinking seriously about getting married. Alexio's parents are from Greece and he sensed that it was going to be hard to get his parents to agree to the marriage. Indeed he was right, and the couple went through a long year of drama and difficulty trying to win his parents over. They feared that Roseanne wanted to marry Alexio because of the money the family had. She hadn't been brought up in their culture or religion, so they perhaps doubted the depth of their daughter-in-law's spirituality, even though she had converted to the Ortho-dox Church. During this time, Roseanne endured a lot of humiliation. The road was rocky for them through this whole period, but after pressure from other family members the par-ents finally, but reluctantly, agreed to the marriage.

Alexio's parents, with all their children now out of the home, had come to have difficulties in their own marriage.

Actually, the problems had always been there, but while the children were at home their needs deflected the couple from looking at what wasn't working between them. Alexio's parents' marriage problems now became yet another worry for him, and he made frequent trips 'back home' to try to help. During these trips, his parents constantly criticized many of his decisions, especially the ones they believed had come from Roseanne. The parents were willing to support them financially to find a house of their own, but their choice of residence was in opposition to what Roseanne was looking for.

After a time, feeling indirectly humiliated and criticized, Roseanne refused to join Alexio on his trips to his parents. This in itself became an issue. Alexio tried to continue visits on his own for a while, but every time he returned, the pressure his parents had put on him and the resentments of Roseanne led to heated arguments and conflicts. This affected other aspects of their relationship. Their marriage was in serious crisis.

Alexio's concerns for his parents were, of course, real and heartfelt. He felt a need to be close to them to help them feel less lonely. But what we have here is a mix of unclarified boundary issues which left Alexio very little energy to nurture and examine his own struggling relationship with Roseanne. She, of course, felt neglected, unloved, and unsure of her position in the whole picture. Alexio, in the meantime, was triangulated between his wife and his parents, and also between his mother and father. In fact, this psychological map of triangles had probably existed for much of his childhood. Now these troubles with his parents were adulterating his own marriage because he had not learned to draw a clear boundary around it. He had not internalized the fact that 'home', now, was not his childhood residence but with his wife, however humble in comparison.

The first thing that Alexio needed to do in this situation was to really listen to Roseanne's concerns and disappointments, and this was not easy to do because Alexio had a reflex of defending his parents. He also tended to receive criticisms of them as criticisms of himself personally. Roseanne needed to learn how to honestly convey her feelings without attacking or criticizing. Both sides of this communication challenge may seem insurmountable; but in fact surmounting it is very possible. How this is done is described in the next chapter.

Once Alexio was able to really understand where Roseanne was coming from, he needed to take steps to change the pattern of his functioning with his parents. Here, he had to learn how to draw a clear boundary without attacking them or giving offence. This does not mean that the parents or other family members were going to take even the most loving and respectful approach with easy acceptance. People can take offence even when none is intended and words are carefully chosen. Changes in entrenched patterns of the family of origin can bring a strong backlash. Alexio needed to step out of being pulled between his parents and his wife. He had to be assertive in a loving way, to make clear that he and his wife were together as a unit and that decisions regarding their home and work were their own. It was a new concept for his parents to come to terms with, but once this step was taken Alexio found the weight of their censure lessen. His role became clearer, both to himself and his parents, and therefore more manageable. Roseanne felt his presence more as a husband, and became a lot lighter and more loving toward him as well as towards his parents. This helped Alexio feel even more confident. With the added strength given to their couplehood, practical issues became more manageable. In time, even the attitude of the parents to all this changed and the relationship between all family members improved.

With respect to parents, it is interesting that one of the psychological purposes of marriage is to complete our childhood and heal our wounds from the growing-up process. We can never forget our parents, but there is almost always some needed finishing work which we are unconscious of and which is bound to surface in the marital relationship. The unconscious childhood wounds not only affect our relationship with our parents; they also affect our relationship with our partner. Effectively, we finish our growing up by dealing with the conflicts and difficulties in our marriage. In this maturing process we differentiate, become more our own true self. We become more present to our spouse and more capable of seeing our parents in a clearer, empathetic way and of discharging our responsibilities appropriately.

The crucial need for couples to resolve issues which emerge in their relationship will be enlarged on in the rest of this book. For now, it is enough just to realize that the resultant maturation enables us to create a new, healthier narrative concerning our childhood. When we are children we tend to see our parents almost as gods, both in their good and negative aspects. When we grow up fully – and this usually has to happen in marriage – then we see more clearly and consciously who our parents were, what they were dealing with; we imagine, and can understand with compassion, their own past. This is a liberating process. It helps us to get unstuck from fused relationships, confused feelings, blaming, resentment, anger and a whole lot of other baggage we may carry from our childhood. We become less defensive with our parents, more centred, more able to care and help them without being shamed into it or acting from feelings of guilt. We clarify our boundaries at the outset so that this important work can get done. We 'find ourselves', and in so doing we increase our capacity to relate to our parents in a healthy way.

Examples of boundary violations with parents include:

- talking about our partner in any way which is not respectful or favourable, whether he/she is present or not

- listening to complaints or criticism from a family member about our spouse (backbiting) without asserting the rights of our spouse or defending him or her

- accepting and acting on advice from parents without consulting our spouse

- deciding to spend family money on relatives or parents without consultation with our spouse

- being neglectful or careless of the respect and love due to the parents

- unilaterally spending extra time and energy with parents which would otherwise be time for the couple together

The primacy of the couple in relation to work

Work is another spiritual principle with practical implications that can be hard to argue with. We need to provide for our family. Beyond this, our identity, our sense of self, may be tied up with our work. Another huge player in creating the image that work should take precedence over our marital relationship is often the mentality of employers. Moreover, the power of the workplace to dictate its own primacy is often tacitly supported by society. The wheels of the economy must be kept in motion, we must remain competitive, we must be productive. A married couple may appear to be small stuff in comparison to all this. But we should wake up to the fact that most of this is just a manifestation of a bloated materialistic attitude, a collective escape from our spiritual and human essence.

According to the Bahá'í teachings, work in an attitude of service is considered an act of worship, but even the spiritual accord given to this kind of work does not give it legitimacy to intrude or undermine the attention and care needed to maintain a healthy marital relationship and family. In fact, a healthy relationship between the wife and husband can become a source of energy and inspiration in pursuing one's talents and career.

On the other hand, when there is an undercurrent of dissatisfaction in the marriage many people turn to work as an escape. We may love our job, give it our all, get commendation for our efforts and talents, and if this is in contrast to how we feel in our marriage we will likely be pulled into it all the more. As with raising children, sacrifice may be required to work long hours for various legitimate reasons when you really want to be together with your spouse, but the decision about this kind of sacrifice should be consciously made by both the husband and the wife in a united way, not unilaterally.

Another issue relating to boundaries is that of workplace parties which do not include spouses. These create a whole other type of venue for relating which would be far more beneficial to families if they were inclusive. Having parties which include spouses could become a means of reinforcing family ties rather than often undermining them. A corollary of this is that spouses should take advantage of these occasions and make extra effort to attend the more inclusive, family-supportive type of office party. Until companies and employers wake up to the need to support marriages in this way, and become more family-oriented in their decisions, we ourselves need to be awake to this need and voice our views to bring about change.

Examples of boundary violations regarding work include:

- taking on more responsibility at work, especially if it takes us away from productive home time, without open consultation with our spouse

- taking on or quitting jobs without prior consultation with our spouse

- feeling entitled to pursue our career at all costs without consultation and agreement of our spouse

- making a decision about whose job or profession is to be put first and given priority without consultation

- getting into investments and taking financial risks without our spouse's knowledge or approval

Personal boundaries

We come into marriage with our own personal boundaries as well as our own relationship (conscious or not) with God. These will have had various degrees of development and will continue to evolve as we move on in life. But what effect do these boundaries have on marriage, and vice versa? What is the relationship of our personal boundaries with the boundary of marriage? Let us start with our personal relationship to God.

God

· · · · · · · · · ·

He hath let loose the two seas, that they meet each other:
Between them is a barrier which they overpass not.

The Qur'án

· · · · · · · · · ·

One of the ways we have come to understand the 'barrier' in the above quotation is that, no matter how intimate this meeting of two seas coming together is, our relationship as an individual to God remains our personal choice and responsibility. As Bahá'u'lláh has counselled (emphasis ours):

For every one of you his **paramount** duty is to choose for himself that on which no other may infringe and none usurp from him. Such a thing – and to this the Almighty is My witness – is the love of God, could ye but perceive it.

Thus, as sacred as marriage is, it cannot be allowed to infringe upon our love for God. Our relationship to God is, indeed, our primary one, and our connection to our Creative Source is our personal responsibility. We are also reminded in the Bahá'í writings that once we come of age, no one – and this includes our parents and our spouse, a political regime or legislature – has the right to keep us from being a believer. Very clearly, our faith, our internal and conscious intention to live under the care and loving guidance of our Creative Source, is our sovereign ground as individuals.

A primary function of marriage should therefore be to further enable the individuals, now acting as a unit, to serve the Will of God. Keeping this purpose alive in a couple's life will help to orient them in times of hardship and guide them in making important decisions throughout their lives.

In response to the love of God, and as a consequence of our faith, we are naturally moved to act and serve the Cause that is so intrinsically important to us. But how we bring this into the society and the world may need to be adjusted according to prevailing circumstances – practical, political, or social – and here we can talk more explicitly about marriage.

Yearning to serve our Creator is an expression of our higher self and this should not be polluted by discord and dissension with our spouse, especially in this age where unity is explicitly the intention of God. Coming to terms with earthly responsibilities is part of our spiritual path and when, in our marriage, we are seeking to promote the spiritual growth of each other, consulting together and achieving unity, the combination of our individual spiritual intentions with the enriching bond of couplehood will bring even greater results.

Shoghi Effendi has clarified that 'the home is an institution that Bahá'u'lláh has come to strengthen and not to weaken'. He further counsels couples to find a balance between serving the Cause of God and their duties to family. The Universal House of Justice makes the connection between family and service even clearer: '. . . every aspect of a person's life is an element of service to Bahá'u'lláh' and this includes 'one's marriage and the bringing up of one's children'.

Here again, it seems that the bond of the marital relationship is instrumental in enabling us to achieve our goal of serving God and humanity. The golden rule of consultation is of paramount importance here too. In making a decision about when to defer to family responsibilities and when sacrifices are required, both wife and husband must be involved. Sacrifices of time spent with family, or of the material resources of the family, will often need to be made, but unity in deciding this is, in our view, the key. Sometimes, in some particular circumstances, a spouse is put in a position where her or his direct service to the Faith is clearly indicated, which may entail an unusual amount of time away from the family. In such cases, it is a family sacrifice that is consciously made.

Examples of boundary violations involving religion or a personal spiritual orientation include:

- spending time, accepting positions or volunteering for service without prior agreement or consultation with our spouse

- donating to religious funds without prior agreement or consultation

- undertaking spiritual discipline at times when involvement in family may be more important

The self

· · · · · · · · · ·

You can never be happily married to another until you get a divorce from yourself. Successful marriage demands a certain death to self.

Attributed to Jerry McCant

· · · · · · · · · ·

Having discussed the challenge that even our higher self faces when we enter into matrimony, what about manifestations of our lower self – the survival strategies and identities we formed when we were younger? We have already described the development of a sense of self and the emergence of ego barriers in the process of growing up. We take this sense of self and these ego barriers into marriage and – except for the stage of romance where self-sacrifice can easily occur – often feel that these are sacrosanct. When it becomes apparent that what our spouse wants is for us to change something that is just 'me', we tend to dig our heels in, rebel, or mourn our incapacities.

Part of our work with couples invariably involves instances where requests for changes in behaviour are brought forward. There is, initially, always a resistance to change. This resistance is at times quite unconscious. The behaviour we are used to is an action which in the past, under difficult conditions, helped us to survive. We have come to identify this kind of behaviour with who we are. No wonder there is a resistance to change. On some level, when we are asked to change these behaviours, we actually feel as though we are going to die (even if our higher cognitive processes understand that we won't).

Psychological literature, in underlining the importance of accepting someone as they are, has sometimes been a source of confusion that creates a barrier to change and personal growth. In recent research carried out in the United States, a significant number of people defined romantic love as when someone accepts and loves us as who we are and that we don't need to change. This is certainly an ego-based romantic notion and it appears to have taken hold. This attitude manifests itself in expressions we hear quite often: 'If you love me you should accept me as I am.' 'If you want to change me then you do not really love me.' 'You want me to be someone I am not.'

· · · · · · · · · ·

You must ever press forward, never standing still;
avoid stagnation, the first step to a backward movement, to
decay.

'Abdu'l-Bahá

· · · · · · · · · ·

These kinds of statements are often emanations of the insistent ego at work and lack of consciousness of **who** we really are and can **become**. Life is all about change. Growth, a sign of life, cannot occur without change. As 'Abdu'l-Bahá said, if we are not progressing we are going backwards. Nothing in life is static. Probably no human relationship requires of us as much change as the relationship of marriage and, therefore, usually no relationship can be as enriching as marriage.

'Abdu'l-Bahá says that the wife and husband must enrich the spiritual life of each other. Enriching involves growth and growth involves change. John Gottman's research into happy marriages showed that one key element in their success was that the partners allowed themselves to be influenced by their spouse. The attitude of being open to change is crucial for the magic of marriage to work. Marriage's healing influence can liberate us from the ego identities we unconsciously developed as we grew up.

In a healthy marital relationship we provide for each other the feedback, space, encouragement and support that is needed for our individual growth. What feeds into this process is the attitude of openness to listening to our partner's requests for change without becoming defensive and, on the other hand, wise and loving ways of expressing our requests and the patience and empathy required for behavioural changes to occur. Criticism is almost sure to trigger resistance. This is where the psychological adage of acceptance really helps. This does not mean that we unconditionally accept all that our partner is. It does mean that we need to fully accept in our partner his or her individual processes of change and growth.

Our true self – our soul – yearns for growth and will often, even unconsciously, work to create troubled circumstances so that its higher qualities can be called forth and brought to light! Marriage is one place where these unconscious forces for growth are hard at work. Thus, even our sense of who we are is 'on the block' in marriage. When the marital relationship holds a central place in our life and we are able to question things about ourselves in a way that has not occurred before, then the psychological fruit of marriage, our authentic self, can grow and ripen.

Boundary violations involving the self include:

- thoughts involving our sense of self and the feelings of entitlement to go on being the way we have been

- the myriad of behaviours that can honestly be defined as 'escape behaviours', as will be explained in Chapter 6 on commitment

Creating clear boundaries around the couple as a unit is indispensable to the health, functioning, growth and happiness of relationships both within the home and in the outside world. It is, however, not enough to build a fortress; we must learn to make it a place of well-being. This leads us to one final note on boundaries before moving on.

The boundaries within the unit, between the couple

Another interpretation of the phrase 'a barrier which they over-pass not' quoted by 'Abdu'l-Bahá in the prayer for marriage could be that each partner in the marriage is an individual in his or her own right, and that there still remains a boundary around each individual self which needs to be honoured and respected. Having respect for each other outwardly as well as inwardly is a vital, subtle and often underestimated aspect of a healthy relationship. These are the boundaries that denote the sanctity and nobility of each partner in this most intimate of relationships.

The intimacy, familiarity and presumption of oneness in marriage can often conspire to work against a sensitive and respectful orientation towards one's partner. This is usually a bigger challenge in marriage than in other relationships. It takes vigilance to remain conscious within the intimate sphere of marriage, especially in times of frustration or conflict. When emotions run high, the risk of crossing these lines of propriety increases. Once the lines are crossed, it becomes easier to cross them again, and this can easily result in a pattern that progressively becomes more intense and hurtful.

That there may be strong differences of opinion, difficult issues or hurt feelings is quite probable, but to resort to acts of physical or verbal abuse must by all means be avoided and considered as unacceptable in a healthy relationship. Our moral awareness may well keep us from moving into physical abuse but still allow for hurtful language to creep into our encounters. This can perhaps do as much harm to our souls, emotions and relationship as physical abuse. The effects can be long-lasting and deep.

In the Bahá'í writings we have been admonished to observe courtesy, for 'above all else it is the prince of virtues'. Some of us may have developed this virtue outside the home quite well but become lax within it. Bringing this prince of virtues into our home is, in our opinion, equally important. On the other hand, this does not mean that we should keep frustrations piling up within us, nor does it mean assuming a 'martyr' attitude and putting up with unacceptable behaviour just to avoid confrontation and conflict. Doing this is also harmful to the relationship, since it leads to distancing and the loss of a crucial sense of connection.

If a pattern of frank and open conversation, clothed with respect and use of proper language, is established within the home, our children will be the direct beneficiaries and their souls will be spared the contamination of foul language. Bahá'u'lláh writes:

> the tongue is for mentioning what is good, defile it not with unseemly talk. God hath forgiven what is past. Henceforward everyone should utter that which is seemly, and should refrain from slander, abuse and whatever causeth sadness in men.

We need to develop the capacity to communicate our feelings, our frustrations, our thoughts, our needs and longings in a manner that is clear, direct, and respectful without being the cause of pain or hurt feelings – the content of what we say may be challenging to the other but the **way** we express ourselves can still be compassionate. Being open to and respectful of our partner's needs helps us to expand our world. We can grow as a result of stretching to understand our partner's needs. Trying to control or dominate the conversation, or proving a point in a proud way, is a violation of the boundary of respect for the other, and in the long term is destructive of the relationship. Crossing this interpersonal boundary can take various forms, such as raising our voice, making facial grimaces, using bad language or sarcasm, not responding to the repair attempts of our partner, making hurtful remarks or jokes about our partner in public, or ignoring our partner. It is best to be heedful of the care with which we address each other early in the marriage and to avoid developing a disrespectful pattern of relating. But we know this is a huge challenge, and most of us need to learn a lot more before we are able to make this 'prince of virtues' such a strong part of our character that we carry it through to this most important of all human relationships. How this can be done is the subject of the next chapter.

5

Mindful Dialogue:

The Special Case of Consultation in Marriage

· · · · · · · · · ·

Say: no man can attain his true station
except through his justice.
No power can exist except through unity.
No welfare and no well-being can be attained
except through consultation.

Bahá'u'lláh

· · · · · · · · · ·

Relating to each other verbally is a huge part of a marital relationship. How we talk with each other – share ideas, make decisions and, perhaps most significantly, work through differences probably constitutes the major portion of our relationship in operation. As with other contributions from our childhood experience, we have all learned to use words in the ways our exemplars used them. These imprints, together with our own creative survival instincts and whatever conscious steps we may have taken to perfect our communication skills, all combine to make up our relating style. What we have learned in these ways may have enabled us to manoeuvre through various situations in life, but they may not help us maintain a relationship which has the high demands of intimacy, care and commitment which characterize marriage.

Conversation

Most of our relating to our partner is through casual conversation: sharing of feelings, ideas and perceptions, informing each other of our past and present experiences, talking about our dreams and hopes for the future, including each other in our challenges at work and in our relationships with others – in brief, enjoying the pleasures of companionship through the sharing of the highs and lows of our lives.

• • • • • • • • • •

The Lord, peerless is He, hath made woman and man to abide with each other in the closest companionship . . . two intimate friends, who should be concerned about the welfare of each other.

'Abdu'l-Bahá

• • • • • • • • • •

This kind of relating occurs quite naturally at the beginning of a couple's relationship. In fact, conversation is often the primary basis of friendship. Just as any friendship needs nurturing, the companionship of marriage also calls for attention and care. This is all the more so in our present lifestyle, because our time together is, in many cases, so limited and often distracted by differing demands and a plethora of gadgets and devices. If we do not intentionally take care of this relational need, we will stop being companions.

When children come into the picture, the need and reason for conversation increases, but the overwhelming demands of parenting may reduce the possibilities for it. Awareness of this need and of keeping the lines of communication alive is crucial, especially if one of the parents is spending more time at home with the children. We often urge parents to get their children to bed at a decent hour (we suggest eight o'clock at least up to the end of primary school), not just for the health benefits to their children but equally for the health benefits to the couple's relationship and their individual sanity. As couples, we need time to talk, reconnect intellectually, emotionally and physically. If our children are up late, taking our attention and causing a buzz, our relationship is deprived of a crucial need. We, and our whole family, will suffer as a result.

Women are generally better at keeping conversation alive in a relationship and we will discuss more on this in Chapter 8, but this does not excuse men from moving into taking shared responsibility for this aspect of the relationship. Usually lacking somewhat in this instinct, men need to take more conscious steps towards keeping the lines of communication alive. Conversation is a family need and men, who are rightly becoming fully engaged in the parenting of their children, will inevitably need to hone their communication skills to be able to relate to their children and teenagers, especially male ones. Joyful, open and lively conversations between parents not only contribute to unity in the family, they provide a model for the children as they grow up, helping them to develop a respectful and open style of relating to their parents and to their own future spouses.

We can create occasions for conversation which are natural and enjoyable, such as going out together as a family or as a couple on dates, going for walks, taking part in joint recreational activities in and out of the home, doing domestic chores together, reading together, driving, shopping and travelling together – these are all natural settings for conversation. In a society which has become overly individualistic and compartmentalized, we will need to pull ourselves into these occasions more intentionally.

Any conversation between a husband and wife which is void of negativity (criticizing, blaming, instructing, demanding) is a meaningful conversation because it contributes to the building of the bridge that connects the two worlds. This important verbal connection lays the foundation for consultation on important issues that arise and which will call for decision-making. Furthermore, this kind of day-to-day flow of comfortable conversation makes it easier to enter into a dialogue at times when difficulties and frustrations occur in the relationship and resolution is needed. We will spend the rest of this chapter on the more challenging requirements of this special kind of consultation that can help resolve issues, but we do not want our readers to forget the crucial context which having a solid pleasurable day-to-day conversation gives to this.

Consultation

• • • • • • • • • •

In all things it is necessary to consult . . . inasmuch as it is and will always be a cause of awareness and of awakening and a source of good and well-being.

Bahá'u'lláh

• • • • • • • • • •

The demands on marriage – as on humanity as a whole – call for a new standard of relating to each other when differences arise and, also, for the making of collective decisions. Thus it is that Bahá'u'lláh has provided us with much guidance on how to relate to each other and consult on an equal footing. Most of the guidance found in the Bahá'í writings on consultation refers to its use in the context of institutions. But this principle – as implied by **'In all things** it is necessary to consult' (emphasis ours) – applies equally to marital concerns, certainly when it comes to resolving issues and making decisions. We will draw heavily from the guidance found in the Bahá'í writings and offer a psychological structure – mostly gleaned from Imago therapy, which reflects the reality of man as a noble and spiritual being. We may be surprised to find that mastering the skill of consultation in marriage, which leads to growth in our awareness and understanding, may very well strengthen our ability to resolve issues in the wider society.

. . . .

Consultation bestoweth greater awareness and transmuteth conjecture into certitude . . . The maturity of the gift of understanding is made manifest through consultation.

Bahá'u'lláh

. . . .

The requirements

In mastering the art of consultation, 'The first condition is absolute love and harmony . . .' writes 'Abdu'l-Bahá, and also, that the participants 'must take counsel together in such wise that no occasion for ill-feeling or discord may arise'. These quotations set down the requirements of consultation in an assembly or institution. In reading that 'no occasion for ill-feeling or discord may arise', many a married couple might say, 'But our discussions are often around conflict and hurt feelings to begin with. What do we do with this?'

First of all we need to recognize that differences between people are not only natural, but good and useful. Conflicts, especially at the beginning of a marital relationship, are bound to occur and should not be a cause of fear or despair. It is inevitable that couples, having come from different backgrounds and upbringing, face differences and disagreements. Moreover, because of the special, intimate nature of marriage, the differences are intensified, often triggering negative feelings or insecurities that can move us into conflict or stonewalling. What we do with these differences is the key to a healthy relationship. In his extensive research on couples in his home-like laboratory research on marriages, Gottman has discovered that one of the important attributes of successful couples is their ability to make quick repair. In healthy marriages, couples do not let issues and differences hang over them unresolved.

Differences in marriage directly lead us into our feelings of vulnerability which, when touched in other contexts, most of us think we can safely sidestep. But in marriage, leaving our vulnerabilities unaddressed leads to further trouble. Here, the feelings that are brought to the surface need to be given due attention. The interest of preserving affinity in marriage compels us to dig deep and seek the truths that underlie the very strong feelings that surface between a husband and wife. This takes special care. Feelings need to be expressed fully but respectfully; they need to be received with grace, acceptance and understanding. In order to help facilitate a movement toward this high standard, clearly inculcated in the Bahá'í writings, the structure we are offering can be used to highlight these principles at each stage in a concrete way. We will refer to this process as 'mindful dialogue' in order to distinguish it from consultation in other contexts. This tool, we hope, can help us move into a new paradigm of relating to each other, a step towards establishing a 'new race of couples'. But first, let us have a closer look at the nature of conflict in intimate relationships.

· · · · · · · · · ·

Family consultation employing full and frank discussion, and animated by awareness of the need for moderation and balance, can be the panacea for domestic conflict. Wives should not attempt to dominate their husbands, nor husbands their wives.

The Universal House of Justice

· · · · · · · · · ·

Intimacy and conflict

Much recent psychological literature on couples therapy posits that a primary source of conflict, especially in marriage, can be found in childhood and the emotional remnants of our earlier experiences. The 'issues' that arise between a husband and wife are often not the substance of their difference but, rather, the trigger. Sometimes it is something very small or seemingly insignificant that ends up becoming a big issue. We get upset because what our spouse does, or fails to do, triggers something that was wounding in our earlier experience, though we usually remain unaware of this. Our spouse has only to do something which we associate with the way our caregivers or other significant people in our life treated us – either in depriving us of what we needed or in demanding something of us which was against our wishes – and we fall off the edge of equanimity into an abyss of emotion which will stymie our attempts to consult effectively. In order to gain insight into the dynamics involved and gain perspective of these trying situations, it can help to understand what goes on in our brains.

Brain science: It's a jungle in there

If you make a fist with your thumb curled under your fingers, you have a useful, simplified, model for understanding some basic brain structures. The fingers represent the neo-cortex, or new brain. This is where most of our reasoning, reflecting and higher functioning takes place. The curled-under thumb represents the limbic area which includes the amygdala and hippocampus. It processes, among other things, memories and feelings. The base of the thumb down to the wrist represents the brain stem, often called the reptilian brain because it handles the same functions that the brains of reptiles handle. This is the lower, often automatic functioning of body systems and reflexes, which can mobilize our body in quick response to perceived danger.

Now, we like to think of ourselves as rational beings and, most often, most of us are. We think about things, make sense of our experience, draw conclusions, share our thoughts with others in usually quite peaceful and reasonable ways. But there is a lot that goes on and a lot that is stored, out of our awareness, in the lower reaches of our brain. While we may be having what seems to be a calm, rational interaction with our spouse, he or she may do or say something which triggers a feeling. The feeling may be a fairly reasonable response to what was said or done but if it is a feeling which has negative early associations, alarm bells start to ring in the amygdala and the message gets sent directly to the brain stem. The nerve cells in the brain stem convey the electrical nerve currents much faster than those of the rest of the brain and mobilize our bodies in an instant to move into emergency mode. That is, we will fall into one of the primitive means of survival: attack, retreat, or freeze. Once this primitive reflex is stimulated, our cortex largely shuts down. Its attenuated functioning, powered by strong negative feelings from the amygdala, will be used to assist the reflexive mode we are in, that is, thinking of ways to retreat, attack or freeze. This is clearly not a state in which one can resolve anything in a peaceful, constructive way. So the question is, 'How can we move from this aroused state into healthy consultation?' This is a critical question. Let's look at it one step at a time.

Developing a new reflex

• • • • • • • • • •

It is incumbent upon all the peoples of the world to reconcile their differences . . .

Bahá'u'lláh

• • • • • • • • • •

Understanding a bit about how our brains function when

emotionally aroused, we can see the limitations of choice we have when our cortex has largely shut down its rational processes. It **seems** that we are limited to flight, fight, or freeze, but fortunately, as humans, we are not. To avoid these automatic responses, what we need to do is to intentionally create new pathways in our brain which will give us healthy alternatives to our reflexes. This is well within our capacity, especially if we adhere in a disciplined way to a structure which provides safety and keeps our reflexes at bay. Our experience has shown that this clear, concrete structure of relating – coupled with regularity – is indispensable for most couples.

· · · · · · · · · ·

Peace is not the absence of conflict
but the presence of creative alternatives
for responding to conflict . . .

Dorothy Thompson

· · · · · · · · · ·

The following practical steps can help us develop an alternative to arguing, falling into anger, swallowing resentment, or keeping our distance. The ultimate goal of this structure is to help us become better listeners and more respectful and clear in expressing ourselves. Use of the structure is crucial in the beginning in order to learn the skills. Once the skills become part of us, the structure falls into the background.

Let us say at the outset that when we talk about doing the work of marriage, learning to relate in the kind of way outlined below is probably the most central ingredient. It is not hard work, but it is new and, in the beginning, it will trip you up because you will not be able to just flow along and be your old practised self. It requires taking on a skill which is new, but it is not rocket science. It is do-able, it is something we can all learn, it needs time and practice in the beginning to get good at it, and once we are past the initial awkwardness and start to get into a groove, it is pleasurable. What follows is really the core of this book and we encourage you to read it as many times as it takes to really get it. To provide more assistance, you can find added material in the appendixes. Once you have put mindful dialogue into action, your life as a couple will become much easier as you enjoy living free of arguments, quarrels, battles, or long periods of heavy silence. We are all capable of becoming kind, compassionate, 'dialogical' grown-ups.

Mindful dialogue

Step 1: Allocate a regular time to talk, or make ad hoc appointments

• • • • • • • • • •

Gather ye together, and for the sake of God resolve to root out whatever is the source of contention amongst you.

Bahá'u'lláh

• • • • • • • • • •

It is most productive for a couple to set a regular time, or times, during the week to talk intentionally to process the issues or perhaps any frustrations that may have come up. This is the most workable way for most couples to clear the slate, come to understand each other more deeply, and keep the channel of affection open. Once mastered, a dialogue of about 20–30 minutes weekly (extendable if needed and with the wish of both parties) can help prevent negative feelings from building up and becoming dangerously explosive and poisonous. Having a weekly date, we will know that there will be an opportunity to be heard on whatever either one of us wishes to bring up. If, on any of these regular dates, we don't find any issues that need to be cleared up, the time can be used to talk about enriching our relationship and finding ways to deepen our connection and joy in life. This regime can help bring a sense of safety and assurance of connection into our marriage.

There are issues that may come up and trigger us but which cannot be left for the weekly meeting to deal with. Unable to wait for the scheduled weekly dialogue, the best alternative is to ask for an appointment. This one small step of requesting an appointment respects the reality of the other to prepare and make time – physically and psychologically – for the encounter. This is hugely preferable to just dumping a heavy discussion unexpectedly on our partner. The invitation to dialogue can be as simple as: 'Something is bothering me. Can we talk?' This gives our partner a chance to assess whether or not they are ready to talk, and gives them time to prepare themselves to listen if they are not ready at that moment.

Whenever an appointment is asked for, the other partner either agrees to talk right away or gives a time, as soon as possible, when he or she will be available. This implies space for the partner to assess his or her readiness and to choose a time when they can be present with full attention. Without specifying a time, the one asking for an appointment will likely go away all the more frustrated, being unsure this will ever get dealt with.

• • • • • • • • • •

My calamity is My providence,
outwardly it is fire and vengeance,
but inwardly it is light and mercy.

Bahá'u'lláh

• • • • • • • • • •

When we are hurt, or suspect our partner has been hurt, there is a natural tendency for many of us to avoid facing it or talking about it. But difficulties in life and in marriage are opportunities for self-discovery, new understanding and stretching our limits to help each other grow in a safe and loving space. Facing and validating the hurts, willingness to listen and to talk, lead to growth and eventual healing. Perhaps this is one of the ways in which couples can contribute to each other's spiritual growth. Thus, a courageous orientation to these troubled feelings can yield wonderful fruits in our relationships. The advantage of having already set a regular time for dealing with frustrations is that it takes away the anxiety and difficulties related to making appointments. But it still takes courage during the scheduled meetings to step through our anxious feelings, whether about bringing up something difficult or listening with attention.

Written dialogues. There is yet one more alternative way to have this kind of dialogue, and that is in writing. Writing has some advantages over oral dialogue, but some disadvantages as well. A main advantage is that it is usually easier to keep ourselves from getting out of hand while we are writing. We can review what we have written and be more objective about determining whether it conforms to the steps and principles of good sending (discussed further below). Also, no appointment is needed and the receiver can read it when ready, re-reading parts that are difficult after taking some more time to calm down. These advantages are significant and can make writing even more recommended when there has been a severe rupture or the feelings are very intense. Added to this, some people express themselves better in writing and can allow themselves to convey more intimate truths. The absence of body language and eye contact in written communication can be positive or negative, depending on what our body language is conveying. Once we have mastered the skill of mindful dialogue, our body language will remain relaxed and open and foster more connection and intimacy. Of course, writing and making the exchanges is going to take more time and this is usually a disadvantage, but not always. One added point: writing can be a good alternative to failed attempts at face-to-face dialogue and also a good entry point for beginners who are unsure of the process. An exercise for a written dialogue can be found in Appendix 2.

Step 2: Establish a sacred space

When we have resolved to meet our differences peacefully and have set a regular time in the week for working through whatever issues have come up for us – also when we make ad hoc appointments to clear away a difficulty which cannot wait – it becomes essential to tune into the sacred nature of what we are about to do, and to get in touch with our own higher self. This is an especially important task because, as mentioned before, our most well-practised survival strategies come to be experienced as our identity. The 'default' pathways in our brain tend to lead to our 'insistent self', our ego, which is geared to making the other wrong. Thus, the need to take some time to call forth our higher self which empowers us to embrace the otherness of the other and is not compelled to move into reactivity and opposition.

• • • • • • • • • •

*'Say: all things are of God.' This exalted utterance is like
unto water for quenching the fire of hate and enmity which
smouldereth within the hearts and breasts of men.*

Bahá'u'lláh

• • • • • • • • • •

Part of the task of bypassing the default pathways in our brain which protect our ego is the development of pathways which lead to our higher or true self. Daily prayer, meditation, and the study of holy writings help us develop and deepen these pathways. On occasions when we are about to talk about hurt feelings, prayer and contemplation before talking about the issue can help us regain access to these pathways to our higher self. Bahá'u'lláh has provided us with a phrase to transform hate and enmity: 'Say: all things are of God.' We can use this 'exalted utterance' to help us prepare the sacred space of consultation This phrase is a profound reminder to us that everything that happens is of God and that we can gain something from it and grow, as long as we have the courage to face it with humility and curiosity.

It makes sense that, if we are going to make headway in these troubled waters, we need good preparation. Many couples therapists now take time, using guided meditation, visualization, taking deep breaths or other techniques, to create a state of mindfulness and to foster a feeling of safety for a couple, before moving into a dialogue around an issue.

Step 3: Reaffirm love

• • • • • • • • • •

. . . and if a man has ten bad qualities and one good one, to look at the one and forget the ten.

Attributed to 'Abdu'l-Bahá

• • • • • • • • • •

There is yet another very helpful step to take before moving into the actual discussion around the issue. This is to express an 'appreciation' of our partner. This can be a general quality that we admire in our partner, a behaviour that is pleasing, a kind action or word from them that warmed our heart recently or in the past, or an aspect of their being that we find attractive. We do this first of all as a reminder of the underlying love that we have for our partner. When we are focused only on something which is troubling us, we tend to forget, or lose sight of, all the good that is in our partner and the love which is actually present for us. To many, it can seem a contradiction to hold something negative in our mind concerning our partner while at the same time acknowledging our love for them. This kind of 'logic' tends to chase out of our awareness all the good our spouse represents for us. If this is the way we think, we will tend to do all we can to make them wrong and true consultation becomes virtually impossible.

'Abdu'l-Bahá says, 'Every one of the friends should highly praise the other'; and this is a good occasion to apply this principle. It can be done no matter how frustrated we may feel at the moment. There is always a quality we can recall that we admire, or something – however small – our partner has recently done that brought us some gladness. Share this. And then our partner can do the same for us. In receiving the appreciation, it is good to simply and graciously accept it as it comes, without trying to correct the other or modify it as we see fit. It also helps to repeat back what we have heard and to thank our partner. This assures our partner that what was said is understood and received. It also provides a reminder that the bond is still there and that discussing a difficult issue is **not going to threaten the connection, but to improve it.**

A second reason for sharing appreciation has to do with its intrinsic importance. The benefits of expressing positive statements about each other go far beyond creating a feeling of safety in preparation for dealing with a difficult issue. Gottman has observed that an outstanding characteristic of thriving couples is that they have five positive interactions for every negative one. Affirmations can be an intentional means of weighing in on the side of positive interactions. In addition to this, there is the well-established behavioural principal that we generally get more of what we concentrate on. If we want more attention, for example, it is good to focus on, and express appreciation for, the occasions that we do get it instead of stating the negative version of what we are not getting.

Many successful couples regularly let each other know the ways in which they cherish each other and are grateful to each other. This is in contrast to those who assume that their partner knows they are cared for and so rarely put their feelings and appreciation into words. We encourage couples to share appreciation daily. This could be in acknowledging very small deeds and actions of our partner that we may take for granted, such as work-related activities, household chores, or the expression of kind sentiments regarding the looks, attitude, behaviour or words of the other. In addition, used as a prelude to dealing with issues involving conflict, it helps set the stage for resolving the conflict peacefully, a result that changes the potential negative experience of differences into the very positive experience of added closeness and peaceful resolution.

In expressing an appreciation for our partner, we need to take care not to append a 'but' statement to it. For example, 'I appreciate how you took the time to play with the kids yesterday. **I just wish you would do it more often.**' The bold face type is the 'but' statement, the 'but' not being explicitly stated. In this case, what the partner will remember is the 'but' statement. In essence, it not only erases the good of the appreciation, it provokes the other, making them more likely to remember what you don't appreciate in them, occasioning such thoughts as 'God, she is never satisfied,' or 'He is just finding a new way to criticize me.' This leads to an attitude of defensiveness and conspires against openness. Thus, it is best to strive to always keep our appreciations completely 'clean'.

Showing appreciation is an art which, if developed and practised, can go a very long way toward making couplehood joyful and growth-promoting. It starts with **learning to look for**, see, and recognize what is good. Because most of us were criticized in our socialization process, we have internalized certain messages around it. We may tell ourselves, 'If I don't see what is wrong or missing and fail to point it out, others might take advantage of me,' or 'If I don't point out mistakes, no learning or improvement will take place.' In fact, very little criticism is welcomed and that which is not welcomed is not constructive. Usually criticism is an expression of our ego self at work, rather than the higher self. There is a place for expressing what troubles us and bringing forth desired improvements, and this is what we are getting to in the sections that follow.

Step 4: A structure for dialogue

Just as a home gives us a feeling of comfort and security, so can a clear structure of consultation help us to calm down and move forward with confidence that good results will accrue. Just as it takes time to build, furnish and decorate a home in a pleasing way, it also takes some time to develop a way of talking to each other which is conducive to resolution and love. A crucial part of an effective process of dialogue is clarity on who is 'sending' (speaking) and who is 'receiving' (listening). There should always be only one at a time who is sending, and it should be clear and accepted by both. The receiver will have a chance to respond after having heard his or her partner out. Attending to this is a matter of efficiency and politeness and this, too, helps create a feeling of safety.

It makes sense that the one who asked for an appointment be the one who talks first and this means that the other should listen intently and respectfully until the sender has completed all they have to express on that particular matter and until it is absolutely clear that the receiver has 'got it'. There is a huge tendency for our egos to jump in and react to what is said, saying or thinking 'that is not true', or 'it wasn't like that', or 'I didn't mean that' or many other varieties of wanting to correct the other immediately. Contrary to what our egos think, this is not a matter of being correct or of winning or losing. This is about **gaining clarity and understanding the point of view and experience** of the other, a place from which we can both move forward with purpose, dignity and unity. The experience and feelings of the other are valid and real to them and should be honoured rather than argued with or refuted. Our own feelings, views or memory of what happened can come later. If we make it about being right, we are almost sure to fall back into heavy feelings and evoke primitive responses.

Having established the importance of always being clear who the sender is and who the receiver is at any point in a dialogue, let us now explore the role of each.

Sending. In sending, we strive to express all we have to say on a particular issue, being completely open, until we have uncovered all the feelings that are bound up in our frustration; this, in a manner which is polite and fair. We usually come from a place of ego because that is what hurt feelings are usually bound up with. The tendency here is to point the finger at our partner, blaming him or her for all the distress we are experiencing. A dysfunctional way of expressing our frustrations is to emphasize the perceived wrongs of our partner while avoiding our own feelings of vulnerability that may lie beneath the surface. In trying to make the other 'wrong', we usually move farther and farther away from gaining understanding and attaining a resolution. A lot depends on the manner in which we express our frustrations.

· · · · · · · · · ·

If the fire of self overcome you,
remember your own faults and not the faults of My creatures,
inasmuch as every one of you knoweth his own self
better than he knoweth others.

Bahá'u'lláh

· · · · · · · · · ·

Bahá'u'lláh counsels us to remind ourselves of our own faults as a means of calming ourselves down. He also reminds us that we know our own self more than we know about the other. Thus, in bringing forward a frustration, we should avoid labelling the other and making assumptions. We can fairly describe what it is they have done or said which is troubling us, without assuming that they were wrong, uncaring, insensitive, aggressive, etc. We can also use the principle of moderation in describing their behaviour. For example, instead of saying 'You were rude and way out of control, shouting and being terrible as usual,' which is descriptive but judgemental, it would be preferable to say something like 'You were raising your voice, using words I find offensive, and making physical gestures which seemed threatening to me.' Even the quite loaded word 'threatening' here is softened by adding that this as coming from your own perspective, implying that someone else might not have seen it that way.

• • • • • • • • • •

. . . in this glorious dispensation we should not belittle anyone and call him ignorant, saying: 'You know not, but I know.'

'Abdu'l-Bahá

• • • • • • • • • •

After describing our partner's offending behaviour as calmly and succinctly as possible we can pause and give our partner a chance to mirror what they have heard. We can gently correct them if they have changed what we said or missed something out. After this, we can go on to say how their behaviour affected us. Here it is important to underline the importance of expressing and owning our feelings. This is what we know better than our partner can, and it is very helpful to let them to know about this. Psychologists call this an 'I message'. Ironically, some spiritually-minded people resist using the first person pronoun in this way but seem to have no trouble using the second or third person pronoun in very demeaning ways.

An 'I message' is a humble expression of the possibility that, indeed, our ego may be getting in the way of having a smooth relationship. For example, saying 'When you raised your voice at me I felt disrespected,' does not label the other, rather, it accurately describes our inner response to his or her outward behaviour, leaving many interpretations open, including 'maybe I am too sensitive'. Even if it is somehow obvious to us that our partner's behaviour was blameworthy, it is better for him or her to come to this conclusion after hearing how their behaviour has affected us. This kind of language is less likely to evoke a reactive response and more likely to encourage some self-reflection on our partner's part which may include a desire to explore where the offending behaviour came from. For example, our partner may reveal that his or her parents shouted a lot and it became a norm in the family. Gaining this insight can be the beginning of a process of modifying their behaviour.

· · · · · · · · · ·

Help him to see and recognize the truth, without esteeming yourself to be, in the least, superior to him, or to be possessed of greater endowments.

Bahá'u'lláh

· · · · · · · · · ·

To summarize, the goal of sending is to uncover and express the essence of what we are experiencing, sensing, understanding, feeling, associating, remembering, fearing and how we are reacting as a result of these; this, in a way that the other can come to understand us completely. For further guidelines and pointers on how to become good at sending, see Appendix 1.

Receiving. In receiving, we strive to understand our partner so fully that we move into empathy. The great tendency of allowing our egos to step in and derail our movement to understanding is hard to avoid in the beginning. As a receiver, we often tend to conjure up a retort in our mind while the other is speaking so that we are ready to put it forward as soon as we have a chance to speak, or to interrupt.

• • • • • • • • • •

The first duty of love is to listen.

Paul Tillich

• • • • • • • • • •

In order to listen fully, we need to develop the capacity of leaving our world behind temporarily, with all its opinions, judgements, and standards of feeling and experiencing – even memories of what we thought actually happened – while visiting the other's world and being open to new discoveries. Listening is an art, a skill that once acquired yields wonderful results. As in acts of praying or meditation, here too we need to learn to quiet our 'self' long enough to hear the voice of the other.

• • • • • • • • • •

. . . we must be willing to clear away all that we have previously learned, all that would clog our steps on the way to truth . . .

'Abdu'l-Bahá

• • • • • • • • • •

Bahá'ís are encouraged to look to 'Abdu'l-Bahá as an example and, as a listener, He was second to none. Here is a perceptive account of the Master's great ability to hear what the other had to say:

To the questioner He responded first with silence – an outward silence. His encouragement always was that the other should speak and He listen. There was never that eager tenseness, that restlessness so often met showing most plainly that the listener has the pat answer ready the moment he should have a chance to utter it.

I have heard certain people described as 'good listeners', but never had I imagined such a 'listener' as 'Abdu'l-Bahá. It was more than a sympathetic absorption of what the ear received. It was as though the two individualities became one; as if He so closely identified Himself with the one speaking that a merging of spirits occurred which made a verbal response almost unnecessary, superfluous. As I write, the words of Bahá'u'lláh recur to me: 'When the sincere servant calls to Me in prayer I become the very ear with which he heareth My reply.'

That was just it! 'Abdu'l-Bahá seemed to listen with my ears.

Truly good listening requires intent absorption – or more, as described above: a merging of spirits. In order for this merging to take place, the leaving of our own 'stuff' entirely behind while listening is critical. In working with many couples, we have observed that this is difficult but entirely possible, even when strong emotions, which can potentially trigger equally powerful reactions, are brought forward. There is a part of our neo-cortex (located at the tips of the third and fourth fingers in the hand model used earlier to describe the parts of the brain) that is capable of over-riding reflex. For example, if a fast-moving object comes toward our eyes, our protective reflex is to blink. But using this hugely important, humanly unique portion of the brain, we can decide not to blink when someone feigns a blow to our head. In the case of dialogue, with conscious effort we can choose to stay with the experience our partner is describing – even though it may feel like a blow to us – without becoming defensive, even if the events being described contradict our memory of them. This does not mean that we agree with what our partner says or how she or he remembers events. Rather, we are staying in our partner's world, disciplining ourselves to stay present and see things as he or she does, according to the way he or she remembers things. Everybody makes sense in their own world, and the feelings they may have are legitimate. Listening well, therefore, puts us into the supportive position of being able to validate our partner's feelings.

What they share with us in these dialogues is of vital importance if we desire to be intimately connected to them.

• • • • • • • • • •

The fact that we imagine ourselves to be right and everybody else wrong is the greatest of all obstacles in the path towards unity . . .

'Abdu'l-Bahá

• • • • • • • • • •

In order to keep our attention on our partner, it may help to internally 'mirror' everything they say, to get and feel their meaning. We can take this even further and, at intervals, verbally repeat to them what we are hearing, or at least the essence of it, and ask them if we are 'getting it'. This outward mirroring, or paraphrasing, not only clarifies for us that we are understanding them as they want to be understood (which is what listening is all about); they receive the added comfort and feeling of safety of knowing that they are being heard. This helps and enables them to go deeper into their experience, revealing even more of their world to us, bringing a closer and more intimate connection. It also helps the sender to understand themselves better and perhaps gain a new and objective perspective of their own feelings as they hear them mirrored back.

• • • • • • • • • •

Do not allow difference of opinion, or diversity of thought to separate you from your fellow-men, or to be the cause of dispute, hatred and strife in your hearts.

'Abdu'l-Bahá

• • • • • • • • • •

After the sender has conveyed all that is in their heart around the issue and has been heard and mirrored by the receiver, if the receiver then wants to respond to things that have been said, a conscious shift of roles is appropriate. This can go back and forth several times, if necessary, but it is important not to get muddled about who is in what role, so that listening is always taking place, protecting the safe and sacred space between husband and wife from the destructive effects of arguing back and forth.

In summary, the goal of receiving is to understand completely the truth about what the other is experiencing, sensing, understanding, feeling, associating, remembering or fearing, and/or what she or he usually does when having such feelings, **and** to convey to the other with words, body language and tone of voice that we are 'getting them', that they are making sense (because all feelings are real and legitimate and everybody makes sense from their own point of view). A further goal is to be able to imagine how they are feeling and to empathize with them. For further guidelines and pointers on how to become good at receiving, see Appendix 1.

Step 5: Arrival

When sending and receiving are completed in a dialogue, meaning that both have had a chance to be fully heard on the issue, we should have arrived at common truth. What is this truth? The first truth is understanding in itself. We see ourselves and our partner more fully, we come to know more clearly what our feelings are about and what triggers our reactive behaviour. Next, we want a different experience which calls for a modification in behaviour. This modification inevitably involves the behaviour of both partners. At this stage in the dialogue, each partner expresses what they can personally do to contribute to a new experience around the issue discussed. Usually we think that if we could get our partner to change their behaviour, then our relationship problem will be solved. We are neglecting the fact that we always make a contribution to the behaviour of our partner, whether consciously or unconsciously.

Let's take a common example of a conflict about household chores. After a dialogue where it becomes clear that the wife, for example, is overcome with feelings of being overwhelmed around shouldering the load of housekeeping and these feelings are validated, the rest of the dialogue could go something like this:

Husband: One thing I intend to do to relieve some of this burden for you is to make sure the kitchen is clean and tidy after dinner.

Wife: One thing I intend to do to relieve some of this burden for myself is to give you the space and authority to take this responsibility on. I will not interfere in this and I will not criticize the imperfections I may perceive in how you carry this out.

This is a process which can take time and many dialogues. Keeping the process of dialogue positive and sacred makes it both growth-promoting and rewarding. Even though the steps which help keep the process of a mindful dialogue safe take time, it is time well spent because it brings us closer together. If we were to cave into that voice within that pushes us toward some kind of time efficiency, we would not make time for prayer or meditation either.

• • • • • • • • • •

Nothing is too much trouble when one loves, and there is always time.

'Abdu'l-Bahá

• • • • • • • • • •

When a dialogue is finished, it is good to acknowledge our partner for being there, show appreciation for their ability to express what is important, for their listening skills, and their willingness to take on new behaviour – whatever the case may be.

Detachment, patience and openness

As has already been mentioned, the courage to face and resolve issues through such conscious dialogues leads to the personal and spiritual enrichment of both. Three spiritual qualities that this kind of dialogue helps us to develop are detachment, patience and openness.

• • • • • • • • • •

No man shall attain the shores of the ocean of true understanding except he be detached from all that is in heaven and on earth.

Bahá'u'lláh

• • • • • • • • • •

Detachment is more clearly important for the receiver, because he or she has to leave all ego attachments behind while visiting the reality of the other. Without this, the receiver impedes his or her capacity to listen.

Although less obvious, the need for the sender to develop detachment is also essential. While the sender is encouraged to fully explore his or her feelings and experience, the letting go of criticism and blame, and using language which reflects ownership of one's own feelings requires detachment. Expressing feelings usually helps us feel more peaceful and whole and often enables us to gain perspective, but we should be aware that these are our own feelings and that we are the one ultimately responsible for them. For example, even if someone does something which is clearly immoral or evil and we may feel hurt or disappointed as a result, our feelings, even in this case, emanate from our own expectations or the trust that we may have put in the person in the first place. It is not wrong to have trust in others but the trust is **ours** and so are the feelings that result in us when we believe the trust has been breached. Thus, using a phrase like 'You make me feel annoyed' is a form of blaming and does not take ownership of one's feeling of annoyance. It is not accurate and, because of this, is not as likely to be well received. Better would be 'When you come home so late without telling me, I feel annoyed.' In this way, you are expressing your feeling and passing on the **information** crucial to your partner without placing the blame on him or her or, by implication, relinquishing your personal power. We are not only responsible for our own feelings, we are responsible for the actions we take based on these feelings. Expressing our feelings with responsibility provides our partner and ourselves with crucial information about our inner workings and a greater understanding of our actions.

• • • • • • • • • •

And if he meeteth with injustice he shall have patience,
and if he cometh upon wrath he shall manifest love.

Bahá'u'lláh

• • • • • • • • • •

Patience is needed because this process requires time and conscious effort. Especially in the beginning, our faults in being less than perfect senders and receivers can exasperate us. Focused, empathetic dialogue, especially when we are disciplined enough to mirror each other when we speak, seems to our rational mind to be extremely time-consuming. Initially, it may also seem rudimentary or even childish to repeat what we hear when the other speaks. But, looking at the big picture, this is most often a much faster means of getting what we really need (as opposed to what our egos want). Couples can spin their wheels for years, trying to discuss the same issue over and over again, despairing more and more over their partner all the while. Meaningful dialogue, where one listens actively without interjections while the other speaks can be over in less than an hour; and a few sessions here and there over time can completely clarify matters and clear the channels that otherwise may block our intimacy and closeness for a lifetime.

• • • • • • • • • •

In order to find truth we must give up our prejudices, our own small trivial notions;
an open receptive mind is essential.
If our chalice is full of self, there is no room in it for the water of life.

'Abdu'l-Bahá

• • • • • • • • • •

Openness, or curiosity, is perhaps an attitude more than a virtue, but it is nevertheless very helpful for both partners to adopt. When receiving, we move into a mode of discovery, letting go of the 'I already know what this is all about' mindset which plagues so many couples' conversations. When we tell ourselves things like 'I know him/her' we are underestimating the power of the higher self, both in us and in our partner. We are all far more than our well-practised reactivity. Our higher self is ready to step forward when a sacred and safe space is created. A useful image to use when receiving is to think of ourselves as visiting a foreign country or another planet. Carrying this image, we are more likely to open ourselves to what is going on, wondering with an attitude of curiosity about how things are done here, how do people talk and feel, what are the customs, what is the history, how do people react, what is important to them and so forth. To the sender, openness can come after gaining experience with this kind of exchange where his or her feelings are brought to the surface, often bringing new awareness of what has been going on internally. We become more aware of our own vulnerabilities and projections. This is likely to lead to questions such as 'Why does this particular behaviour trigger me this way?' or 'Where does this sensitivity come from?' rather than, 'What a dolt he or she is to make me feel this way.'

Why can't we just be our natural selves when talking?

A question that we often hear around mindful dialogue is: 'Isn't this artificial?' or 'This doesn't feel natural,' 'I don't feel like I am being myself,' etc. Our answer is 'Yes, it is artificial', and 'No, it does not feel natural in the beginning'. The development of every new skill is, to start with, artificial and contrived. The movement of becoming aware of, and developing, any new skill goes through a process which psychologist Thomas Gordon has characterized as a step-wise movement from:

1. being unskilled and unconscious of the need for the new skill;
2. being still unskilled but now conscious of the fact of being unskilled;
3. being skilled and conscious of being skilled; and, finally,
4. being skilled but unconscious of being skilled.

In the last stage, we are unconscious of being skilled because we have mastered it so effectively, and used it so much, that we have internalized it and it feels a natural part of who we are.

Those who quite understandably ask 'Isn't this artificial?' are coming from a place of having internalized certain other ways of relating. In the case of communication, most of how we relate is totally unconscious, because these skills were developed at such an early age that we have no memory of how we learnt it. Thus, we experience our present way of relating – no matter how unhealthy or dysfunctional – as natural and part of our identity. For the same reason, there is a concomitant tendency to feel extra uncomfortable when stepping into a new way of relating. People learning a second language as adults are usually faced with this psychological resistance to expressing themselves in the new language – a resistance which children at a young age do not experience at all.

Consciously overcoming our resistance to learning and using

these new skills is well worth the effort. The practice of these skills is conducive to a kind of mindfulness that can help us live fully in the moment with our partner and move to higher spiritual levels. Not only do we become more self-aware, but while engaged in this way with our partner, we both move into a feeling of connectedness. Deep understanding of each other's world creates unity. Individually, it is through this consciousness of our actions and reactions that we can become intentional beings and live more purposeful lives.

Developing this kind of discipline in communication takes commitment. In the next chapter we will look at the dynamics of commitment and its meaning in marriage.

6

Commitment versus Escape

· · · · · · · · · ·

There is no place for you to flee to in this day.

Bahá'u'lláh

· · · · · · · · · ·

In the last chapter we presented mindful dialogue as a tool for transforming differences and conflict into spiritual growth and intimacy. Earlier we discussed the primacy of the couple with respect to other human relationships and the need to develop and maintain clear boundaries in order to best maintain this sacred relationship. Mindful dialogue is a skill which, once developed, will help a couple in many areas of their relationship, including the establishing of clear marital boundaries. Now that we have been introduced to this skill and have an idea of the importance of establishing the boundary of marriage, we need to look anew at the great tendency we have to avoid doing this work and thus the propensity to move out of the boundary so essential to the safety of the marriage itself.

It is perhaps part of our nature that once we have established a boundary we want to break free from it – this is nowhere more compelling than in marriage. When things are going well we are usually quite happy to stay where we are with each other, but when trouble starts to appear we tend to want to get away. If we lack the inclination to address problems, or have no means for bringing up what is troubling us, the felt need to escape will be almost impossible to overcome. Even when we have some idea about the need to consult, there is still often a stronger urge to escape than there is to bring forward the issue, or issues, at hand.

The sanctity and purpose of marriage

· · · · · · · · · ·

> . . . the union must be a true relationship, a spiritual coming together as well as a physical one, so that throughout every phase of life, and in all the worlds of God, their union will endure.
>
> **'Abdu'l-Bahá**

· · · · · · · · · ·

Although marriage is a social arrangement made in this physical world, all the religions have ordained it; for this alone we can conclude that it serves a spiritual purpose. 'Abdu'l-Bahá has asserted that the law of marriage is eternal and will continue for ever. Marriage is eternal in another sense: our souls continue to remain in communion with each other throughout all the worlds of God. In marriage, our souls unite to help us fulfil our spiritual purpose on this planet. Thus, marriage serves personal, physical, social and ultimately spiritual ends, all of which are linked in this life.

Marriage in the larger picture

In addition to the enrichment of the spiritual life that a husband and wife can provide for each other there is another purpose for marriage underlined in the Bahá'í writings; this is the rearing of children who will grow to be awake to their spiritual nature and be able to project this into society. These can be seen as being profoundly linked, since our own spiritual growth as a couple will have a direct and deep influence on the children we raise. The family unit in all its diverse aspects becomes a building block of the society at large and, ultimately, of the whole world. All of this points to the sanctity of marriage.

• • • • • • • • • •

Are you running away from something you don't want?
Or running away from something you're afraid to want?

Anonymous

• • • • • • • • • •

Bahá'u'lláh has repeated many times in His writings that 'There is no place to flee to in this day.' In other words, achieving unity as a people is no longer optional. The commitment of marriage is a microcosm of this overarching call. Committing ourselves to love and stay with our partner for a lifetime, for the sake of our own spiritual growth and the higher good of our children, holds within it many of the challenges and promises of achieving unity in diversity on a global scale. As we shall more clearly see, in marriage there is also nowhere to flee. Many psychologists are saying now that if we fail to hold together as a couple, if we fail to move through the challenging psychological work of marriage which 'grows us up', we are bound to take our same unfinished psychological issues with us into our next relationship and to encounter the same kinds of problems. Moreover, our children will also carry this same unfinished heritage with them, and face the same kinds of issues in their marriages. No wonder, then, that Bahá'u'lláh has stated that He 'abhors' divorce.

• • • • • • • • • •

Marriage, like a submarine, is only safe if you get all the way inside.

Frank Pittman

• • • • • • • • • •

There is perhaps a relationship between the gravity of our need to stay together as a couple and our compulsion to escape. The issues of our childhood are painful ones and our ego, which has assured its survival by bypassing these sensitive areas, will feel it a matter of life and death NOT to deal with these issues. One side of us recognizes the importance of marriage while the other side often has a crying urge to escape. This is the impetus of our insistent self and it has a myriad strategies for carrying out its design. Thus our conscious and resolute commitment to do the work of marriage is crucial.

Ironically, while the work of marriage may seem painful and therefore something to avoid, as soon as we step into doing it the pain dissipates and the renewed and deepened intimacy which results is hugely rewarding. On the other hand, sidestepping the anticipated pain of doing the work leaves us with a gnawing agony which keeps replaying in the background of our lives, no matter what we do to try to numb it or escape from it. The patterns of escape that we develop, while protecting our ego, conspire against our growth, minimize intimacy, and conduce to distancing or conflict in our marital relationship. Let us, therefore, have a close look at the kinds of things we do in our attempts to flee, become conscious of them and come to see the importance of closing these escape routes so that we can attend to our partner in such a way that we maintain an intimate connection conducive to growth.

The great escape

· · · · · · · · · ·

It wasn't a suicide attempt, it was an escape from everything awful.

Anonymous

Murder is born of love, and love attains the greatest intensity in murder.

Attributed to Octave Mirbeau

· · · · · · · · · ·

When we feel beaten down by our marriage, when the demands or perceived deficiencies of our partner seem to be too much for us, we have the urge to get out, to escape from what seems to be a painful, even torturous, trap. The great escape is one which puts an end to having to deal with our partner as a partner. The most apparently final version of the great escape in its most extreme form is to kill oneself. Yet the great spiritual teachers and Manifestations of God have all said that even this is not an escape, that we will have to face ourselves and our unfinished business in the worlds beyond this one. Another version of the great escape is to murder one's partner. While suicide and murder may seem too extreme to even talk about, the fact is that a significant number of suicides and murders in our society are directly linked to marriage and romance. Furthermore, we must assume that the number of contemplated suicides and murders far outnumbers the actual attempts. Also, many behaviours such as physical and mental abuse, or unhealthy lifestyle choices, may reflect some kind of death wish on our partner or ourselves, a death wish which is triggered by the special kind of difficulties we encounter in the sometimes maddening confines of marriage.

• • • • • • • • •

Getting divorced just because you don't love a man is almost
as silly as getting married just because you do.

Attributed to Zsa Zsa Gabor

• • • • • • • • • •

Another version of the great escape, which is more easy for most of us to relate to and to seriously contemplate, is divorce. This has become increasingly adopted by couples almost everywhere. Here again, the already high frequency of divorce in our societies indicates an even higher number of contemplated separations or divorces. Probably a majority of us have considered this as an option, even if only momentarily, though perhaps we may have not verbalized it or overtly threatened it.

• • • • • • • • • •

Each divorce is the death of a small civilization.

Attributed to Pat Conroy

• • • • • • • • • •

Death and divorce are terminal forms of escape. They spell the end of working on the marriage, of solving the unresolved issues and all the rewards that come with this. Other extreme, but still very common, forms of escape are affairs (sexual or emotional), addictions, eating disorders, neuroses, depression or other mental disorders. These are also generally increasing in frequency and are also often linked to feelings of failure or hopelessness in our marriages. As a means of escape, they do not necessarily spell the end of a marriage but their indulgence makes any hope of functioning well as a couple impossible.

All the aforementioned forms of escape are, in a way, different versions of divorce, different ways of not following through on our commitment, of not being truly connected to our partner. For productive work to move forward in our marriages, we need to decisively close all these kinds of exits. But there are many, many other kinds of escape from the challenges of the most intimate kind of relationship which marriage is conceived to be.

Lesser escapes

• • • • • • • • • •

The place of the father in the modern suburban family is a very small one,
particularly if he plays golf.

Attributed to Bertrand Russell

• • • • • • • • • •

Lesser escapes are harder to put a finger on. We lived for years in rural areas and found a favourite escape of husbands there to be fishing. Fishing is a healthy way of connecting with nature, slowing down, finding peace of mind. It can be a good form of recreation, of recovering perspective. But when used as a way to avoid the pain of unresolved or unaddressed issues in our marriage it becomes an escape, an impediment to the deeper satisfaction of resolution. A man might always be able to find a rationalization for getting away to fish, but he needs to be honest with himself when it becomes a pattern and his wife feels abandoned or unfulfilled. Akin to fishing is golf, a favourite American male version of escape (and increasingly one for females as well), and other 'pastimes'. The expression 'golf widows' shows that, on some level, a lot of people (most probably wives) have recognized the effect these forms of escape have on marriage.

We perceive in many wives a perhaps even more subtle form of escape: housecleaning. Houses need to be cleaned, and keeping them clean is a matter of orderliness and hygiene. It is hard to fault this. But it nevertheless can become a form of escape, a way of being in a world which is predictable and manageable while avoiding meaningful and loving connection in a seemingly unmanageable relationship. In places where traditional roles around domestic chores are still largely adhered to, no woman feels the need to explain herself for keeping the house spotlessly clean all the time. But, here again, if in fact it is used as a way of avoiding the hard realities of an unsatifying marital bond, it can often be a form of escape.

· · · · · · · · · ·

I love sleep. My life has this tendency to fall apart when I'm awake.

Anonymous

· · · · · · · · · ·

This opens up a wide range of activities which we could all do well to reflect deeply on in order to uncover possible forms of escape. Going out with the guys, visiting Mother, watching TV, sleeping, jogging, going to the bar, shopping, community service. Even serving humanity or God can be twisted by our egos into a way of getting out of doing what God wants us to face in our marriage. The latest and most alluring, segregating activity of all is perhaps spending time on the Internet.

All these things can be seen as healthy, or at least okay. Also, there is good in a couple having time to themselves, doing things independently. It is healthy for a relationship to breathe, to have closeness and apartness. But while doing these kinds of things away from our spouse, it is good to ask ourselves: How do I feel about my partner? How does my partner feel about what I am doing right now? Is my love and affection strong? Is the relationship alive and life-giving? Is our marriage receiving enough attention and energy to thrive? And when we finish with our interludes apart, do we reconnect joyfully with renewed energy? If the answer to any of these questions is negative, then we are probably escaping the work of marriage through these other activities. We need to be honest with ourselves and, if we have any doubts, we would do well to have a good talk with our spouse about this. The possibilities of escape are almost endless.

With this wide, almost endless number of ways we contrive to escape, it is time to look more closely at what we are really trying to get away from.

Intimacy

· · · · · · · · · ·

The people we loved the most – our Higher Powers – hurt us the most. Our emotional intimacy issues were caused by, our fear of intimacy is, a direct result of our early childhood experiences. Our lives have been lived in reaction to the intellectual paradigms our egos adapted to deal with emotional trauma.

Robert Burney

· · · · · · · · · ·

The word 'intimacy' comes from the Latin word *intimum*, which means 'innermost'. Intimacy, as we have described in Chapter 1, is our earliest experience in this world. The womb world, and the early connection to our mother, were extremely intimate encounters. We all have a deep yearning for intimacy, this way of being with another where we can relate from our innermost being. As we grow up, we inevitably go through painful episodes of disconnection. Thus there is a connection, in our implicit memory, between intimacy and pain. Because of this association we develop a fear of intimacy, despite our innermost yearning for intimacy and feelings of oneness. We unconsciously seek ways out of intimacy to protect ourselves. The long-term commitment in marriage provides the milieu, a place where we can explore our fears and break through to achieving our innermost yearning for oneness.

Long-term commitment

• • • • • • • • • •

*No matter how free divorce, how frequently marriages break
up, in most societies there is the assumption of permanent
mating, of the idea that the marriage should last as long as
both live . . . No known society has ever invented a form of
marriage strong enough to stick that did not contain the 'till
death us do part' assumption.*

Margaret Mead

• • • • • • • • • •

There are several studies which directly relate to the wisdom of
commitment over the long term. The first, carried out in Oklahoma, United States, asked currently married respondents: 'Have
you ever seriously thought your marriage was in trouble?' Thirty-
four per cent said 'yes'. Those who said yes were asked, 'Are you
glad you are still together?' Ninety-two per cent said that they
were glad they were still together.

• • • • • • • • • •

*It is necessary but insufficient to stay married for the
children's sake. It is also necessary to stay happily married for
the children's sake.*

Frank Pittman

• • • • • • • • • •

A finding from the large-scale National Survey of Families and
Households (NSFH) in the United States is consistent with these
findings from the Oklahoma survey. As part of a report entitled
Does Divorce Make People Happy?, a team headed by Linda Waite
examined longitudinal data from the NSFH. Two-thirds of those
who were very unhappy in their marriages at some point but who
stayed together were happy five years later. We don't know what

happened to those couples, but it certainly shows the value of staying together through difficult times.

Our society has tried to accept divorce as inevitable in most cases where a couple seem to be incompatible. We have done our best to try to live with divorce and accept it. As a result of this growth in tolerance to separation and divorce, we have tended to turn a blind eye to the significant psychological and social consequences that research is continuing to reveal. We will have a more in-depth look at divorce later in this book, but the fact that children of divorced parents are twice as likely to divorce as children from intact families is sobering indeed. Many studies point to the much greater likelihood that children of divorced parents, whether or not the parents remarry or stay single, will face greater psychological, financial and social problems as adults. This is irrespective of the social class or educational attainments of the divorcing couple. As for the couple themselves, most will remarry but their chances of success in their second marriage are considerably less than in the first. Each successive marriage becomes more likely to end in divorce.

Commitment revisited

• • • • • • • • • •

Passion is the quickest to develop, and the quickest to fade. Intimacy develops more slowly, and commitment more gradually still.

Robert Sternberg

• • • • • • • • • •

When we start to understand more about our ego's compulsions to escape, and become more aware of what it is we are trying to escape from, we see the wisdom of commitment on another level. Many people clearly want to have a close, caring relationship with someone of the opposite sex, yet resist the whole notion of marriage, trivializing it as just a piece of paper. Yet commitment has a deep purpose with both a psychological and sociological dimension. The marital ceremony is a symbol of our commitment made inwardly, to each other, to God, and outwardly to our society and to the world. Analogously, many of our Bahá'í friends have told us that when they first came into contact with the Bahá'í teachings and became enthralled by them, they resisted moving into commitment, saying things like 'I am not the type who joins a religion' or 'religion is not for me' or 'I will just use these teachings in my life, I don't need to join anything to do that'. We are missing the point with these ego-born rationalizations. When we really connect with our soul's longing, when our higher self has awoken to its larger purpose, the most fitting thing to do is to commit ourselves, inwardly and outwardly, to the path that God has so graciously laid out for us. We make serious, long-term commitments like this at times when we feel connected, because on some level we recognize that the path of maintaining connection is truly challenging and our lower self will forever strive to avoid it. A deeply inward and courageously outward expression of commitment can orient both our inward being and our outer circle towards this significant move.

· · · · · · · · · ·

At the gate of the garden some stand and look within, but do not care to enter. Others step inside, behold its beauty, but do not penetrate far. Still others encircle this garden inhaling the fragrance of the flowers, and having enjoyed its full beauty, pass out again by the same gate. But there are always some who enter and, becoming intoxicated with the splendour of what they behold, remain for life to tend the garden.

Attributed to 'Abdu'l-Bahá

· · · · · · · · · ·

Our higher self has vision and is able to commit itself, conscious of the fact that our lower self will, when alarmed by feelings of alienation, seek ways out. The Prophet Muhammad has said, 'Do men think when they say "We believe" they shall be let alone and not be put to proof?' The strength of our inward commitment and the power of our social world to 'remind' us of the commitment we have made, while maddening at difficult moments, is actually an enduring gift. At times we need something to carry us through once the romantic notions fade or become obscured.

• • • • • • • • • •

If men or women contemplate an escape, they do not collect all their powers for the task. In none of the serious and important tasks of life do we arrange such a 'getaway'. We cannot love and be limited.

Alfred Adler

• • • • • • • • • •

Having said all this, we want to underline an important point. Commitment in marriage, to us, means far more than just staying together as a couple or hanging in there on a slender thread. What we understand as commitment to marriage is the **commitment to the work** that makes marriage enriching and life-giving.

Signs of conscious commitment in marriage

• • • • • • • • • •

Lay the foundation of your affection in the very centre of your spiritual being, at the very heart of your consciousness . . .

Attributed to 'Abdu'l-Bahá

• • • • • • • • • •

1. We see marriage as a spiritual path, attending to it as a spiritual task and service.
2. We are concerned about the well-being of our spouse

and occasionally inquire about her/his feelings concerning our relationship.

3. We see marriage as a dynamic, growing process which we seek to actively feed and enrich in diverse and novel ways.

4. When in conflict, we can remember the love we have for our partner.

5. We understand that our experience and perception of reality may be, and often is, different from that of others, including our spouse, and we honour this.

6. Resolution of conflicts is given high priority. The time and effort needed to resolve the conflict is made.

7. When marital difficulties seem beyond our ability to resolve, we get help from appropriate sources.

8. When immersed in marital difficulties, we don't 'leak' our problems to others.

9. We are willing, at times, to defer to a decision other than the one we believe to be correct, for the sake of unity in the marriage.

10. We appear in public as being clearly married (through words, body language and, perhaps, by wearing a ring or other symbolic conveyance) and, when not with our partner, still carry the aura of being married.

11. We close the door completely to considering or imagining anyone as a possible or better mate to us than the one we have married.

12. We consciously avoid any opportunities (in person or through the Internet) that might lead to an opening to exploring other relationship options.

PART III
MARRIAGE IN TRANSITION

7

Sex and Affection

· · · · · · · · · ·

*. . . marriage must be a union of the body and of the spirit
as well . . . this connection between them is a spiritual one,
hence it is a bond that will abide forever. Likewise do they
enjoy strong and lasting ties in the physical world as well.*

'Abdu'l-Bahá

· · · · · · · · · ·

If you are amongst those who have come to read this chapter
first, it is important for you to know that it is almost impossible
to isolate the physical and sexual relationship of a couple from the
dynamics of other aspects of their life together. In other words,
if you don't have time to pay attention to the rest of the content
of this book, which is about creating a deep connection and
enjoyable communication between husband and wife, reading
this chapter will not help you to have a fulfilling physical and
sexual connection with your spouse. Enjoying the pleasures of
physical connection takes attention, care, openness to learn, and
skills that impact on and are interwoven with all other aspects
of the relationship.

Our body is the throne of our spirit and the seat of our emotions, and therefore its health and pleasures are integral to maintaining emotional and spiritual well-being. Our spiritual and emotional connection is directly affected by our physical connection and vice versa. When two human beings commit themselves to partnership throughout all the worlds of God, they become united and intimates in all aspects of their life. The marital bond interweaves and integrates the physical, emotional and spiritual realms of our being. While the physical aspect of our marital relationship is necessarily temporary and therefore ultimately less important than our spiritual connection with each other, it is, nevertheless, very important to our marital life in this world.

One significant aspect of our physical being – our sexuality, in its most healthy, fulfilling expression – finds its legitimate place in the sanctity of marriage and becomes both a conduit and reinforcer of the marital bond. Through misuse, abuse and manipulation, it can also lead to distancing and troubles in a relationship. Our sexual connection in marriage is often a good reflection of our relationship as a whole. A dearth of physical and sexual connection is usually a sign of trouble in the relationship and should not be allowed to go on without being addressed. Here, too, doing the work of marriage concerning sex brings growth, closeness and abundant rewards.

Is there a place for sexuality in a spiritual life?

· · · · · · · · · ·

How many a man hath . . . denied himself the things that God hath decreed as lawful, imposed upon himself austerities and mortifications, and hath not been remembered by God, the Revealer of Verses.

Bahá'u'lláh

· · · · · · · · · ·

Humans are unique in so many ways. One of the functions we share with animals is the need for procreation. Thus we engage in sex, as do animals. But sex seems to complicate the life of a spiritual being. Many with a conscious spiritual orientation try to deny or overcome the desire for sex. Catholic priests are celibate; in many Buddhist traditions monks are celibate. Many Hindu gurus promote celibacy. In other circles, sex is permitted but confined to marriage. But even within marriage, sex is often viewed as something somehow shameful for the spiritual human being. For a creature which is essentially spiritual, having a body with sexual desires has often been seen as somehow unholy.

In a seminar we gave to single people, we received a question anonymously from a young man: 'My fiancée has said that we should strive to be as pure as possible and only have sex when we want a child. What do you think?' This question exemplifies the perspective we have just outlined, where sex, although permitted, is somehow unseemly to a spiritual being and should be kept to a minimum. The conclusion for someone holding this perspective, but acknowledging the need to procreate, is to have sex only to have offspring, which is actually the norm for animals.

But humans are not animals. We share the need for sexual intercourse in order to procreate but, for us, sex has come to mean much more. In many traditions, this 'more' was seen as somehow unacceptable from a spiritual point of view but, keeping to our theme that marriage has become an expanded institution with higher requirements in this age than in former times, let us look at this 'more' and understand its many implications.

· · · · · · · · · ·

The sexual embrace can only be compared with music and with prayer.

Attributed to Marcus Aurelius

· · · · · · · · · ·

The sexual revolution opened us up to sex, to see it not as something dark and unruly, not as something to feel guilty about, not as something to repress, but to enjoy as fully as we can. But this has also opened a Pandora's Box and we have not been able to put the lid back on. So taken have we become with the fascination of sex, so much have we become victimized by this fascination, that we have overlooked what was actually useful in this wild experiment. In becoming overly liberal concerning sex, the meaning of sex for the human creature, and its ramifications, have eluded us.

• • • • • • • • • •

His sexual attitudes are permissive rather than puritanical,
even though his emancipation from ancient taboos brings
him no sexual peace.

Christopher Lasch

• • • • • • • • • •

What is healthy sex?

'Abdu'l-Bahá has told us that the power of attraction and love permeates the universe at all levels. In terms of physics, a polar attraction between objects exists at the supra-galactic level and the sub-atomic level. Chemically speaking, molecules are bound by an attraction between atoms with a negative value to those with a positive value. Plants have stamens and pistils which effuse elements of attraction in order to procreate. Animals are differentiated to a greater degree, having the ability to move. Aside from the natural desire of social animals to be together in family or community groups, hormones become a source of attraction as a means to ensure procreation.

With humans, who have the added factors of consciousness, free will and imagination, this power of attraction has become much more complex. We are social creatures, therefore what is allowed, what is lawful, what is acceptable in any given society to some degree governs our choices of behaviour. The social needs of humans are deep, and growing in complexity with each passing generation. This is partly related to the growing complexity of human society, and it is also related to our individual psychological, intellectual and emotional yearnings which expand in concert with our societies' growth and development. The revolution in social technologies has further fed into our human sexual appetites, interests and possibilities.

In all areas of life, the structuring of human behaviour has been carried out through socialization which is imposed upon individuals through various social institutions. Historically, governments and religions have all, to some degree, put some restraints on what is 'okay' concerning sexual behaviour. These restraints have evolved, in part, to meet the need of the human infant to be cared for by a father and a mother who will stay with it, care for it, teach it and socialize it for the many years it takes for a human infant to reach maturity. This has been the case for humans for millions of years now, and has resulted in the development of a sexuality which always potentially transcends that of the animal or the purely hormonal sexual drive.

· · · · · · · · · ·

For all our 'sexual liberation', we've made sex profane by keeping it mundane.
Without some positve spiritual direction, sexual novelty eventually degenerates into boredom and emptiness.

David Schnarch

· · · · · · · · · ·

The primary sex organ of the human being, as testified by many psychologists and sexologists, is the brain. Our rich imaginations, fantasies, conceptualizations and mental associations have transformed human sexuality tremendously. The primitive pleasure of sexual release has, for humans, evolved into the possibility of sexual ecstasy which, we must assume, no other known creature experiences. To modern man, this has become fascinating to an extreme degree, and it is equally fascinating to explore what really works best, both for the enrichment of our sexual experience and the protection and development of our offspring.

The first requirement

One of the surprises to many which was uncovered in the extensive research project described by Robert Michael and his associates in *Sex in America* (1995), was the finding that, as a group, the most sexually satisfied couples were evangelical Christians. It had been supposed by many that these would be the most repressed sexually. How can this finding be explained?

As humans, we have evolved from relying on sex for mating into developing romantic circuitry and finally utilizing attachment circuitry. In the past, the romantic drive was not encouraged as a means of finding a partner – partners were most often chosen by parents or other elders – and the sex drive was sanctioned only within marriage. The waning of religious constraints on our societies in the 20th century opened us to a huge surge of liberalization and experimentation with both these drives. One of the most frequent causes of sexual problems nowadays is the huge emphasis put on the sexual relationship. There are high expectations of it, and in some cases a lot of experience with sex prior to marriage. Sex, as portrayed in the media, becomes something to do early in a relationship, rather than an expression of love in the context of mature commitment.

Within this context of sexual 'awakening' and liberalization, the evangelical Christians in the United States have been one significantly large enough group to maintain a reasonable degree of traditional structure to marriage and the teaching of limiting the sex drive to married couples. We can imagine that the opening up of sexual thinking had its positive influence on this group within their marriages. Their adherence to their religious standards has, mostly, held them back from experimenting with sex outside the parameters of marriage. Apparently, it has worked quite well! Time and again it has been proved that promiscuity and wild sexual experimentation are not conducive to healthy or even satisfying human sexual functioning; safety and commitment are. The conditions of safety and trust in a relationship, especially for women, have been cited by specialists in sexual relationships as being important criteria for a fulfilling sex life. The spiritual and emotional commitments and connections we make with our partner have their counterpart in our physical and sexual connection with them. Thus, the first condition for a healthy and truly satisfying sexual connection is a commitment, with absolute faithfulness, to a relationship that will endure, according to Bahá'í teachings, even beyond this world.

The other requirement

Of the three circuits related to pair bonding, the brain's sexual circuitry resulting in the sex drive is the most purely physical and animalistic. In *Why We Love*, Helen Fisher has explained that the romantic drive is much more powerful and intense than the sex drive; the brain's romantic circuitry has links to some sexual functions but can work more or less independently. The powerful feelings of love engendered by the activation of the romantic circuitry can add incredible intensity and a whole new dimension to sexual experience. However, it is apparently the attachment circuitry, which comes into play in the long-term commitment of a couple to each other, that brings the greatest amount of sexual satisfaction. One of the reasons for this is that our sexuality can become linked to growth in mindfulness and maturity.

· · · · · · · · · ·

*Your feelings have a bigger impact on genital function and
orgasm than do physical sensations.*

David Schnarch

· · · · · · · · · ·

Research is showing that a couple of generations ago people
were having more sex than they do at present. We may, however, remember some of the history around sexual relationships
in earlier times. This might include the fact that women usually
had little hope of enjoying the sexual experience. Sex was widely
viewed as something that men need and that women, in their
subservient position, needed to accommodate to, often without
enjoyment. While these roles were not very exalted, they were
clear, and this conduced to more sex taking place.

But we have come to expect more from our sexual partnership.
Gender equality, as we have stated before, brings into marriage
very significant changes. What was previously simply a matter
of playing a well-defined role becomes open to negotiation
between husband and wife. The usual assumptions no longer
hold. The huge benefits which the achievement of intimacy
yields to couplehood and, by extension, to the whole family,
make it necessary for every couple to expand their horizons,
and to honour the refined and very sensitive nature of intimacy
between a man and a woman in marriage.

The requirement of commitment naturally finds its
foundation in feelings of love, emotional connectedness and
open communication. In the sexual arena too, the new age will
be an age where the feminine qualities must come to the fore
so that there will be a balance between feminine and masculine
qualities, leading to the enrichment and maturity of both.
Commitment creates the context for this process, since this kind
of growth takes a lifetime and a willingness to learn at every step
of the way. This rarely occurs at the outset of a relationship.

· · · · · · · · · ·

It takes a long time for a human being to mature sexually.
David Schnarch

· · · · · · · · · ·

Nature wills

As in other areas of our personality, we come into marriage with different baggage and dispositions in relation to physical contact and sex. It is fascinating to observe that, here too, nature provides the opportunity for the amazing act of balancing and brings together two different and sometimes opposing elements that would provide the best fit for the growth and development of each. The opposition of the elements that have been brought together often becomes apparent after the romantic stage in a marriage, after we have been given a taste and a sample of what is possible. Romance provides us with a vision towards which we can aspire. Aside from the uniqueness of each individual, there are often gender differences in sexual attitudes and appetites. To complicate things, these physical and sexual needs evolve and change as we go through different stages of our life.

Marriage is the milieu for fulfilment and evolution in this facet of our life. As was previously mentioned, marriage gives us the opportunity to grow up and finish our childhood. This extends to the physical and sexual aspects of our life as well. Maintaining a healthy and affectionate physical connection requires the same kind of qualities of spirit as do other aspects of our marital life, and yields similar benefits. As the welfare and happiness of our spouse is of paramount importance to us, learning about their healthy physical needs should find a prominent position in our orientation. Interestingly enough, as we have already seen in other areas of the marital relationship, consciously setting out to discover and fulfil the physical and sexual yearnings of our partner leads to the awakening of lost parts of our own self.

Why can't it all happen naturally?

· · · · · · · · · ·

Love is a choice you make from moment to moment.
Attributed to Barbara De Angelis

· · · · · · · · · ·

Our physical connection is often thought of as something that should just happen or come naturally. Why do we need to examine it? Why talk in terms of 'doing the work of marriage around sex'? The above-mentioned factors which affect our sexual relationship help us realize that the so-called instinctual sex drive is far from simple and natural to human beings who are engaged in a meaningful relationship.

During romance, if we are fortunate enough to have this phase endure past the engagement and wedding, sex, like other aspects of our relationship, **does** seem to be the most natural and yearned-for experience. The pumping of love hormones, the newness of the relationship, the falling away of protective walls we have built up around us as we grew up, and the anticipation and hope for fulfilment of all of our wishes, are often naturally reflected in our early physical and sexual interactions. This natural expression of love in sexual encounters acts as a catalyst to strengthen and solidify the relationship.

Research is showing, however, that a very significant percentage of married couples gradually fall out of having sexual relations. As mentioned above, in this time of so-called sexual liberation the present generation of couples are apparently getting less sex than did their grandparents. Many a married couple live their lives with unfulfilled sexual needs. Research also clarifies that the breakdown of sexual relations in a marriage is a good predictor of a complete breakdown of the marriage. Why should such a pleasurable experience as sex fall to the wayside in marriage?

In Chapters 2 and 3 we wrote about the second stage of a relationship in marriage and its challenging dynamics. In the power struggle phase there are a whole range of factors which tend to tie us up in knots and keep us from getting close emotionally and, therefore, physically. Around this time in the life of a couple, the realities of everyday life set in. There may be children to be looked after, work to be done, fatigue from these and other daily responsibilities which can wear us thin. There are a whole range of emotions that are churned up during the power struggle: sadness, resentment, rejection, confusion, incompetence, disappointment and fear. These negative feelings do not conduce to physical closeness. We may still feel some sexual urges, but the negative feelings will tend to dampen or eliminate our desire to move into showing any physical affection, at least to our spouse. In addition, the many differences two people may have around their sexual appetites and in the ways they find pleasure, some of which can be purely gender-based, come to the fore. Beyond this is the baggage we carry with us around sex from our childhood socialization, from the myriad images we have soaked up through the media, and from whatever sexual experiences and impressions we may have had before marriage.

All of this has a direct impact – quite 'naturally' – on a couple's sexual relationship. If we do not attend to this, it should come as no surprise that our sexual life will diminish or deteriorate. In a healthy relationship, the physical and sexual relationship becomes enhanced over time rather than diminished. Consciousness about these challenges and a willingness to communicate and learn from each other lead to an enriched, dynamic and sustainable physical and sexual bond in which the sexuality of each is celebrated and honoured. Let us examine some aspects of this positive and pleasurable work.

Towards a fulfilling sexual connection in marriage

· · · · · · · · · ·

. . . while the urge to eat is a personal matter concerning only the hungry person, the sex urge involves for its true expression another individual. It is this 'other person' that causes all the trouble.

James Thurber and E. B. White

· · · · · · · · · ·

We have said this elsewhere, but it bears repeating because it is somehow a surprising point about intimate relationships: perhaps the most primal challenge to having a truly close – as opposed to enmeshed – relationship with another is the realization that they are, indeed, an 'other'. During the first two stages of marriage – romance and power struggle – we project onto our partner in a big way. While projecting, we are not really accepting their 'otherness'. During romance, we bask in the projection that they are us or, at least, that they are there for us. During the power struggle, we are all about making them us through every device imaginable. We have explored earlier the dynamics around our resistance on an unconscious level to otherness. This is a significant barrier to moving into mature love. Let us have a look at one very concrete manifestation of otherness around sex and see how we can move forward and grow with the inevitable differences between partners.

Men and women

· · · · · · · · · ·

Women need a reason to have sex. Men just need a place.

Attributed to Billy Crystal

· · · · · · · · · ·

It is evident that the marital relationship benefits from sexual contact. Perhaps not as clear is the fact that both men and women also individually benefit psychologically as well as physiologically. The quality of a relationship is often a good indicator of the partners' general health.

Research has shown that healthy sexual activity in committed relationships boosts self-image and self-confidence. In men, research shows that regular sexual intercourse is conducive to success in the workplace, better physical health and longer life, including lower rates of diabetes and even cancer (because having sex bolsters the immune system). Researchers have also found that having sex twice or more a week – compared to men having sex once a month or less – reduced the risk of fatal heart attack by half.

For women, a fascinating study has found that semen acts as an antidepressant and also helps protect the vagina from harmful bacteria. Oxytocin, a hormone that is related to sexual function in a woman's body, increases endorphins which help reduce headaches, arthritic pain, and PMS symptoms. Surges of oxytocin also promote sleep. Other research in this arena has shown that sex is generally linked to lower blood pressure and overall stress reduction, and helps maintain a healthy weight in both men and women.

While having a healthy sexual relationship in marriage benefits both men and women, what sex means to each gender differs markedly. Without understanding the nature of these differences, we run the risk of moving into conflict around divergent expectations and sensitivities. Although gender differences are not universal and there are always exceptions, knowledge and information about these is vitally important. Understanding differences, whether gender-based or purely idiosyncratic, helps us move out of the patterns of blaming and personalizing that often occur around sexual issues, and opens us to finding ways and means of expanding our sexual manner of relating for the purpose of achieving compatability and mutual fulfilment.

• • • • • • • • • •

You know that look women get when they want sex?
Me neither.
Attributed to Steve Martin

• • • • • • • • • •

Testosterone is the main hormone which fuels the sex drive, especially in men. It is present in both men and women but much more so in men. Research on brain and hormones has shown that the amount of testosterone pumped into a man's circulatory system is, on average, ten to thirty times that of a woman's. This is the amount men need to live a happy and healthy life. Since this is the hormone that motivates us toward sexual activity, it makes sense that research reveals that a man tends to think about sex more often than a woman does. With all this natural ammunition in their body, men are usually more inclined to use sexual contact as a means of expressing their love and energy, and to perceive it as a means of creating connection – or even restoring ruptures when they happen – in a relationship.

• • • • • • • • • •

Among men, sex sometimes results in intimacy;
among women, intimacy sometimes results in sex.
Attributed to Barbara Cartland

• • • • • • • • • •

The findings on sexual desire and inclination in women reveal quite a different reality. When asked if they would be content to be held close and treated tenderly without moving into sexual play, 72 per cent of the 90,000 women questioned said 'yes'. Half of the sample were under 40 years old. For women, sexual inclinations are closely linked to physical tenderness, physical affection and emotional closeness. It is no surprise then that in order to have a healthy sexual life they want to feel good about the connection in the relationship. In other words, the sexual connection for women is an extension of emotional and physical, non-sexual connectedness. While for women feeling emotionally secure and receiving abundant physical affection from their partner makes them sexually responsive, for men it works the other way round. When a man feels sexually connected to his wife, he feels more secure, has more energy and becomes a more willing partner, motivated to do the work of relationship in other areas of couplehood. This is a manifest wonder of nature at work: men for women and women for men doing exactly what is needed to complete the circle and take their sexuality to a mature and enriched level.

How can the two worlds meet?

In the realm of physical and sexual connection, as in other domains of marriage, we are called to move into a more conscious mode of relating. Breaking through differences starts by becoming aware of the nature of differences in a safe, non-judgemental way. Working through sexual differences requires a simple yet fundamental procedure: a mindful dialogue in which we can express and empathize with each others' feelings and needs in a meaningful manner.

Mindful dialogue is in itself a form of verbal intimacy which moves us almost immediately into emotional intimacy. A meaningful dialogue about any subject of importance, in which both partners feel heard and respected, goes a long way towards increasing closeness and a desire for sexual intimacy. Most affairs, as we will discuss later, start with these kinds of sharing and verbal intimacy outside of marriage. It is because of this natural tendency that we strongly recommend to couples: one, **not** to get engaged in sharing deep feelings and emotional concerns with anyone of the opposite sex other than their spouse; and, two, emphatically do so with their spouse.

• • • • • • • • • •

I'm too shy to express my sexual needs except over the phone to people I don't know.

Attributed to Garry Shandling

• • • • • • • • • •

A meaningful dialogue, especially around sexual experiences, fears and concerns, which is not about criticizing and blaming but rather about exploration with an open attitude, significantly contributes to intimacy and closeness. But there is often a huge fear, usually because of feelings of shame or inadequacy, that keeps us from moving into discussions about sexual intimacy. These kinds of feelings, which affect our experience of sex, are especially tender ones; and the need to keep our dialogues about sex safe and *without* criticism is, if anything, more important than in all other dialogues. Rising above this fear, taking extra care to prepare spiritually for these dialogues, priming our feelings of compassion for one another and listening with intent make these encounters very rewarding.

As always, in a mindful dialogue our discussions around sex involve learning to let go of our purely subjective experience and opening up to learning about what is happening in our spouse's world. Again, for humans, our sexual world is far from being purely physical. We have dreams, expectations, vulnerabilities and inner experiences. Some of what we are carrying within ourselves around the topic of sex may be very unhealthy introjections of messages we received while growing up in an unhealthy social or even family environment. Some may carry confusion and trauma concerning early – and sadly even childhood – sexual encounters. If we don't visit these areas with our partner, many things may remain hidden and unresolved and become sources of frustration to our sexual connection. If they have no chance to be aired or to have light shed on them, they act as an impediment to our marital relationship and can come to manifest themselves in unhealthy and destructive ways. The marital relationship is the one most exquisitely designed to help us finally come to understand and break out of the many dark, unexplored areas of our psyches which prevent us from benefiting fully from the legitimate pleasures of sexual connectedness, a gift that is the exclusive domain of married couples.

• • • • • • • • • •

The proper use of the sex instinct is the natural right of every individual, and it is precisely for this very purpose that the institution of marriage has been established.

Shoghi Effendi

• • • • • • • • • •

From dialogue to action

The information and insights gained in dialogue, when both have had a chance to express themselves and feel heard, lead to a deeper understanding and greater compassion for each other. This can help us move out of our rigid disposition and will naturally prime us to adopt new behaviours to enrich the relationship. Becoming aware of the need for new behaviour, even the willingness to adopt it, however, does not make it occur right away nor does it happen perfectly in early attempts. There is almost always a need for a number of such safe dialogues to reinforce the process by providing more information and appreciation of the advances, no matter how small. This is why commitment and active patience are implicit requirements of this journey.

• • • • • • • • • •

The art of love . . . is largely the art of persistence.
Albert Ellis

• • • • • • • • • •

Our standpoint goes against the common assumption that the differences in sexual energy and desire in partners are absolute and nothing can be done about it. This common assumption leads couples to settle into patterns in which, even if one is getting his or her way, the encounter or lack thereof is not fulfilling to either. Here again, we are called to move beyond doing what we think should happen 'naturally'. This is in keeping with a main theme of this book: what we achieve by consciously stretching into a new behaviour to meet the needs of our spouse is the recovery of parts of our self which were repressed or left undeveloped early in our lives. It takes some time, at first, to bring these natural latent urges to life, but what we achieve is, in its broader sense, more truly natural. Let us review here some of the latest findings and insights of experts in this field which point to a new outlook on sexual relating.

• • • • • • • • • •

. . . intimacy is nature's latest 'experiment' (because it uses the part of our brain that evolved last), and we're still trying to understand what it is and how it works in long-term relationships.
David Schnarch

• • • • • • • • • •

High or low libido?

Marriage provides the ideal milieu for physical and sexual needs to be fully expressed and enjoyed. Commitment to marriage entails an implicit and often explicit promise of faithfulness.

Our yearnings for physical and sexual affection are going to be expressed and met within the framework of the trust and commitment embedded in this promise. The assumption is that a partner's love and care for the other's welfare will make her or him responsive and available to the human needs of the other, including those of a sexual nature. Dr Willard B. Harley, in discussing ten basic emotional needs that show up in a marital relationship in his book *His Needs, Her Needs* (2001), points to the emotional need for sex as an exclusive one because we will be dependent on our spouse to meet it and have no other ethical choices.

• • • • • • • • • •

You can give without loving, but you can never love without giving.

Anonymous

• • • • • • • • • •

If we remain mindful of this ethical premise to a healthy married life, then we have the motivation to find the ways and means of meeting each other's needs. Creating a bridge between the two worlds becomes a necessity. A difference in libido, for example, is usual; but each partner, in their own way, is fully responsible for creating what is fulfilling to both. Alison Armstrong, in her seminars *Celebrating Men, Satisfying Women*, says that in a successful marriage the partners must always respond positively to the other's request for intimacy and move into sexual connection without necessarily feeling the urge or desire to have sex at that point (she gives exception to what she calls 'pumpkin hours', the time period that women need to sleep without interuption). She believes that in understanding the difference sex makes in creating a healthy relationship, one must develop a new willingness to provide sex on an 'as needed' basis with an expectation, of course, of moving into an enjoyment of the process over time. For some this will take learning, and this learning will take place through engaging in the sexual experience. Pat Love and Jo Robinson, in their book *Hot Monogamy*, say that sex is, itself, the most powerful aphrodisiac; in other words, having sexual relations opens one up sexually.

Connecting to and honouring the sexual yearnings of a partner with higher libido is a positive stretch for the one with lower libido, and brings rewards for both. But how can one just go along without desiring it? How can we avoid a build-up of resentment? And what would be the role of the one with more needs in making it possible and easier for their partner to make this stretch?

One of the reasons women often have less desire for sex is the way their minds and bodies work. John Gray, in his book *Mars on Fire, Venus on Ice*, talks about the significance of hormones in determining human behaviour, but with a new twist. While he reaffirms that testosterone is the hormone that keeps men sexually active, he says that what evokes sexuality in women is, in fact, oxytocin, generally called a bonding hormone. Oxytocin increases during sexual activity, peaks at orgasm, and stays elevated for a period of time after intercourse. In women this hormone is also released when they talk, share inner feelings, care for others and feel cared for. Some other activities that can also contribute to the release of this hormone in women is getting their hair done, manicures and pedicures, massages, even working in the garden or shopping. According to Daniel G. Amen, in *The Brain in Love*:

> there is an amnesic effect created by oxytocin during sex and orgasm that blocks negative memories people have about each other for a period of time. The same amnesic effect occurs from the release of oxytocin during childbirth, while a mother is nursing, to help her forget the labour pain, and during long, stressful nights spent with a newborn so that she can bond to her baby with positive feelings and love.

The world out there is still largely founded on masculine principles: it is a problem-solving, competitive milieu, one which is conducive to the production of testosterone. According to John Gray, most of our daily encounters, including driving, are testosterone-producing activities. All of this conspires against the production of oxytocin in women who have become more actively involved in this world. Because of the multi-tasking capacities of the woman's psyche and the connective and inclusive way her brain operates, by the end of the day most feel overwhelmed and exhausted both physically and emotionally. Cooperative activities are what women need to raise their level of oxytocin and to feel good as a woman. According to Alison Armstrong, for women to become alive to their sexual energy they need to find ways of letting go of the male energy they call upon in the workplace. This may entail getting out of their heads and into their bodies. Going to yoga after work, having a hot bath, or dancing, are among the many ways a woman can effectively do this, and much of this can be helped along or initiated by their husbands. Women do not as naturally or as easily reside in their bodies as men do, but once they do, they find it quite naturally a feminine place. This is something for women to awaken to, and their husbands are most definitely the ones best placed to facilitate this. Higher oxytocin not only affects a woman's sexuality; it has also been linked with a feeling of generosity which naturally is extended toward one's partner, especially if the partner has been active in facilitating the oxytocin-producing activities.

The antithesis of this is seen more and more in the media. Nowadays there is a fashion for portraying women as sexually aggressive in movies, TV dramas, commercials, etc. This is yet another example of attempting to extend the masculine idea of sex and make it the norm, rather than honouring the feminine and allowing for difference. The more women try to fit into this strange fantasy, the more they will find themselves losing their feminine energy in an effort to adopt to a male-oriented milieu.

This trend not only strains women to emulate men, but creates false expectations in men. This is a compartmentalized view of sex rather than a dance and balance between the masculine and feminine.

For men with a higher libido, awakening to the need of their wife for such activities or conditions and stretching into facilitating them is a good start. For some women, the mere involvement of their husband in family and household chores, thereby reducing their stress and feeling of responsibility in the home, goes a long way to help them relax and be more present for their husband emotionally and sexually. In addition to this, a major step forward for the male is stretching into greater emotional connection and also feeding the relationship with greater amounts of non-sexual physical affection. Holding hands, embraces, hugs, cuddles, expressions of love, sharing of inner feelings and appreciation, all affect a woman's sense of herself as a woman. Efforts in these areas are a clear manifestation of love to a woman, and this is conducive to increasing levels of oxytocin in her body, making her more responsive sexually. Women more commonly find that their sexual confidence and competence blossom when they feel loved and appreciated.

These efforts are not only beneficial to the partner with lower libido, but are equally important for the one with higher libido, because it helps them to get in touch with repressed and unknown parts of themselves. It especially awakens men to areas that have been lost as they grew up in a competitive male-oriented society.

• • • • • • • • • •

A fellow ought to save a few of the long evenings he spends with his girl till after they're married.

Kin Hubbard

• • • • • • • • • •

Crossing the bridge to the other side

Everything we have said above points to the need for us to stretch our sense of who we are and what we can do. When we take the high road of conscious behaviour rather than falling into the trap of a familiar, easy and instinctual disposition, the bond connecting us strengthens. We develop as individuals, just as the bond between us grows. A deep appreciation of the other comes into focus. This also reactivates the romantic and sexual circuitry, resulting in deep and intense feelings of spiritual oneness as well as physical connection. The romantic feelings engendered in this process are much more awake and aware than they were at the romantic stage of our relationship, because now we see the other, know each other better and more intimately, and our own sense of self has also grown.

Sex therapist David Schnarch has written that the best sex comes with maturity. In other words, despite the decline in sexual hormones, he says that sex doesn't get really good until we move into our forties. This, of course, requires that we have done the work of marriage, which includes the often necessary explorations into our sexual relationship. Seen from this perspective, sex is not something to let go of as we move through middle age and beyond. Rather, as we age and continue to transcend the limits of our survival mechanisms, we move into ever closer domains of intimacy. This intimacy works through the various aspects of our partnership: verbal, emotional, sexual and spiritual. Each of these support the other and conduce to a feeling of wholeness, of completion.

In this chapter we have touched upon differences between men and women which have to do with sexuality and sexual contact. Our differences around sex are just part of the picture. The design, originally propelled by sexual polarities, of male and female coming together and forming a union, has its struggles. But we have begun to see the wisdom of the Creator in ordaining the seemingly crazy mix of man and woman coming together to form an eternal bond. In the next chapter we will look at the differences between men and women in other spheres of encounter and how we can meet these struggles together for our further enrichment and development.

8

Gender Dances

· · · · · · · · · ·

The world in the past has been ruled by force, and man has dominated over woman by reason of his more forceful and aggressive qualities both of body and mind. But the balance is already shifting; force is losing its dominance, and mental alertness, intuition, and the spiritual qualities of love and service, in which woman is strong, are gaining ascendancy.

'Abdu'l-Bahá

· · · · · · · · · ·

The Bahá'í writings clearly establish the equality of men and women. This principle, along with many others found in these writings, has gradually come to the fore as humanity has stepped further into the modern age. As these principles are gradually taking hold, the edifice of human society has become shaken. The particular principle of gender equality has been revolutionizing our world on many levels and continues to do so right down to the very roots.

Effects of the movement toward equality

. . . .

I asked . . .
why women, after centuries of following their men,
now walk ahead.
He said
there were many unexploded land mines since the war.

Anonymous

. . . .

When Bahá'u'lláh first promulgated the principle of gender equality, females were at an extreme disadvantage around the world. It seemed, outwardly, that they were definitely **not** equal (meaning inferior) and the whole idea of equality was met with resistance, especially by males. Expounding on this principle in 1912, 'Abdu'l-Bahá stated that

> At present in spheres of human activity woman does not manifest her natal prerogatives, owing to lack of education and opportunity. Without doubt education will establish her equality with men.

In the United States and many other countries, more women than men are now gaining acceptance into universities, so much so that some of these institutions have contemplated lowering requirement standards for males in an attempt to equalize the gender ratios in classes! In symphony orchestras around the world, women used to be almost completely absent, even though they would audition for places. When many orchestras recognized that a strong prejudice was influencing the selection process, auditions started to be held incognito, with both males and females kept out of sight of the selection committees. Ever since, the number of women being selected has soared!

● ● ● ● ● ● ● ● ● ●

Women belong in the house . . .
and the Senate.

Anonymous

● ● ● ● ● ● ● ● ● ●

In science, engineering and law, although women have made many inroads these fields are still relatively more dominated by males, not because females have not proved their abilities but because many women often retreat after attaining high positions in these professions in favour of having children or changing to fields which seem to suit their female sensibilities and desire for human interaction. In other words, the social context is often still driven by male attributes and this affects the degree to which women feel comfortable within it.

Effects of the movement towards equality on marriage

We have asserted before that marriage lies at the foundation of human civilization. What has been the effect of the movement towards equality on this institution? In a word: Huge! Marriage has been revolutionized by the impact of the movement toward gender equality. This has challenged marriage severely, and couplehood within the home is still far from having attained a sense of equilibrium. Let us explore the impact that the movement towards recognizing gender equality has had on this foundational union.

● ● ● ● ● ● ● ● ● ●

I refuse to believe that trading recipes is silly.
Tunafish casserole is at least as real as corporate stock.

Barbara Grizzuti Harrison

● ● ● ● ● ● ● ● ● ●

The traditional role of the female in the home can be seen as being central. Cooking, cleaning, nurturing children: these have been considered her sphere. Unfortunately, this role was often not regarded highly by men. Though the wife was doing hugely important and demanding work and having a mighty influence, especially on the children, this was all done under the good graces, as it were, of the husband who was doing the presumably more important work of supporting the whole operation financially. In some ways the wife was seen as a kind of servant. Making big decisions was usually up to the man, who did not usually feel it necessary to consult his wife and take her views into consideration.

. . . .

My husband makes all the important decisions: will our country go to war next year, will the dollar rise or fall, and so on. I just do the minor stuff: shall we move house, what school our children will go to, their choice of career or life partner . . .

Anonymous

. . . .

Men, in this context, managed the home in the same power-oriented way that things were handled in the workplace, with the lucky exception that men who were considered underlings in the workplace still usually held the superior position at home. Mastering and fine-tuning a way of relating to each other as husband and wife, where the voice of each is equally heard, was not even considered. This suits the male psyche, because relating as equals is not something that men have ever been strong in. Relating to a woman as an equal is inherently frightening for a man who senses his inner fragility and weakness. Dominating by force, staying confidently in control, helps men keep the lid on feeling inferior or vulnerable. Broadly speaking, domination has historically been a male survival mechanism.

The shift towards gender equality has changed all this.

Outside the home, the greater role played by women has been in the context of a still largely male-dominated milieu. The way things are done in the workplace has been shifting, but very slowly. We are still living within a power-oriented society, and many of the natal strengths of the female do not sit well in this environment. Within the home, of course, the call has been raised for husbands to be more present; take more hands-on responsibility for domestic work; and most significantly, be more involved as a father to his children. The psychological literature now points to the role of the father as being hugely significant and helpful to the healthy development of children. Men have been struggling with this but have been learning a lot.

The movement towards equality, which has not yet shifted the power orientation of society as a whole, has already brought about a massive shift of orientation within the home. But some of the emerging patterns have not been expressive of true equality. We will explore two such patterns below, but first we want to enlarge on a theme that has cropped up already in various sections of this book: the differences between male and female, especially as they pertain to the marital relationship. Without a clear understanding of gender differences we cannot really begin to make marriage work, and a working vision of a relationship of equals in marriage will continue to elude us.

Emotional needs of men and women

· · · · · · · · · ·

The source of all life and knowledge is in man and woman,
and the source of all living is in the interchange and the
meeting and mingling of these two: man–life and woman–
life, man–knowledge and woman–knowledge, man–being
and woman–being.

D. H. Lawrence

· · · · · · · · · ·

Amongst the many physiological differences that exist between men and women is the difference in the structure of the brain and its function. While the male brain is larger, the female brain has more neurons and neural connections. The corpus collosum, which connects the left brain to the right brain, is significantly larger in females, leading many to believe this provides the physiological basis for women being better at multi-tasking, less linear and more holistic in their thinking. Based on his extensive work with couples, psychologist Willard Harley wrote his book *His Needs, Her Needs* about the different needs of men and women. According to Harley, there is a 'top five' list of emotional needs that surface with regularity amongst women and which differ from the 'top five' for men. The number one emotional need for most women, he found, is affection. Women need their spouse to assure them through words and affectionate deeds that they are loved and cared for. The next emotional need of a woman is for him to talk to her. The need to engage in conversation is frequently a primary need for women but rarely one for men. Another important need for women is for her husband to be honest and open with her so that she can trust him. Next, she often needs to feel financially secure and comfortable, and finally she needs her husband to be a family man and a good father.

· · · · · · · · · ·

Women always worry about the things that men forget;
men always worry about the things women remember.

Anonymous

· · · · · · · · · ·

In the list of emotional needs for men, according to Harley, the number one is sexual fulfilment. The next emotional need of a man, he found, is for his wife to be his recreational companion. He also often needs his wife to be good-looking and attractive, and to provide a comfortable and peaceful home for him. Finally, he needs to be admired and to feel that she is proud of him.

As with similar findings – those that John Gray, Alison Armstrong and many others in this field have explored – the differences uncovered by Willard Harley are not written in stone. Any given man or woman can be different from the norm of their gender on any given trait. These are just generalized differences, and perhaps as our societies move toward balance between masculine and feminine characteristics these could change. Understanding the differences at this point, however, can help us make sense of the troubles that emerge in marriages. It can help us get beyond negative labelling or our tendency towards enmeshment where we attempt to make the other like us. We **are** different and difference is not, in itself, pathological. However, because so many of these differences are generalities, we need to explore them further with our own particular spouse and our own self to discover what is true for us.

$\bullet\bullet\bullet\bullet\bullet\bullet\bullet\bullet\bullet\bullet$

He is half of a blessed man,
Left to be finished by such as she;
And she a fair divided excellence,
Whose fullness of perfection lies in him.
William Shakespeare

$\bullet\bullet\bullet\bullet\bullet\bullet\bullet\bullet\bullet\bullet$

We have talked about gender differences related to affection and sex in the previous chapter. What we would like to do here is look more closely at two other gender-related needs mentioned above which call for a special kind of attention in marriage. This is the need most men have for acknowledgement and admiration, and the need that the great majority of women have for verbal companionship. These needs are often viewed negatively by the opposite sex.

Admiration

● ● ● ● ● ● ● ● ●

And each man stands with his face in the light
Of his own drawn sword,
Ready to do what a hero can.
Elizabeth Barrett Browning

● ● ● ● ● ● ● ● ●

The need for admiration is usually much stronger in men than in women. Men like to do things for people, and getting recognition for this garners a sense of satisfaction which makes them want to do even more. Most men love to feel like a hero, to be looked up to. This does not make men bad, any more than the desire for fond physical affection makes a woman bad. Given the backdrop of the shift towards gender equality discussed above, this craving of men to feel admired, probably most especially by one's partner, has put men's psyche in a perilous position. As women have become equal breadwinners, men's pride of place as sole provider has been usurped. As men have taken on more involvement at home and in the domestic arena, they have found themselves falling far short of their wives' higher expectations and standards. Women, in their quest to improve their husband, have many ideas and ways of expressing these to him. In doing this, they believe they are helping him, but in almost all cases the husband receives this as criticism, feeling that he is not measuring up and perhaps never can. The resulting disappointment and dissatisfaction in the woman results in her husband coming to believe (but not wanting to acknowledge) that he is the source of her unhappiness. An emotionally defeated man will not make a good husband.

Many men have, in the interest of being enlightened males who shouldn't need the recognition of their wives, swallowed this often primal need and just try to push on, leaving their tank of admiration need empty. Not only does this make a man very vulnerable to another woman who may start to fill that tank, it leaves him with little fuel to fulfil the needs of his wife in a healthy way, so adding to her frustrations and hence to the criticisms or 'negative vibes' she sends his way.

· · · · · · · · · ·

Behind every successful man is a surprised woman.
Maryon Pearson

· · · · · · · · · ·

Recognizing this need in men can help women in their encounters with their spouse. Giving praise is generally helpful for building self-esteem, especially in children. With men, it touches a primal nerve devoped through the ages of their being protectors and defenders of the family unit or clan. It doesn't mean that men need to be applauded constantly, nor that their shortcomings should be ignored; it does mean that encouragement and acknowledging their efforts and goodness will be far more effective in improving their behaviour than the negative statements, belittling and criticism that are often used for this purpose. Issues around failings that trigger a wife are best dealt with by using a safe structure such as mindful dialogue.

· · · · · · · · · ·

We must ever praise each other.
'Abdu'l-Bahá

· · · · · · · · · ·

Conversation

· · · · · · · · · ·

One must talk. That's how it is. One must.
Attributed to Marguerite Duras

· · · · · · · · · ·

The need to engage in conversation is frequently a primary need for women but rarely one for men. First of all, there is a difference between men and women in the way they converse. Women tend to look at each other when talking; men tend to face, together, in the same direction, especially when talking about personal things and as equals.

· · · · · · · · · ·

Given the cultural barriers to intersex conversation, the amazing thing is that we would even expect women and men to have anything to say to each other for more than ten minutes at a stretch. The barriers are ancient – perhaps rooted, as some paleontologist may soon discover, in the contrast between the occasional guttural utterances exchanged in male hunting bands and the extended discussions characteristic of female food-gathering groups.

Barbara Ehrenreich

· · · · · · · · · ·

These gender differences around conversing are, in the generalized sense we have earlier explained, valid. It is definitely helpful at times for women to realize that conversation can be easier for her husband if she doesn't approach him face on. All kinds of rich and meaningful conversation can take place without having to face one another – for example, while walking together or lying side by side in bed.

· · · · · · · · · ·

It is not what we learn in conversation that enriches us. It is the relation that comes of swift contact with tingling currents of thought.

Agnes Repplier

· · · · · · · · · ·

But what of the woman's need for eye contact when talking about something which troubles her? She yearns for face-to-face relating in such instances, as to her it is a sign of deep caring. Actually, it signals the same for men, it is just that men are less often ready to receive this kind of intimacy. One of the difficulties men have here is to know how to respond. Most men need to learn that when their wife shares her feelings what she needs most is to feel heard and validated, not corrected or to have a solution proposed. This is often difficult for men, but it is extremely important. Men, because of wanting to be the knight in shining armour, have a strong inclination to want to solve the problems his wife presents. This is not usually what she wants. Actively engaging in listening can, by itself, be tremendously fulfilling. Without knowing this, the knight will often get knocked off his steed.

• • • • • • • • •

Don't have sex man. It leads to kissing and
*pretty soon you have to start **talking** to them.*

Steve Martin

• • • • • • • • •

A woman is usually curious and wants to know what is going on in the mind of her man. Specifically, most women also want to hear from their partner after sharing their inmost feelings and, when this is the case, beyond the important step of validating his wife, the husband should step into sharing his feelings (as opposed to his advice and solutions) as well. While men struggle with this, if his partner learns to keep it safe for him and to take the time the man needs for his blood to flow from his hearing centre to the speaking centre of his brain, he can quite success-fully come forward with what is going on in there! This gives satisfaction to the wife and becomes illuminating to the husband who can, over time, greatly increase his emotional intelligence through this process.

● ● ● ● ● ● ● ● ● ●

The difficulty with this conversation is that it's very different from most of the ones I've had of late. Which, as I explained, have mostly been with trees.

Douglas Adams

● ● ● ● ● ● ● ● ● ●

Conversing at this deep level is thus not just a primary need for most women, it is a central need of the relationship. As mentioned earlier, while it is usually more difficult and awkward for men, it is essential for them to learn the skills of verbal intimacy, especially as they become more involved fathers. A good part of parenting is about relating verbally to our children at a deep level, being able to listen and talk to them in such a way that they are fully heard, understood and validated, and have a male model for expressing themselves as well. The secure attachment thus established helps keep the channel for parental guidance open and gives children the best possible foundation for their healthy growth and maturation.

● ● ● ● ● ● ● ● ● ●

One has to grow up with good talk in order to form the habit of it.

Attributed to Helen Hayes

● ● ● ● ● ● ● ● ● ●

'Abdu'l-Bahá foresees a civilization in which the balance shifts more towards feminine ideals, moving away from its overly masculinized orientation. In this process, it makes sense that this is going to be generally more challenging for males than for females. But the added difficulty a husband may have in doing this is not a valid excuse to avoid it; nor does it give his wife – or any other female – licence to disdain or look down on him. Rather, greater tact, understanding and patience are called for. As both husband

and wife learn to bridge this gender divide around communication, the other limiting divisions – such as age, nationality,
ethnicity, health, degrees of education or wealth – which we find
between peoples around the world will be more easily overcome.

Two types of problematic family patterns emerging around equality

In our experience with couples, we have come to observe two
prevalent, but still troubled, styles of couplehood emerging from
sincere attempts to integrate equality into the couple's relationship. The first of these styles carries a vestige of the more traditional
mode of marriage, with the male – this time more inadvertently –
still finding ways of dominating the female; in the second we see
more of a reversal of roles, where the female has gained ground
and found her voice but has inadvertently overwhelmed her husband in ways that result in his retreating from some healthy male
strengths, the loss of which are felt by both husband and wife.
Although there are many ways in which couples lose connection
with each other, we are highlighting these two patterns because
they represent attempts at attaining a more egalitarian couplehood. Most marriages we see have elements of these two major
types of relating. Both of these approaches run into trouble eventually, and because of this we will attempt to profile these styles,
point out what we see as problematic, and what has helped those
couples who exemplified these patterns to move into more consciously refined styles which bridge the gender divide. We want
not only to describe how this is so; we hope to clarify how both
male and female strengths can not only live well side by side, but
influence each other in ways that help both of them to integrate
new strengths which are then bequeathed to the relationship and
the rest of the family.

Profile One

· · · · · · · · · ·

Women have served all these centuries as looking-glasses
possessing the magic and delicious power of reflecting the
figure of man at twice its natural size.

Virginia Woolf

· · · · · · · · · ·

Let us take the case of a man, a husband, who has a keen and insightful intelligence and an earnest sense of spirituality. This husband has enlightened views on women, an abiding belief in equality. He is successful in life and sees himself as a family man. The biggest challenge he faces is that his wife is unsure of his love and, at times, ambiguous about her feelings for him. She is also intelligent and spiritual, but feels, despite her husband's enlightened views, oppressed and overwhelmed by his bearing. Moreover, because of these ambiguities and resulting tension in the air, their children show signs of anger towards both of them. The husband, ever confident in his own abilities and spiritual ground, feels secure in his direction and is positive, in the face of difficulties, that all will be well. The wife, far from having attained her husband's summit, is full of fear, and while she has always been there to support and serve her husband and children, feels uncertain about the family's foundation. She rarely talks about it, but she is often confused, concerned about the children, harbouring feelings of guilt about not feeling stronger and happier in a family situation that appears quite ideal.

From the husband's perspective, although he handles finances pretty much by himself, he has sought to consult with his wife on important family matters and decisions. He has learned to do things around the home, things his father would have never done, and he pays attention to his children, guiding them in ways that he believes are important. This husband lives a good life, serves his community, and maintains a devotion to his family. He senses unhappiness in his wife but falters in addressing it, taking it more as a sign that he must persevere, be strong and push ahead. His hope and belief: things will work out in the long run.

• • • • • • • • • •

The world has never yet seen a truly great and virtuous
nation because in the degradation of woman
the very fountains of life are poisoned at their source.

Elizabeth Cady Stanton

• • • • • • • • • •

It is the husband's very strength that is the failure in this family. To some degree, even his spiritual strength has become a hindrance to the family's unity. This man, full of goodness and energy, tends nevertheless to overwhelm his wife. His confidence and ability to convince has, in a significant way, left her out. When she has had views different from his, he has almost always convinced her of the rightness of his. And his views are well thought out, not necessarily conventional arguments that more conservative males often fall back on.

• • • • • • • • • •

Men will often admit other women are oppressed
but not you.

Sheila Rowbotham

• • • • • • • • • •

This has left his wife feeling unheard. Though he listens to her and considers her views, he does not really hear her. She, for her part, in the interest of peace in the family, gives in to his views and follows his ways, even at times when she believes him to be too severe, too extreme, too overbearing and insensitive to the children. In fairness to him, had she had a stronger sense of self and expressed her views with more inner power and conviction, he might have heard her. Her sensitivities, so full of value, have been left unheeded, the feminine voice left unheard, because despite his forward-looking beliefs this man was reared in a masculine world.

In a masculine world a man learns to wrestle, figuratively, with others. It is a kind of match or contest which the stronger one wins even though the weaker one may yet make a point. In this world, men are not trained to hear the voice of feminine softness. Nor are they taught that this voice needs to feel safe before it is able to really speak out. In his masculine brain, this husband firmly believes that a person can be frank with him, that it is safe to say anything to him. In his world, the man does not believe he is easily offended, though he does still get offended, even outraged, when he feels that his wife is not really with him. At these times, instead of really exploring why she is unhappy he tends to belittle her, not realizing the force of his words and manner on her sensitive being and self-doubting stature.

What is problematic here is that the husband has not really turned the corner in learning how to honour and relate to the feminine and create space for the emergence of her voice. While he believes in equality, it is still more an equality on his own terms. In rare instances, if she stands her ground and then gives him time to wrestle with what she has said, he may be able to hear his wife. There are two reasons why this doesn't happen often: first of all, most women have not had a model for taking this kind of stand in a powerful way; secondly, taking stands in such a way is more masculine and ultimately not often attractive to the man. She may make the point, but ultimately lose the connection and disrupt the peace in the family. Sensing this double bind is perhaps her unspoken reason for caving in and not asserting herself.

The problems that actually surface as a result of this bound-up position of the wife can be many and varied. The feminine voice is crucial, both to the relationship and to the family. If it is held down – even when this is not the intent of the husband – the wife and the family will suffer. Her sensitivities and emotions build up. This can cause mental problems such as insomnia, depression or anxiety. Even physical health problems related to these anxieties can arise. Other problems that commonly surface relate to the children who, on some level, are likely to also build up a kind of resentment. They, too, need to be heard and are inherently sensitive. Lacking the benefits of both the masculine and feminine working in concert within the home, problems can appear at various stages of their development. Lacking their own voice and power, but afraid of rocking the boat, the children may also hold on to their anxieties. These are almost sure to show up in adolescence if not before. Problems that appear with children often become the focus of concern for the parents, while the central problem is most often with the relationship between the husband and the wife.

What can a couple exemplifying this kind of profile do, before the inevitable problems become too big to ignore? The husband needs to let go of control and, with humility and authentic interest, softly make inroads to discover the inner reality of his wife. At first the wife may not be open, having developed a long pattern of assuming that the husband will get his way no matter what she does or says. Thus, the willing husband needs to be patiently and kindly persistent, not only to develop a receptive attitude to her feelings and opinions, but to actively invite her input and show curiosity about her inner life. This includes honouring her point of view even when it is at odds with his.

While outwardly accepting his confident assurances of 'Of course I love you!', a woman in this kind of scenario internally questions the love of her husband. Feeling love is central to a woman's psyche, and feeling valued is one way a woman can feel she is loved. Thus, he needs to be sincerely interested in her inner reality and value her sensitvities. Rather than convincing her of his love and his opinions, he needs to assume a posture of learning in her presence. In this process he needs to pay attention, first of all, to her feelings, her point of view, then open up to the possibility of doing things very differently.

The wife, in this scenario, needs to dig deep to find her sense of worth. She may for a long time have been convincing herself that her sensitivities are nonsense, that nobody would really understand, that she is not as informed, that her contributions are trivial, etc. She needs to acknowledge her value and the importance of bringing it forward. A healthy motivation for regaining her sense of self-esteem and value can be the recognition that her children need her strength and input to develop their own sense of self. Even if she does not see or feel the value of her own self, she can recognize that her children have been suffering, and that she needs to show up in a larger way in her relationship to her husband.

If either husband or wife have trouble moving forward in their respective areas or wonder how they can actually do it, we would suggest the use of the structure of mindful dialogue often referred to in this book. It provides a way forward which is safe for both and, if practised as proposed, empowers the husband and wife to bring their feelings out in a safe and peaceful way, illuminating new horizons and possibilities of how to be with each other and learn from each other's different point of view.

Profile Two

• • • • • • • • • •

Just think, if it weren't for marriage,
men would go through life thinking they had no faults at all.

Anonymous

• • • • • • • • • •

Here we start our profile with the wife. This is a woman who, like many women around the world, has engaged in the struggle for more recognition of the female voice. In a world which has not made it easy, this woman has found ways to speak up, make herself known and become successful. In the process, she has managed to find a husband open to her abilities and respectful of her intelligence, one who is 'on the same page' as her with respect to important social issues. On top of this, he is quite an enlightened man, a capable professional, ready to settle down and start a family.

· · · · · · · · · ·

My wife has a slight impediment in her speech.
Every now and then she stops to breathe.

Jimmy Durante

· · · · · · · · · ·

These two capable people are, of course, both quite engaged in the world but, being resourceful, use their problem-solving abilities and skills in time management to balance the many demands of working in the world and bringing up three children. Like many women in similar situations, she seems better able than her husband to stay on top of the myriad of concerns they face daily. With her usual feminine strength in multi-tasking, she pushes forward in many areas, working tirelessly to take care of the many duties in and out of the home, often losing patience with her husband's tendency to want to drop his load or to miss important details around the children's needs or household chores. She is doing more than her share and, in many ways, she lets him know it – not often kindly. In any case, her husband feels like he is living in some kind of storm that won't blow over. Amazed at her abilities and believing, as an awakened male, that he should support this, he does his best to support her projects and do a half-decent job of doing his share. His entreaties to take a break are often

193

met with scorn and his approaches to be intimate dismissed as being untimely and, because of his respect for her boundaries, he retreats . This retreat has taken him more and more into his own world.

· · · · · · · · · ·

Some of us are becoming the men we wanted to marry.
Gloria Steinem

· · · · · · · · · ·

This tendency to retreat greatly upsets his wife. She gets on his case more intensely and he, feeling his insufficiencies more keenly, becomes less proactive. She has started to lose respect for him and feels that she is on a merry-go-round gaining in speed and unable to get off. She does not feel loved and cared for by her husband, believing that his own welfare is more important to him than she or the children are. Their sex life has become almost non-existent as she finds herself wearing thin with all the duties of work, the children and the household. Moreover, her unpleasant and unhappy behaviour puts a cap on his sexual desires towards her and he stops pursuing. She, on the other hand, no longer feeling pursued, takes it personally, as a sign that he doesn't really care or that she is not attractive. Feeling shunned, she works all the more and in her criticisms, body language and facial grimaces, communicates to him his insufficiencies. She pushes on more than him and has managed to garner successes outside the home and to keep her children achieving well at school and involved in other activities.

· · · · · · · · · ·

I am woman! I am invincible!
I am pooped!
Anonymous

· · · · · · · · · ·

She feels that if she stops, it will all fall apart because she is the only one who is taking real ownership for all the things that need attending to. Thus, she sends outward signals that she is going to press on no matter what. Her husband, out of a feeling of honour for her integrity, and ever impressed by her capacities, feels he must heed these signals. Beyond this, he has been dancing to her tune – or at least at her tempo – for so long that he has lost contact with, or has repressed, many of his own needs for connection. Most dangerously, in trying to determine what she wants from him, he has lost his inner locus of control, and lacking this, he loses his ability to act and take charge in the ways that she actually craves. They are in a double bind; both are unhappy in their marriage, yet both feel they somehow have to live with it. Outwardly, they appear to be a successful family, but her feelings of resentment are increasing, staying rather blind to his many attempts to catch her cues and be more responsible in the ways she wants.

What she really needs is a husband who will take charge, but not necessarily in the ways she imagines or even realizes – rather, someone who will step in, take her off the treadmill and help her to slow down. In the maze of activities which engage her mind incessantly, she has become lost and disconnected. She needs someone to lift her out, give her perspective, force her to relax and take some time out, to feel connected.

In this relationship, the female's voice has drowned out the male's or, perhaps more accurately, has usurped the masculine. The woman is covering both bases and this is wearing her very thin. The overpresence of the masculine within her is crowding out the feminine, the softer side of herself that longs to be held, taken care of, and taken away from her myriad responsibilities. Women have a tremendous capacity to cover all bases, but this is not necessarily in her, or the relationship's, best interest. Moreover, those around her all end up dancing to her tune – and one song, no matter how compelling, does not fit all. We all have our own melodies which need to be developed, heard, and become part of the symphonic richness and harmony which every family – including the human family – can produce.

· · · · · · · · · ·

No woman is required to build the world by destroying herself.

Attributed to Rabbi Sofer

· · · · · · · · · ·

What can be done to bring about a healthy equilibrium to this type of family? For his part, the man needs to become awake to, and validate, his own emotional needs. Because he has internalized her many reproaches, he may have come to regard his needs as pathological. It is okay to want to be spoken to respectfully, to want physical intimacy, to have time alone with his wife, to want to have her join him in a kind of recreation he enjoys and which fills his spirit. This is the place for him to take more initiative and be more assertive, a good place for him to facilitate the activation of oxytocin in her system. As explained earlier, oxytocin helps women to feel relaxed, connected and more generous. He could give her a massage, take her dancing, or encourage her to go to yoga – or other activities which would fill her spirit – while he looks after the children and shoulders responsibility for household chores. By doing things like this, by helping her get into her body, her bonding reflexes can come to the fore and they will start to feel reconnected. A man who feels more connected to his wife feels more successful, and therefore more energized and ready to do more for her, and more of what she values.

· · · · · · · · · ·

Instead of getting hard ourselves and trying to compete, women should try and give their best qualities to men . . .

Attributed to Joan Baez

· · · · · · · · · ·

For her part, the wife needs to let go, step back, breathe and do less. She can start by saying less, especially to her husband, but also to her children. Rather than criticizing her husband, she needs to look for the good that he exemplifies. Of course, she has to get out of her reptilian brain to see this. When aroused, many women have the remarkable ability to verbalize it all and lay it out to their tormentor in vivid detail. We have discussed the male need to feel admired and appreciated; what a woman delivers in her aroused reptilian state is the antithesis of this. Once she moves out of reactivity and expresses appreciation to her husband, he can start to feel his healthy masculinity and start to hold her – physically and figuratively – in ways that feed her feminine spirit. She needs to get back into her body, listen to its message, and allow herself to be comforted.

· · · · · · · · · ·

Respect a man, he will do the more.

Attributed to James Howell

· · · · · · · · · ·

The reciprocal actions of her showing gratitude and vulnerability, and him stepping in to comfort and taking her away from her endless chores, is the beginning of deep healing for both of them. Men's needs are voices to be heard, not repressed. When men are in touch with these and put them forward, the natural feminine sensitivity and desire to relate and be loving can also come to the fore. This brings balance to the relationship, which is what each of them most deeply wants.

The dynamics of dominance

What we have seen in both of the above profiles are portrayals of the dynamics of dominance. Dominance is an old-world-order dynamic which is dying hard and, in the intimate chambers of matrimony, fails more utterly and obviously, perhaps, than it does in the world at large. One may still be able to run a corporation or even a country through domination – especially in this immature, power-oriented world – but a marriage of equals will come to ruin unless we transform this insidious trait.

· · · · · · · · · ·

Men weren't really the enemy – they were fellow victims
suffering from an outmoded masculine mystique
that made them feel innecessarily inadequate
when there were no bears to kill.

Betty Friedan

· · · · · · · · · ·

The new story of domination in marriage is the need to be right and in charge. It is not a domination of sword or physical might, rather it has morphed into a spiritualized version of it. This is how the male psyche, raised in an over-masculinized world, has learned to survive and this is how the female psyche can get pulled in and lose itself.

· · · · · · · · · ·

The world of humanity has two wings, man and woman.
If one wing is weak, then the bird cannot fly.

Attributed to 'Abdu'l-Bahá

· · · · · · · · · ·

The first profile portrays a subtle hold of male dominance through the husband. The second shows a manifestation of male-energy dominance working through, and embellished by, the female. What is similar in both scenarios is that one of the wings of the marital bird has been left dormant and not gained strength. This bird of marriage soon starts to lose its grace and its flying begins to labour; unless it learns the use of both wings, flight will become well-nigh impossible.

The essence of the weakness of the wing in the preceding metaphor is the loss of an inner locus of control. We are all noble creatures of God, rich in unique and valuable inner resources which are our sacred ground. Each of us needs to guard this ground in ourselves and respect it in the other. Being open to the influence of the other, stretching into new behaviours to meet the needs of our partner, and striving for unity are all essential parts of couplehood. However, this all must come consciously and from a deep and strong sense of a self who is exercising his or her power of choice, as opposed to a floundering submission, despair or fearful acquiescence.

Simply caving in to the other is not a noble sacrifice but rather a loss of nobility itself. Marriage is the coming together of two potentially whole people who choose to live, learn and evolve together. What we want is to stay in touch with our noble essence **and** be open to the enriching possibilities that our partner presents to us. This means not only accepting the perspective of the other as legitimate, but inviting it and encouraging it because this is what we need to become whole. In consciously daring into new behaviours we connect with our hidden resources and develop new capacities; we can feel new energy surfacing from deep within. Far from losing our inner locus of control, we strengthen it and expand on it.

· · · · · · · · · ·

Love is the will to extend oneself for the purpose of nurturing one's own and another's spiritual growth. Genuine love is volitional rather than emotional.

Scott Peck

· · · · · · · · · ·

The demise of family shakes us to the core. This can, and should, wake us up, especially now that alternatives to power orientation in the family are coming to the fore. Domination, in all its subtle manifestations, is not the way forward; this realization will ultimately be seen as a real gift to humanity. When we drop our power orientation and learn to give up the ego's need to feel right, our marital relationship gains and integrates more of the feminine strength of nurturing, sharing and learning together that has been kept on hold for so many centuries. Accessing and practising this richness in couplehood enables the great family of humanity to learn the beautiful weave available when diversity and differences are honoured and allowed to contribute to the fabric of civilization.

9

Troubles in Marriage

· · · · · · · · · ·

The troubles of this world pass, and what we have left is what we have made of our souls.

Shoghi Effendi

· · · · · · · · · ·

That there are troubles in marriage is something to be expected, just as there are troubles in life. This is not, in our view, a pessimistic or negative outlook. Tests are there for growth and can, in a very healthy way, be welcomed. Yet there is a side of us that feels put upon when difficulties are encountered. This probably comes from our pre-dethronement existence when we felt ourselves to be the centre of the universe, when everything seemed geared to our wishes and when, if anything did seem amiss, all we had to do was cry and our caregivers would come running to take care of the problem. In romance, as we have already seen, this dormant yearning to be perfectly cared for can be reawakened in a powerful way. As we move into commitment with the loved one who occasioned this reawakening, we carry the beliefs that he or she is fully capable of keeping us in this exalted state and that his or her apparent failure is some kind of demonic refusal to do what they have implicitly promised and are capable of. Thus, when things go wrong, we not only feel wronged, but direct our incredulity at our partner.

· · · · · · · · · ·

Because the superior man faces all difficulties, he experiences none.

Attributed to Lao Tzu

· · · · · · · · · ·

The preceding chapters have all been geared to helping us understand this dynamic from a psychological and spiritual point of view. Beyond just understanding, we have offered tools, the most central of which is mindful dialogue based on the Bahá'í teachings on consultation and recent advances in psychological understandings of couplehood. What follows now is a discussion of some of the extreme problems that can be encountered in marriage. These can also often be prevented and handled through the use of the understandings and tools we have offered earlier, but because they are both extreme and prevalent, it is worthwhile to have a special look at them here.

One last note. When encountering these kinds of difficulties in marriage, no matter how extreme they may seem, we should know that there is almost always something that can be done to solve the problem. Divorce lawyers are not the first people to be turned to and, hopefully, we can avoid seeing them.

Troubles around anger, resentment and entitlement

Anger is an extreme way of responding to hurt feelings. Some people move into an anger response as soon as any negative feelings are touched. It helps to know that anger is a secondary emotion, which means that when we feel angry there is always another, more primary, feeling beneath it. For example, we may feel humiliated, embarrassed, fearful, ashamed, jealous, put upon, unjustly treated, ignored, disrespected, demeaned, intimidated and so forth. Not having learnt to be in touch with our feelings and to express them in a fair manner, we move into showing anger in inappropriate ways. We all feel angry at different times for different reasons and this in itself is natural and human. Our feelings of anger at social injustices are indeed positive and necessary to make us move in the direction of change. Violent and harmful expression of anger, however, is not healthy, nor is it productive, especially within the home.

● ● ● ● ● ● ● ● ● ●

The success tactic of babyhood crying for attention gets imprinted:
'When you are frustrated, provoke the people around you.
Be as unpleasant as possible
until someone comes to your rescue.'
Harville Hendrix

● ● ● ● ● ● ● ● ● ●

The unhealthy expressions of anger can be hot or cold. Hot expressions include speaking loudly or yelling, swearing, insulting, hitting, throwing things, tearing things up, breaking objects, slamming doors and so forth. Cold expressions are shutting the other out, going completely silent, keeping or making distance, refusing to relate or accept advances, repair attempts or apologies. These ways of expressing anger are not only arrogant, intimidating, harmful and humiliating; they are inadequate ways of conveying your true feelings and futile in terms of getting what you really want in the relationship.

A common element in all this is disrespect and disregard for the dignity of the other. The only one who feels good is the one who is expressing the anger, and even this is only temporary. While expressing anger we are exemplifying an attitude of entitlement: 'We can say or do whatever we want, no matter how hurtful to the other, because we have a right to make our obvious superior bearing clear to this other for whom this fact seems to have not penetrated because of their inferior apprehension.' Contrary to the general assumption and previous psychological thinking that we need to 'get our anger out', research shows that the more we allow ourselves to move into anger, the deeper it gets and the more likely we are to do it again. The hurt, wounded reactions of our partner are also more likely to be deepened and repeated.

· · · · · · · · · ·

I first learned the concepts of non-violence in my marriage.
Attributed to Mahatma Gandhi

· · · · · · · · · ·

The good news is that, even if losing our temper or giving the silent treatment has become an entrenched pattern or if we have come to think of it a part of our character, we can do something about it. The habit of moving into expressing anger in an inappropriate way can be reversed. Everyone, with the possible exception of psychotics, has the ability to hold themselves back from expressing anger in a disrespectful manner. To illustrate this, just imagine that you are really upset by someone, but that person is in a critically powerful position in relation to you. For example, an armed, intimidating border guard in a foreign country, who can keep you from getting in or out of his country, maddens you. You may be an easily triggered person, raging inside, but it is amazing how quickly you can learn good manners in such a situation. Similarly, when engaged angrily in a private relationship, the fact that we can shift almost immediately from expressing anger, cold or hot, to a more normal mode of conversation when a third party suddenly appears on the scene, also indicates our ability to control anger.

• • • • • • • • • •

My wife has trouble opening jars.
Apparently, that involves a different set of muscles than
slamming doors.

Anonymous

• • • • • • • • • •

Thus, a common context for showing anger is when we are in a relative position of power. It is often only towards those perceived weaker that we feel entitled to move into anger. This is why we keep our cool at work when our boss may do something humiliating or degrading to us. Later, carrying these same feelings home, we may well let it out on our spouse or children. Of course, this is not because the family members are the cause of our anger, but rather because they are in a weaker position. All this underlines the fact that we have the power to decide to hold ourselves back from moving into an anger response.

• • • • • • • • • •

I found one day in school a boy of medium size ill-treating a
smaller boy. I expostulated, but he replied: 'The bigs hit me,
so I hit the babies; that's fair.' In these words he epitomized
the history of the human race.

Attributed to Bertrand Russell

• • • • • • • • • •

Pause request

• • • • • • • • • •

Jealousy consumeth the body and anger doth burn the liver:
avoid these two as you would a lion.

Bahá'u'lláh

• • • • • • • • • •

How can we make the shift at the critical moment when we feel angry, and what can we do with our angry feelings? When there is an obvious, recognized trigger point – an action or words from our spouse – we can start by acknowledging it by expressing it directly in a way that is not intimidating. We can simply say 'I am really angry now', then explain in measured terms what the trigger is and what the underlying feelings are. Verbalizing what is going on with us is far preferable to acting out in aggressive or passive–aggressive ways. If said in a way which is not threatening, it can often be received with empathy and understanding, leading to amends being made. If, however, our best attempts of expressing ourselves in a calm way is received defensively and eventuates in an argument, it would be better to use a process akin to the one described below.

When we are already in a discussion and feelings of anger begin to well up, we need to recognize the point at which our anger arousal mechanisms are moving out of control. Bodily symptoms of losing it usually include a higher heartbeat, sweating, tension in the muscles or stomach. For most of us, these are signals that we have already started to move into an anger response. They can serve as signals for us that it is time to stop! We can prime ourselves to actually visualize a big red 'Stop' sign, which would mean that our lower self is about to usurp our true self. We need to come to a full stop before a collision occurs that is bound to cause injury to all.

Couples therapist Terry Real, in *The New Rules of Marriage*, suggests that couples use a simple hand signal that either partner can show at any time to indicate a time-out. We suggest that couples who are prone to bouts of anger come up with an agreement about a signal that they both feel comfortable with. This signal – a word or hand signal – would indicate, in essence, 'I am getting angry. I need to contain it and get some space. I will be back to you in twenty minutes.' It is important that the intent of the signal is not that '**you** (meaning your partner) are getting angry so I need to get out of here' or '**you** are making me angry' . It is an 'I' message in intent. A 'you' message, even if it is conveyed only in your body language, is only going to stir your partner's anger up more, even if it is obvious that they got angry first and are further along the rage spectrum. It is also important that this signal connotes that you are coming back, because it helps the other feel more settled and secure, knowing that they are not losing you. This helps to prevent them from getting riled any further. After the twenty minutes are up, the one who signalled the time-out should get back to his or her partner. If still not settled down enough, a further, longer period can be requested.

Self-soothing

Using a time-out approach like the above raises the question: 'How do I use the twenty or so minutes, apart from my spouse during a time-out, to calm myself down?' Any approach to overcoming an anger response is going to call for some kind of self-soothing or self-regulation. Mastering the art of self-soothing is indeed a necessary skill for all of us to develop in the process of maturation and growing up. There is a range of activities that we can learn to do in order to hold on to our extreme feelings and avoid crossing the boundaries into hurting others, whether physically, verbally or emotionally. Finding ourselves some space is a good start in order to help us move into doing things which help us calm down. Often, some physical exercise helps burn up the hormones that have been released into our blood stream, but we need to discover what works for us. We should also watch the messages we send ourselves about the other during these times. Rehearsing in our mind how rotten the other's behaviour was, or repeating things like 'He or she makes me so angry,' only serves to keep us aroused. We need to remind ourselves that it is not their fault that we are angry. Their behaviour may have been less than appropriate, but a self-righteous response on our part is our choice. To know that we have a choice should help us calm down. The choice is between letting our lower self get out of hand, or calling forth our higher self which seeks peaceful resolution. We need to remember that our partner is, in essence, a good person and that everyone makes mistakes, then move into reflecting upon what may have been our contribution to the blow-out. A letter on behalf of the Universal House of Justice draws attention to this:

> You ask how to deal with anger.
>
> The House of Justice suggests that you call to mind the admonitions found in our Writings on the need to overlook the shortcomings of others; to forgive and conceal their misdeeds, not to expose their bad qualities, but to search for and affirm their praiseworthy ones, and to endeavour to be always forbearing, patient, and merciful.

If we have caught ourselves early enough and are effective at self-soothing, we may well be able to come back to clear up the issue. If we have mastered the skill of mindful dialogue we should be able to get in touch with the primary hurt feeling that is coming up and be able to express it to our partner in such a way that he or she can hear it. If, after invoking a time-out, the issue is still stirring our anger up, it is probably best to hold off talking about it until the regularly scheduled dialogue time, or at least a later date.

The reason we may need to hold off talking about the issue until we have settled down is that the conversation is not felt as safe any more and the ability to really communicate becomes severely impaired. Interesting research has shown that this kind of stress actually affects the neurons behind the ears, reducing the sense of hearing. Continuing with a quarrel will not lead anywhere.

• • • • • • • • • •

They must then proceed with the utmost devotion, courtesy,
dignity, care and moderation to express their views.

'Abdu'l-Bahá

• • • • • • • • • •

Responsibility

At a high level of maturity we become conscious of the fact that
nobody has the power to make us behave one way or the other.
We need to take 100 per cent responsibility for our actions at
times of feeling aroused. Feelings lead to thoughts, and thoughts
can lead to choices of hurtful behaviour. Hurtful behaviours tend
to magnify negative feelings and these feed back into our thoughts
and subsequent actions. This cycle occurs almost instantaneously.

Thoughts of entitlement to behaving angrily justify our
action. To change our behaviours we need to start thinking
differently about the rights of others. With conscious effort
we will be able to exchange the reflex of wanting to hurt the
other, when filled with negative feelings, into the intention of
expressing our hurt feelings in an appropriate manner. Of course
we also need to know that we will have a chance to be heard by
the one who means the most to us.

Extreme care needs to be taken not to repeat unhealthy
patterns of expressing anger. Anger is seriously damaging to the
marital relationship and deeply affects the whole family. The
above time-out process often works, but if you or your partner
cannot make it work, you should definitely get some professional
help.

For a partner who feels victimized by inappropriate expressions
of anger, it should be clear that tolerating this is not a virtue and
not recommended. Often we hear that one partner, in the name
of keeping peace, puts up with the angry expressions of the other.
But holding the peace by allowing the other to be emotionally,

verbally and – God forbid – physically abusive, is a double-edged sword, not good for either of the partners and definitely harmful to the children who often witness these occasions or sense the fall-out. Sometimes this attitude of tolerance is done under a false assumption, so let us have a more realistic look at this.

Forgiveness or resentment?

• • • • • • • • • •

Guilt is anger directed at ourselves – at what we did or did not do. Resentment is anger directed at others – at what they did or did not do.

Peter McWilliams

• • • • • • • • • •

An attitude which prevents many of us from bringing up frustrations and working them through is the internal voice – sometimes coming from religious sources – which says 'This isn't important,' or 'I shouldn't be bothered by this,' or 'I should be forgiving, I'll just forget it.' Another attitude which hampers resolution is the so-called martyrdom complex, a self-righteous kind of orientation: 'I will suffer and keep quiet to avoid conflict for the good of my family.' Unfortunately, in most of these cases, most of us are not really engaged in authentic forgiveness; rather, we are burying a hurt which festers as resentment and which sooner or later (sometimes years later) surfaces in some form of vengeance. In the meantime, it inevitably cools the connection between husband and wife. The form of this resentment can be very subtle and completely out of our own awareness and intention. It gets deposited deep in our psyches, gaining interest all along and waiting for an occasion to be cashed in, mostly for our own benefit. Holding on to what bothers us often eventuates in an explosion, which is what we may have been trying to avoid in the first place. Unless we are truly able to forgive, or not even take offence in the first place, let us be honest with ourselves in admitting the hurts and work on them.

• • • • • • • • • •

He that cannot forgive others breaks the bridge over which he must pass himself, for every man hath need to be forgiven.
Edward, Lord Herbert of Cherbury

• • • • • • • • •

It is far more spiritually healthy to express our feelings fairly and honestly in the safe structure of a caring dialogue, and learn where the feelings come from and what can help modify them, than to pretend that we can sacrifice our needs for the peace of the family. In practising respectful, clear communication, we gain insight and new experience which may eventually and authentically move us beyond reactivity into a truly spiritual radiant acquiescence. Having gained certainty, through experience, of being able to resolve issues peacefully, we can actually move into the sublime state of not taking offence in the first place. Knowing that through positive pro-active behaviour we can change things for the better, we may eventually achieve the elimination of all negativity in this sacred relationship. The great majority of us will have to go through a long-term and disciplined process to get there. Fortunately, there are many joys to be experienced with each successful step taken, and the discipline we develop can start to feel a welcomed and natural part of our lives.

• • • • • • • • • •

To forgive is to set a prisoner free and discover that the prisoner was you.
Lewis B. Smedes

• • • • • • • • • •

Thus, the crucial place for forgiveness, we believe, occurs after having brought up the issue as best we can. We can then forgive each other and – often as importantly – ourselves, and move on with love and compassion for our partner, free of resentment and clear of ill-will. While we say 'each other', forgiving is essentially a unilateral act. Forgiving can take courage, the more so because it is done alone, after having gained understanding through dialogue; it is done in our own heart and, often, only with the help of God. Forgiving in this way, as it devolves on us, is a spiritual act. While it helps give the other a cleaner psychological space in which to live and grow, it primarily helps our own spiritual growth and is not dependent on the other forgiving us for our contribution. We can still have high standards for our marriage without carrying a grudge or seeking revenge or endlessly listing or revisiting the history of wrongs wrought by our partner. Forgiving helps clear the way forward for ever more conscious relating, living and loving.

· · · · · · · · · ·

*Anger makes you smaller, while forgiveness
forces you to grow beyond what you were.*
Attributed to Cherie Carter-Scott

· · · · · · · · · ·

The trouble of infidelity

· · · · · · · · · ·

*Maybe our trouble is that we live in the twilight of the old
morality, and there's just enough to torment us, and not
enough to hold us in.*
John Updike

· · · · · · · · · ·

The most painful of issues we have witnessed in working with couples is infidelity. Torture may be a more apt descriptor of the emotional wreckage it causes. Yet, sadly, infidelity in different forms abounds.

To manage the complexity of modern life and the multitude of issues facing couples takes consciousness and skill. The issues that call for a couple's attention have increased, and so there is also an increased likelihood of more of them being left unresolved. This means there are going to be more unmet needs for physical, emotional, intellectual and spiritual connection. This is a common scene within marriages.

Outside the home, the environment is ripe for opportunities that could temporarily fulfil some of these needs. Workplaces where men and women work long hours together, trips needing to be taken for business and research that lead to short-term separations, a multitude of internet outlets that make available, at the touch of a key, others to take the place of one's spouse – all these are potential dangers to a couple's sanctuary. From the apparently innocent advent of social networking, to hotlines constantly providing names and addresses of available people within a ten-kilometre vicinity of your whereabouts, our social reality has been revolutionized. This calls for a higher level of responsibility from all of us.

It is clear that huge numbers of people are not yet conscious of this. While moral rectitude is perhaps the major bulwark against having an affair when there are troubles or insufficiencies within the marriage, many people of high principle and devoted religious upbringing have nevertheless succumbed under these circumstances. Even in marriages that seem to be doing okay with few major problems, the spiritual pollution and lack of morality in the surrounding social milieu takes its toll. In such cases the spouse, having held high expectations regarding their unfaithful partner's morality, is all the more dismayed and heart-broken. In addition, the rising prevalance of the 'emotional affair', whose damaging and severely demoralizing effects are only now being recognized, is further eroding the sanctity of marriage.

· · · · · · · · · ·

*I'm tempted to go to all the buildings downtown and put
up a sign, 'DANGER ZONE: Men and Women at Work.'
Today's workplace is the most common breeding ground for
affairs. It's the proximity and collegiality – the intimacy of
working together, not bad marriages, that is the slippery slope
to infidelity.*

Shirley Glass

· · · · · · · · · ·

Affair-proofing your marriage

Prevention is the surest means of addressing this pressing issue of
our times. The first line of defence against affairs is the forming
and maintaining of a clear, strong marital boundary, as described
in Chapter 4. Clarifying and reestablishing the boundaries may
be a sure step towards preventing this cataclysm. It should be
made clear by each partner at the outset that there is no place or
tolerance for unfaithfulness in a marriage.

Infidelity has infected our society to such an extent that we
see many married people who consciously or unconsciously
carry with them an expectation that their partner will have an
affair. This is bad news to start with, and for several reasons. Not
only is such thinking likely to result in the reality, but it is also
an underlying manifestation of low self-esteem. That we could
contemplate that our partner, the parent of our children or
children to be, would commit an act of such disrespect towards
us is a sure sign that we have become disconnected from our
noble centre.

Thus, we urge engaged or newly married couples to develop
a strong inner conviction that faithfulness in marriage is the
unnegotiable standard. Awareness of and vigilance about the
boundaries must of necessity go hand in hand with the clear
agreement that the couple will address and earnestly attempt to

work through every issue that may come up in their marriage, and that the feelings and needs of both husband and wife will be given attention and not dismissed. This, furthermore, entails an agreement that failure to resolve issues by themselves will mean taking steps towards getting professional help (more on this later). These conditions, we believe, are basic requirements of the marital covenant. Whether or not they are explicitly stated or implicitly understood in our marital vows, we believe that an awareness of the peril of unfaithfulness in these times of confused morals and troubled marriages makes it necessary to clearly define the lines and make known the consequence of stepping over them.

Nevertheless, in our work with couples who have become the victim of this infectious disease and have come to realize the gravity of the rupture in the family that has resulted, we do strive to help them survive and heal this horrendously painful episode. Sexual infidelity is a clear ground for divorce in the Bahá'í writings, as it is in most other religious teachings. But infidelity need not spell the end of marriage. Divorce, no matter what the cause, wreaks a havoc on souls that is so profound that we need to be very sure that there is no other option before proceeding (more on divorce later).

Despite the pain caused by infidelity that couples go through, we have observed that a marriage can weather the storms of past infidelities if the couple do a lot of work and there is a lot of capacity for change and forgiveness. This assertion may seem to contradict our original counsel not to tolerate infidelity, but it doesn't. Most couples have not made the demand of fidelity explicitly clear, and fewer still carry through on keeping the work of marriage an ongoing high priority in their life. Let's have a look at some recent research on the causes of affairs, so as to be in a better position to prevent them.

The justifications men give for having affairs

• • • • • • • • • •

*Infidelity flows from a belief that women have the power
to make you feel like a man if you only find a woman that
thinks you're perfect; if you can only find a woman that you
haven't hurt or disappointed yet.*

Frank Pittman

• • • • • • • • • •

Contrary to what many think, an American study of men who
have had affairs reported that only 8 per cent of the men cheated
on their wives primarily because of sex. Compare this with the 54
per cent of men who said it was because they felt under-appreci-
ated or uncared for in their marriage. Another 11 per cent listed
lack of communication; 10 per cent, no longer sharing the same
values; and 12 per cent, the wife's problem with losing her temper.
Furthermore, only 12 per cent of the cheating men said that their
mistress was more physically attractive than their wife. Other
research has indicated that only 28 per cent of cheating men felt
more wanted, loved and appreciated by the other woman.

• • • • • • • • • •

*. . . when you're cheating on her, you're cheating on your
children as well
. . . they can and will pay the price for it.*

Phil McGraw

• • • • • • • • • •

One drawback of self-reporting research such as this is that we
don't get to hear from the other party, in this case the wives of the
men who had the affairs. From our experience, we can assume
they would all have had a lot to say! Nevertheless, the men's self-
reporting is quite revealing and confirms much of what we and

many other therapists working with couples have observed, and which was discussed in the previous chapter. Men feel increasingly pushed down in their marriages. Feeling this way is **not** an excuse to go out and have an affair, but the fact that the majority of men cite this as the main motivation for seeking outside company is nevertheless telling.

· · · · · · · · · ·

Men's affairs in particular are often the cause of troubled marriages and not the effect. In my data, 56 percent of men who entered into affairs said they had 'happy' or 'very happy' marriages, compared with 30 percent of women.

Shirley Glass

· · · · · · · · · ·

Husbands roaming freely in the world seem to be prone to infidelity. In cases where a man has some consuming passions which take him away from the home quite a lot, the wife should at least have some occasional presence at those venues. Beyond this, we have to be vigilant about the many opportunities that abound in the workplace. That men and women work side by side in the workplace is not a problem in itself. How they work together and what they share about their personal life and struggles, and what they convey through body language, is what we need to be careful about. Few of us have the knowledge or sensitivity to manage this. Men, especially, often lack the understanding of what women get from even seemingly innocent attentions that men pay to them. That these may be innocent from the man's point of view is not sufficient when it comes to protecting a marital relationship. Men need to become clued into the very many subtle aspects of making contact with women, and the best source of information on this is their wives. Men can learn a lot from their wives in this respect if they are open to it and willing to be completely transparent about the kinds of interactions that take place away from the home.

The justifications women give for having affairs

• • • • • • • • • •

For men, the strongest predictor for having an affair is their attitudes and values about monogamy.
For women, it's marital unhappiness.

Shirley Glass

• • • • • • • • • •

While it is not quite as clear why women have affairs, one thing is quite apparent: women are having affairs more and more often; in some places the numbers are reaching those for men. One major reason cited for women having affairs is as a way of getting back at their husbands for their affairs. Perhaps similarly, if women are abused in their marriage they can get pushed to breaking point and go out to have an affair in retaliation. Importantly, a woman needs to feel she is the most important person in her husband's life and she likes to be paid attention and talked to on a regular basis. She also needs to feel that she is physically and sexually desired. Lacking this crucial input from her husband – and women are often not that good at expressing these things to their husbands in the kind of explicit language men would understand – they may roam, both as means of getting the attention they long for, but often as a clear message to their husbands that the marriage is over!

Repeating patterns

• • • • • • • • • •

Adult children of parental affairs are at particular risk to repeat the pattern . . . Some adult children of parental affairs have huge agendas, or needs, that could never be met by any spouse – and they bring them, like baggage, into the marriage.

Dave Carder

• • • • • • • • • •

One factor that cannot be overlooked as contributing to affairs is our own family background. If either of our parents have been involved in an affair, the likelihood of affairs occurring in our present marriage is greater. This does not mean that we are fated to repeat the patterns of our parents, but we are strongly inclined to repeat what is 'familiar'. This is very unconscious, and the tendency is strong even if we have no knowledge of our parents' indiscretions. One way of safeguarding against repeating these patterns is to bring more consciousness into our marriage by doing the kind of work recommended in previous chapters.

The internet

• • • • • • • • • •

Those who flee temptation generally leave a forwarding address.

Lane Olinghouse

• • • • • • • • • •

Pushing the button to become a friend with an old friend or suitor on a social networking site **can** be the beginning of an affair! Reconnecting with old friends via social media has been one of marvellous gifts of technology, but lack of consciousness about how this may come to impact our marriage has proved to be fatal. Seeking out old flames on these sites has become a growing interest, and while certain kinds of roaming the internet (for example, pornography) can be a violation of the marital boundary, social networking seems to be the one most profoundly loaded with pitfalls. Couples therapists are finding increasing incidents of affairs which have started in this way. As we recommended in Chapter 4, opening up our various internet explorations and correspondence to our spouse can be very helpful in keeping our marriages free of intruders. The internet is often too easy and too private a medium for moving into relationships in ways which can be extremely damaging to and even destructive of our marriages.

Emotional affairs

A few words need to be said about emotional affairs, which can be as destructive or even more destructive than sexual affairs. An emotional affair is the having of romantic feelings for someone other than your spouse without there being sexual – or sometimes even physical – contact. Both men and women are vulnerable to having emotional affairs and the occasions for the possible occurence of these have increased greatly in recent decades. The workplace is a common venue for the development of inappropriate feelings for another, but evening classes, clubs, workshops, societies, committees, contact with neighbours, and social media all create many, many possibilities for 'crossing the line'.

Because there may be no explicit moral code against it, people can fool themselves into believing that it is completely innocent and platonic and that any reprimands from their spouse are purely a result of unfounded jealousy. Even when secrecy is not the issue – as it often is – the emotional drain on the marriage, in terms of the time taken in these liaisons and in the often excruciating pain felt by the betrayed spouse, can result in a complete breakdown of the marriage. This is a very real danger, not to be toyed with.

· · · · · · · · · ·

Secrecy is the protection; alcohol is the barrier buster; and availability lights the fire.

Dave Carder

· · · · · · · · · ·

Emotional affairs often start innocently, but the secrecy which is often involved (which is in itself a sign of shame around the liaison) prevents the partner whose feelings are the most vulnerable to being hurt from pointing out the potential danger. Any weakness in a marriage creates an opening for a liaison to occur. A common example, as we saw in the case study in Chapter 4 (pp. 79–81), might be in a workplace where the husband works long hours. The overtime he puts in usually puts stress on the marriage, so that his wife is not as likely to receive him with welcoming arms when he comes home. He feels not understood and not appreciated. These feelings can start to leak out to a female co-worker or underling who greatly admires how he handles the challenges of the workplace. She sympathizes with him, and he feels good at finally being understood and respected. This all adds fuel to the development of a liaison, one which is very unfair to the wife who only sees her husband when he is tired out and has nothing much to give in terms of energy. His co-worker, on the other hand, has his company during prime time, so everything works much better. In this scenario we see the need for both clearer boundaries and clearing whatever issues may exist around working long hours.

In some cases, an old flame is found and reconnected with. This is especially dangerous because the romantic circuitry already exists for this person, it only needs to be reaccessed. Still, when we feel the need for love, even people from the past for whom we had only fleeting fantasies can become a serious liaison in no time. When we already feel vulnerable, our imagination that a certain other person would have been better for us can very easily delude us. This danger is augmented if the other person is also feeling a lack in their love life or marriage and is reciprocating the contact. The very fact that the other is open to emotional or romantic contact with a married person is, in itself, a sign that they are not aware of the proper boundaries of marriage. This is also a sign that the other (and perhaps we ourselves) have not developed a mature orientation to marriage, a fact which is borne out by the 90 per cent failure rate of marriages that start out with this kind of liaison.

Separate dwellings

One increasing factor in our world which increases vulnerability to affairs is the trend for couples to live temporarily apart for reasons of work, study, one partner initiating immigration in another country, having to care for a sick parent, and so on. There is nothing inherently wrong in this; living apart temporarily can be a practical solution or an inevitable means of solving a family's two-career conundrum or economic concerns, or for taking advantage of new opportunities. Being apart, however, is a significant test for couples, most especially for the one who leaves the home environment. We are, as we have stressed before, pair-bonding creatures. We have a significant yearning to have a partner to be with, to interact with, to have a physical, emotional, intellectual and spiritual connectedness with. Stepping away from this tends to create a hole which longs to be filled. There are, fortunately, many things we can do to keep the feeling of bondedness alive: we can talk regularly with each other and with other family members, even by video. This can take care of some of our need for emotional, intellectual and spiritual connectedness. Being able to hear our partner's voice and see their face even takes care of some of the physical connectedness. But touch and sexual connection are lost completely, and we have talked about the importance to the relationship of this dimension and how it is tied to feelings of secure attachment. If in addition to this we are not doing enough to stay connected in the other aspects of our relationship, a real vacuum forms. Because of these factors, many couples who previously had strong marriages and were sure that their relationship could weather temporary physical separation are later dismayed to find the geographical distance between them resulting in a complete break-up.

Affairs, whether emotional or sexual, are described by Harville Hendrix as catastrophic exits, ways out of doing the work of marriage. Catastrophic exits can, and often do, bring a marriage to collapse. We need to learn to close these exits completely and unambiguously, so that our energies are turned towards our partner and the marital relationship. We also need to develop the skills around relating to each other, so that the energy and time we put into the relationship are productive. As mentioned before, dealing with an affair requires professional help. Also, if you find a couples therapist who is willing to work with you as a couple without the offending partner agreeing to an immanent end to the affair, find a different therapist. No real work can be done while an affair is still in process, and we know very well the difficulties this entails when the affair is romantic in nature. The work, in all cases of affairs, is excruciatingly hard but many important lessons will be learned as it moves forward.

The trouble of addictions

Another exit which is catastophic to marriage is addictions. There are, unfortunately, many things that humans can become addicted to (alcohol, drugs, sex, gambling, pornography, danger, etc.) and sadly, most of them probably make marriage unworkable. It can be tricky to decide when an oft-repeated action becomes an addiction, but one working definition useful for our purposes here might be: a repeated, compulsive action which causes a functional problem within the marriage and for which attempts to quit have failed. Addictive behaviours usually stimulate the reward circuits of our brain, making us eager to do it again and again. Of course, addictive substances add the factor of chemical dependence to psychological dependence, making such addictions even more difficult to overcome.

A primary symptom of every addiction is denial. The one addicted is rarely ready to acknowledge that he or she has a problem, because such an admission not only shows 'weakness' but puts the possibility of continued indulgence in the addiction at risk. (Actually, it is denial that is the weakness, whereas acknowledgement of dependency is a crucial step towards recovery.) The bottom line for an addict is to keep the gate open to further indulgence, and this starts to become the pivot which everyone close to the addict must circle around. Thus, unless it is dealt with, not only does the dependence of the addict on his addiction deepen; the rest of the family moves into co-dependence. This is why many experts think of an addiction as a disease infecting the whole family.

• • • • • • • • • •

If addiction is judged by how long a dumb animal will sit pressing a lever to get a 'fix' of something, to its own detriment, then I would conclude that netnews is far more addictive than cocaine.

Attributed to Rob Stampfli

• • • • • • • • • •

Some get stuck in unhealthy habitual behaviours which become a source of frustration for their spouse but which have not yet reached the stage where they are clearly an addiction or dependency. While it may take an expert to determine when that line has been crossed, this kind of troublesome behaviour should be addressed in a different way from an addiction. The approach is to bring it up using the structure of a mindful dialogue, in the same manner as we approach any other frustration in our marriage. This can move into a request for a change of behaviour which is not all-or-nothing, but a moderation of the repeated action. A behaviour change like this is given as a 'gift' to one's partner, not as a response to an ultimatum. The giving of this gift shows willingness to change a behaviour for the sake of compassion for our partner's feelings and for the relationship; it is a real gift of love. It also prevents the habitual behaviour from getting out of hand and moving into a full-blown addiction. Concerns around this behaviour can be revisited at times, especially if it escalates again or if it becomes clear that a greater attenuation of the behaviour is needed for the well-being of the relationship or the family as a whole. An ongoing struggle with this, if it becomes or remains a serious issue, might indicate a need to get professional help.

When it is clear that an oft-repeating behaviour **is** an addiction, a whole different approach is required. We recommend that the spouse of the addict – or suspected addict – reach out for help first. Find someone who is an expert on addictions, preferably relating to the particular substance or behaviour that engages your partner. This person can first of all help you with your co-dependency issues, which usually include the enabling behaviours that spouses of addicts often fall into. Enabling behaviours include covering up for your spouse's behaviour, making excuses for it (these excuses are often learned from the addict), swallowing the heavy feelings you have around the addictive behaviour, minimizing the extent to which the behaviour is a problem, being overly tolerant, nagging or complaining of the behaviour without there being any change, and so forth. Sometimes joining a support group such as Al-Anon (for spouses of alcoholics) can help you with your co-dependence and find more effective ways of working with the addiction. An addictions counsellor will also help you find the most productive ways of getting the addicted spouse into treatment. Because of the seriousness of addictions, it is usually necessary that an addict be in treatment for the addiction before any couples therapy can move forward in a productive way. Once the addict is in treatment, however, it is highly recommended that couples therapy begin. Couples therapy will help both husband and wife understand where the vulnerabilities to addictions – or to addicts – originate, and how to support each other to overcome them.

· · · · · · · · · ·

She goes from one addiction to another. All are ways for her to not feel her feelings.
Attributed to Ellen Burstyn

· · · · · · · · · ·

The trouble of mental disorders

The subject of mental disorders is very complex; it is not for amateurs. We emphasize this because one common tool used by couples in their power struggle is to label their spouse as being pathological in some way. If they have perused diagnostic manuals or read articles about some psychological pathologies, they suddenly become experts, and add these labels as weapons to their arsenal to 'bring their spouse round'. There are disorders which make being in a healthy relationship almost impossible and these need to be addressed, but we should never become our partner's analyst. Rather, if we genuinely and earnestly suspect a mental disorder which needs to be addressed, we should turn to a specialist who is competent in this area and learn from him or her how best to proceed. The worst tactic, even if a diagnosis of a disorder is accurate, is to bring it up in an accusing way during an argument or moment of frustration.

Most disorders which make for difficulties in marriage have components which we can all identify with. For example, a narcissistic disorder is a condition where a person basically appears to be incapable of empathy and is never truly interested in the needs of other people. However, at any given moment in a power struggle, these very same lacks are present in all of us, almost without fail. We are all guilty of putting our own interests above the interests of others and are all to varying degrees narcissistic, especially while quarrelling, and we should not be in the business of labelling others in this way. Much more helpful is to examine our own propensities in this direction and explore our frustration as a projection. Having said all this, there is a point at which truly valiant efforts to make a marriage work fail utterly because of an unaddressed disorder and it is necessary and appropriate to get professional help in order to learn how best to move forward.

The trouble of one partner unwilling to work on the marriage

What can you do, alone, when you see clear problems in your marriage and want to work on them, but your spouse refuses? Much has been said in this book about how a couple can make a marriage work, but if only one is willing to do the work, what then? Can something be done unilaterally, to make a difference?

• • • • • • • • • •

Whether you married the right or wrong person is primarily up to you.

Zig Ziglar

• • • • • • • • • •

Marriage busters

The first step in working by yourself on your relationship is to determine if there are any of the above catastrophic marriage busters: affairs, addictions, or mental disorders. These are the problems that definitely require professional help and that, without therapeutic attention, will spell the end of your marriage in one way or another. If you have determined that the above-mentioned marriage busters are not present, what is needed next is to step away from looking at or analysing your spouse, and turn your gaze toward your self.

A fearless self-inventory

In a dysfunctional marriage, there are always two parties contributing in different ways and to varying degrees. Looking honestly and objectively at your own contributions takes courage and an open mind. Rather than excusing your partner for their failings, the shift of focus to yourself means that, up to now, all your best

227

efforts at repair have failed and you, for now, are the only one you can effectively work on. So sit down, do some studying, and examine what it is you are doing that your spouse finds difficult to cope with, things that you are doing or not doing that may contribute to the trouble in your marriage.

Beyond the things we have already described in this book that add or take away from a healthy relationship, in the re-examination of your behaviour and attitudes we recommend looking at what Gottman calls the 'four horsemen' that attack a relationship and spell trouble for one's partner: criticism, contempt, defensiveness and stonewalling. Similarly, what Willard F. Harley calls love busters give vital information on the things that poison a relationship. These include: selfish demands, disrespectful judgements, angry outbursts, annoying habits, independent behaviour, dishonesty.

· · · · · · · · · ·

Many of the faults you see in others, dear reader,
are your own nature reflected in them.

Anonymous

· · · · · · · · · ·

Another helpful source for discovering your own contributions to trouble in marriage is to examine your projections. In this, you do look at what bothers you about your spouse, but only to discover how and in what way those very things that frustrate you about him or her live in **you**. This takes a lot of honesty, and an ability to move beyond defensiveness and self-pity into honest search. The exploring of projections is an enriching means for self-discovery. For example: a major issue for you may be what you perceive as self-centred or selfish behaviour in your spouse. Take a moment to ask yourself, 'What are some ways that I may be self-centred? How might this trait live in me?' To really gain the most from exploring this, it helps to assume that this trait **does** exist in you in some form, then dig deep to find it. If in all honesty this fails to bring anything up for you, there is still another step to take. Ask yourself, 'How might the inclination to be self-indulgent have been shamed out of me as a child?' This can help bring a buried projection out of the shadows. Many behaviours that anger us about others are things that we gave up, with resentment or fear, as children. Virtues are great to develop, but if we are shamed into a virtue we do not really own it ourselves. In these cases, we will tend to react strongly against others who seem to ignore these virtues, and will feel self-righteous about it because we had to suffer to develop it.

· · · · · · · · · ·

Hell is oneself, Hell is alone, the other figures in it merely projections.

T. S. Eliot

· · · · · · · · · ·

The concept of projection is a profound and enduring one in psychology. We have often observed in our work with couples that what one complains about in the other is usually present in the one complaining, but shows itself in a different way. In other words, what one partner yearns for in the other is, in reality, what the other wishes for as well.

· · · · · · · · · ·

O Son of Being!
How couldst thou forget thine own faults and busy thyself with the faults of others?

Bahá'u'lláh

· · · · · · · · · ·

Another way of examining your part in the dysfunctionality of the relationship is to imagine what your spouse would have said had he or she been asked about what behaviour of yours bothers them. The complaints of a partner, even when not put forward in the loving ways we have encouraged, can nevertheless be a useful reference for improvement and modification of our own behaviour and are better not dismissed or explained away as high expectations, extreme sensitivity, stress, physical symptoms such as PMS, or excused as being a disease, disorder or the result of an unhappy childhood. To the degree that you can pay attention to these complaints in an objective manner and identify your own contributions to troubles in your marriage, to that same degree you can improve the relationship without the direct support of your spouse.

Feelings of resentment towards each other lead to behaviours which aggravate the relationship and frustrate both partners. Becoming aware of, and changing, some of your own behaviours which may be a source of resentment for your partner can go a long way towards changing the interactions between the two of you. In doing this, you may find that – quite 'magically' – things get better. It may even create an opening to discuss things about your relationship you were never able to discuss before. But there is still much more you can do on your own without bringing your spouse 'on board'.

Love boosters

One recurring theme in this book has been that husband and wife are different and that this seemingly obvious statement is not easily accepted by us at a subconscious level. If a couple master the mindful dialogue described in Chapter 5, they will come to learn truths about each other in ways that have been eluding them – often for years – because our brains and our survival mechanisms have been trying desperately to fit our spouse into the category of our own self. One important learning from mindful dialogue is usually that what we **do** in the name of love to our partner is often not **received** as love. Our partner is looking for something else from us to feel loved and cared for, leaving our best efforts to be a good partner without much effect. Your partner may not be willing to enter dialogue about your relationship, but they may be willing to answer one simple question put to them directly: 'What word or action would tell you that I care?' or 'What can I do differently to show you my love?' If your spouse is vacillating or not even clear about what they want or their own needs, then understanding the generic divide between the basic emotional needs of men and women discussed in the previous chapter might help you. This can orient your actions in ways that will usually bring joy and satisfaction to your partner and assure them of your love and care.

It is, of course, ideal for both the husband and wife to do this together and meet each other's needs, but barring the willing participation of your spouse, working unilaterally can go far to transforming your relationship. Success in this almost guarantees that your spouse will eventually come round and reciprocate by moving in to meet your needs. This may be hard and selfless work, especially doing it alone, but the rewards are well worth it.

Wife and husband are usually taking part in a dance of behaviours. They interact and affect each other's behaviour directly. These steps may have become long term, quite habitual or even second nature. The change in the steps of one forces the other to move differently. If this does not succeed in immediately bringing your partner round to coordinating their steps with yours, it at least confuses their steps so that they will have to make some changes to survive in the dance.

If you manage to leave off your patterns of love busting and work hard to gain credit by learning and using your partner's language of love by meeting his or her primary emotional needs, and your partner still remains cold to you, you might consider the possibility that he or she is involved in an affair. **Only emotional involvement with another partner can keep** a person resistant to the love advances of a spouse who is informed about his or her emotional needs.

Troubles around money

• • • • • • • • • •

Delight not yourselves in the things of the world and its vain ornaments,
neither set your hopes on them.

Bahá'u'lláh

• • • • • • • • • •

In marriage, there is usually one who is a saver and one who is a spender (this is another instance of minimizer/maximizer). In extreme cases there is usually one who is very serious about money while the other is likely to be irresponsible and carefree. Because of this, money is often a source of conflict. Some couples get really tied up about money, so that the issue surfaces at frequent intervals for years or decades. Even when a couple gets into what seem to be serious money troubles where debts have become unmanageable, there are ways of dealing with the problem that need not be an endless source of frustration or a cause for divorce.

• • • • • • • • • •

The one with the most toys wins.

Anonymous

• • • • • • • • • •

When money becomes a serious issue in a marriage, the first step, as always, is to step out of counter-productive reactivity. If the reptilian part of our brain has been activated – and for many of us, troubles around money trigger exactly this kind of reactive state – then we have already driven off the road leading to unity and resolution. We all bring with us patterns that we have developed in reaction to the approach taken in our family of origin relating to money.

• • • • • • • • • •

I have enough money to last me the rest of my life, unless I buy something.
Attributed to Jackie Mason

• • • • • • • • • •

We also live in a world which, at least on an unconscious level, is dominated by the perspective of 'the one with the most toys wins'. Unthinkingly, unconnected to our spiritual essence, we can tend to let the tide of society carry us away into the vacuity of this vain existence. We are being endlessly enticed to do this, so that without gaining and maintaining a spiritual perspective we can become almost hopelessly lost in debt or material encumbrances. The earnest voice of our spouse can often wake us up to our excesses or compulsions in these areas. One potential sign of trouble around finances is when either the husband or wife is not fully included in financial decisions. Sometimes, one partner is severely lacking in information about what the family resources are and how they are being used. This deficiency needs to be remedied so that full participation of both can take place.

• • • • • • • • • •

I'm living so far beyond my income that we may almost be said to be living apart.
Attributed to e.e. cummings

• • • • • • • • • •

A helpful way of approaching finances and related decisions is to step back, explore the large perspective of our lives, and move into a discussion of our vision for marriage and the place of money in it. When they really settle down and reflect deeply on their lives and the role of money, the vast majority of couples find that their differences are not great, that their higher selves yearn for what is most important: a united family that is materially self-reliant and uses material means in the service of its spiritual aspirations.

• • • • • • • • • •

Together make mention of noble aspirations and heavenly concepts . . .

Attributed to 'Abdu'l-Bahá

• • • • • • • • • •

There are responsibilities – providing for our family, serving others, giving to charity, providing hospitality, and so forth – which call for care in handling our financial resources. On the other hand, many see value in having things in their life which are beautiful and conducive to physical comfort, perhaps even luxurious. Bahá'u'lláh tells us that this is acceptable provided we do not lose sight of what is most important and we are in no way attached to these things:

> Should a man wish to adorn himself with the ornaments of the earth, to wear its apparels, or partake of the benefits it can bestow, no harm can befall him, if he alloweth nothing whatever to intervene between him and God . . .

God leaves us with a wide swathe of possibilities. It's our attachments that tend to scuttle a helpful discussion around money. Some of us are attached to the things that money can give us, some attached to the money itself. These are the spenders and savers, respectively. Once again, in marriage these maximizing and minimizing orientations tend to bring us into despair, but with increased consciousness on our part they can be enlightening. Once we are clear on all this we can move into earnest dialogue around what steps are important in the short run. Our differences can either be fuel to endless conflict or, given a healthier perspective, a way to learn from each other, becoming more complete and balanced – and in the process, even closer to each other and to God. Bahá'u'lláh writes, 'Whatsoever deterreth you, in this Day, from loving God is nothing but the world.'

There are literally millions and millions of people who are saddled with debt they find themselves unable to keep up with. Here again, when we finally start to take earnest stock and see trouble staring us in the face, we may need to reach out and get help. Fortunately, there are good resources out there that have sound practical advice to help couples out of strained financial situations. The earlier you recognize the need and reach out, the healthier.

· · · · · · · · · ·

My problem lies in reconciling my gross habits
with my net income.
Attributed to Errol Flynn

· · · · · · · · · ·

Troubles of children

While parenting issues and problems are largely beyond the scope of this book, a few words need to be said about the alarming increase in certain mental and physical health problems of children and which are directly related to the subject of marriage. These include: oppositional defiant disorder, attention deficit hyperactivity disorder (ADHD) and its subtypes, higher risk of other forms of mental illness, sensory disorders, asthma and allergies. In his book *Kids Pick Up On Everything: How Parental Stress Is Toxic To Kids*, David Code refers to research from many sources that indicate that one of the main contributing factors to all of these problems is stress, and that one of the main contributors to childhood stress is the level of parental stress.

Code goes all the way back to illuminating research done by a pioneer in family therapy, Murray Bowen, in the 1950s. He and his colleagues observed schizophrenic children in their family settings and noted that there was observable emotional distance between the mother and father of these children. Other observers had thought that this distance in the couples' marital relationship was a result of the children's mental disorder, but Bowen determined that this emotional distance – which he described as 'emotional divorce' – had existed prior to the children showing any symptoms of mental disorder. In this same research, it was observed that when the parents spent more time interacting with their troubled children, the children got worse!

Moving forward to more current research on stress, Code makes two main points. First of all, the present-day trend of parents to intensely hover over their children to protect them from trauma and make them as successful as possible, is failing. It appears that, by many measures, this increased focus on children conspires against both the parents' and the children's mental and physical health. The competition to dote on children, look after all their needs, have them excel, be top students, get into the best colleges and universities, etc. is making the children sick. The second main point, a corollary to the first, is that the parents' neglect of their marital relationship engenders problems for their own and their children's well-being. The research that Code refers to is the measurable factor of stress, and this stress, he points out, is passed directly on to the children at a level of which is beyond their capacities to handle. Of course, one of the stress factors for parents is their need to have their children turn out so well. The energy and resources that this consumes also contributes to the decline of their marital connection. What Code is pointing out is that trouble in the marital relationship is directly passed on to the children in a measurable way.

As we have pointed out in this book, the health of the marital relationship is fundamental to the well-being of both the husband and the wife. We have also stated that taking the time and consciousness to make this relationship work well is of greater benefit to our children than trying to apply parenting techniques or spending extra time with them. A significant factor in the above-mentioned physical and mental diseases of children, all of which have increased alarmingly in the last two decades, is their level of stress which is, in turn, greatly affected by their parents.

• • • • • • • • • •

The most important thing a father can do for his children is to love their mother.

Attributed to Rev. T. M. Hesburgh

• • • • • • • • • •

Not only in this book, but in virtually every seminar, presentation and workshop we have given to parents and couples, we have made the point that the first principle of good parenting is to have a loving and healthy relationship as a couple. Now we see that there is an abundance of research that corroborates these statements. The marital relationship is clearly hugely important to our children and this should serve to wake us up to the need to tend to it as masterfully as we possibly can.

Troubles of divorce

• • • • • • • • • •

Truly, the Lord loveth union and harmony and abhorreth separation and divorce.

Bahá'u'lláh

• • • • • • • • • •

Because of the vast incease in the number of divorces over the last several decades, much has been done to 'normalize' it. By this, we mean finding ways to live with it which do not demonize the couple for breaking up, helping the couple to do the best they can to make the break-up as trouble-free as possible, and encouraging the divorced couple to continue their responsibilities as parents and to help their children make the many difficult adjustments required. So much has been done in these ways that we may have stopped hearing about the trouble that divorce really entails, its effect on the children and the wider problems it causes for society. Let us, therefore, review what research is showing us about the negative effects of divorce despite the massive steps that have been taken to help broken families make the adjustment. Those who are apprised of the multidimensional aspects of this information almost universally feel strongly that our whole liberated approach to divorce needs to be closely reexamined.

· · · · · · · · · ·

When there are kids involved, there's no such thing as divorce.
Attributed to Carl Whitaker

· · · · · · · · · ·

First of all, divorce is extremely stressful, both in terms of going through with it and living with its aftermath. The event of divorce, according to studies, is second only to the death of a spouse in its overall stress rating. Once divorced, two households need supporting instead of one. Taking care of the needs of the children, which become greater because of their hurt and confusion, is onerous on many levels even when cooperation between ex-spouses is high, and effective cooperation is the exception rather than the rule. UCLA Professor R. H. Coombs reviewed more than 130 studies on the effects of divorce on well-being. Here is a summary of his findings from 1991, as well as findings from other studies:

Adults

- Divorced people have higher rates of clinical depression than married people, and 5 to 21 times the risk of needing formal psychiatric care.

- Divorced men and women have more strokes, acute infectious diseases, respiratory and digestive illnesses, severe injuries, cancer (married cancer patients also have higher rates of recovery) and, not surprisingly given all this, lower life expectancy.

- Divorced men are 2.7 times more likely than married men to commit suicide.

Children

- Rates of clinical depression are higher among children of divorced parents. Coupled with low socio-economic status in early childhood, divorce increases the long-term risk for major depression.

- Children brought up in single-parent families (not all of these because of divorce) are three times more likely to have children out of wedlock, twice as much chance of being high school drop-outs, 1.4 times more likely to be unemployed after schooling, 2.5 times more likely to be unmarried teenage mothers (these are not figures for low-income families alone but include the broad spectrum of society in the United States). Following the next generation of increased numbers born out of wedlock, there is a 5 times greater likelihood of poverty compared to those raised within intact families. These same children, born out of wedlock, have 2 to 3 times more likelihood of having psychiatric problems during their teens.

- Children of divorced parents have higher chances of behavioural problems than those of non-divorced parents (which includes a mix of happy and unhappy relationships), are more likely to have reported cases of abuse and, after controlling for factors such as IQ, race and family background, do worse in school on average than their counterparts coming from intact homes.

Another factor getting more attention in recent times is how much satisfaction is gained – or not – by those who have divorced. There are definitely some who in the long term are no happier after their divorce than they were before. There are couples in very troubled marriages who seriously contemplate divorce, but for one reason or another decide not to. A significant number of these report, five years later, that they are doing much better and are glad the marriage did not break up.

Finances

Because of high court costs and legal fees, policies have been adopted in some areas which decrease the costs of obtaining a divorce. These policies include 'no fault' divorce and opportunities for mediation without a lawyer, which can help a couple settle many of their disputes out of court. Without these measures, the cost of divorce can be astronomical; even with them the costs can be very high.

The financial costs of divorce and many problems related to family maintenance after court settlements continue for years after a couple part ways. Most divorces since the 1990s have been instigated by women, and many of the former husbands express their resentment by withholding payments for family support. Even when feeling an obligation towards their children, they remain reluctant to pay support for their children to their former wives.

Interestingly, those couples who marry and opt to stay married – whether because they are able to successfully work through their interpersonal struggles or merely able to persevere – end up four times richer, on average, than those who don't marry or whose marriages don't last. This points partly to economies of scale, although most married couples still have children to provide for as well. The two main factors here appear to be that people who marry in the first place, and especially those who are able to keep the marriage going, are the kind of people who make plans, work towards them, and have better than average skills in relating. The second factor is that marriage tends to affect us in very good ways: married men make more money than unmarried men with similar levels of education and work experience, by a factor of between 10 and 40 per cent. They tend to work harder, drink less and take fewer drugs than their single counterparts. The division of labour and shared decision-making in marriage makes for more successful financial outcomes.

In the United States, 'divorced' households consumed 627 billion gallons more water and 73 billion kilowatt more hours of electrical power than 'married' households. The cost of these utilities for the 38 million extra rooms used by divorced families costs a total of 10.7 billion dollars. So, even for the sake of conservation and energy footprints, staying married carries benefits.

• • • • • • • • • •

Nearly every major social problem has deep roots in the failure of adults to form and sustain healthy marriages . . . the disconnection of childrearing from marriage ranks high on the list of what ails our society and our communities.

William J. Doherty

• • • • • • • • • •

Common law couples

While we hear a lot about divorce statistics, we rarely hear about the break-up of cohabiting couples with children, couples who have never married each other in the first place. Here, both parents are present as in marriage, but statistics show that the unmarried couples generally do a worse job of parenting in the ways that can be measured. These relationships are much less stable than marriages. In the United States they last an average of two years, and figures are at least as bad in most European countries. In America, about half the unmarried couples with children decide to eventually marry, but these marriages are more likely to end in divorce than those who married without cohabiting first. Sixty-six per cent of the cohabiting couples who marry later will break up by the time their children are ten; this is twice the number of those who married in the first place. Marriage makes a difference; a lot more should be said about the break-up rate of cohabiters.

Remarriage

· · · · · · · · · ·

Instead of getting married again,
I'm going to find a woman I don't like and give her a house.
Attributed to Groucho Marx

· · · · · · · · · ·

Most divorced people in North America remarry. This is good news because it shows that, despite failure in the past, marriage is still important in most people's minds. The bad news is that most of those who remarry have still not worked through the issues that brought their first marriage to an end. Most still carry the myth that they just married the wrong person or were too young, or other rationalizations. The truth is that unresolved issues, as well as the choice of partner, tend to be a repeating pattern. In addition, most of these couples are now bringing not only child-hood baggage, they are bringing unresolved stuff from their first marriage, and often also children, which create the very compli-cated 'blended family' scenarios. Thus, the bad news is that an even greater percentage of second marriages fail. The majority of these still remarry and a still greater percentage (70 per cent) fail in their third marriages.

Troubled marriages

• • • • • • • • • •

For the sake of the children
a ninety-year-old couple decide to get a divorce.
They go to the judge and say, 'Judge, we want a divorce.'
The judge says, 'You've been married 70 years and now you
want to get a divorce?
Why did you wait so long?'
The couple say in unison, 'Well, we wanted to wait until the
kids were dead.'

• • • • • • • • • •

All of this research paints a pretty bleak picture of divorce, but of course these are mostly statistics and don't point to individual exceptional cases, of which there are many. Some divorces are handled quite well, some single parents do an exceptionally good job even with minimal support, and some people remarry and are successful in their new relationship. There are also children who manage quite well in the new arrangement, although a majority of even these children are still emotionally scarred in ways not immediately apparent and are bound to face similar challenges in their own marriages. All of this needs to be weighed against the harm, both for the couple and the children, of staying together when the couple's relationship remains in conflict or emotionally distant, which can be equally damaging to all.

In citing all this, we are not saying that divorce should be avoided at all costs. The only sure and healthy way forward for a family is for a husband and wife to learn the skills of couplehood. Sometimes on this journey, a couple may need to reach out for help.

The trouble of lost love

· · · · · · · · · ·

Happy marriages begin when we marry the ones we love,
and they blossom when we love the ones we marry.
Attributed to Thomas Mullen

· · · · · · · · · ·

What can be done when one partner has lost all feelings of love for the other? This, it seems, is a question of romance. We have stated elsewhere that the vast majority of Americans would not consider marrying someone that they weren't in love with. The other side of this would seem to be that, if this love is lost, what is the use of hanging around? We have observed this kind of thinking quite often, even when the couple have young children with all the added complications and pain that a divorce would entail. To many, envisioning any kind of future with a partner they no longer have romantic feelings for trumps all, no matter how poor the prospects of a life apart may seem.

To gain some perspective on this question, we need to look at what happened to the love that was there. This has actually already been explored in earlier chapters but let us make some clarifications here. Whenever we fail to attend to our marriage in a healthy way, the feelings of love we have for our partner get pushed more into the background. One version of this, more common to women when they don't receive love and attention from their partner, is to give more of themselves and do more in an effort to 'earn' love. This can go on for years, with the wife believing in her heart that she is giving her all for her husband and marriage. Finally, living on an empty tank for so long, the wife gives up, thinking she has given everything she possibly can, to no avail, and now her feelings of love are completely gone. Another version, more common to men these days, is to 'put up with' tirades of criticism or even anger from their wife, keeping as low a profile as possible, being as cool and calm as they can so as not to awaken the dragon. This, too, can go on for years until finally the husband realizes he has had enough, that he deserves more, and that he no longer loves his wife at all, at least not in a romantic way. These may seem to be extreme scenarios, but we have observed these in real life and they serve as good illustrations for the subject at hand.

• • • • • • • • • •

What counts in making a happy marriage
is not so much how compatible you are,
but how you deal with incompatibility.
Attributed to Leo Tolstoy

• • • • • • • • • •

In both these cases there is a feeling of being let down by the partner over a long period, a feeling that they have given a lot, deserved more, and are finally depleted. What they come to, in their own minds, is that staying together is now pointless, especially since they have no romantic feelings left. It may be that, finally coming to this point, their partner starts to wake up and move into doing the things that they neglected to do all these years, or mollifying their negative mien, but learn that their efforts are to no avail. It is too late.

Is it too late? Many behavioural psychologists would say there is no big problem here. Just stop ruminating or fixating on internally voiced, black and white messages that this is impossible. When we feel down or defeated, studies have shown that our brains tend to repeat messages that are really a very distorted way of seeing reality, and these bring us down even more. The first step is to recognize the distortions, correct them in your mind, and you will start to feel better, and ready to take some realistic steps to do things differently so you can get a different result.

What is real here is that in neither case did the complaining partners who reported no feelings of love move out of their well-practised survival mechanisms to do something that could have made a real difference. They seem to have been suffering for a long time doing the same kinds of things, hoping that their partner would somehow understand that something is very wrong. Doing or saying the same kind of thing over and over again is what has worn them out. This leads them to assume that they have done all they could do. The blamed partner, at this time, is often taken by surprise at the impact of their behaviour. In reality, the partner who lacks loving feelings has made a huge contribution to this by keeping the other in the dark for such a long time. Taking ownership for this contribution is the second step.

· · · · · · · · · ·

Love never dies a natural death.
It dies because we don't know how to replenish its source.
Attributed to Anaïs Nin

· · · · · · · · · ·

The third step is new behaviour. Part of the new behaviour will have to include non-acceptance of what had been the status quo for so long, the way each of them behaved that contributed to the demise of loving feelings. The other part of the new behaviour is to give loving gestures to each other and also to receive them. Doing things for one's partner that are registered as loving gestures in the partner's world wins their love. It is quite a simple formula really. Only our resistance, born of a usually self-righteous resentment, makes it difficult. If both partners are stretching into this kind of awakened behaviour, love will show its head again and grow. And if you review what we have written in the divorce section, renewing the love in one's marriage is almost always far preferable to breaking up the family, no matter how much effort it may require. At the beginning of the relationship we had romantic feelings that moved us to behave and talk in very loving ways. This process can now be reversed: behave and talk in loving ways and the loving feelings will come to the fore.

Arthur Aron, a researcher and lecturer at the University of California Santa Cruz, undertook an experiment which gives an indication of how powerful this formula can be. He would put a man and woman who were chosen randomly, and who had never met before, in a private room. He gave them detailed instructions, such as to exchange intimate information; gaze into each other's eyes without talking for two minutes; 'tell each other what you already like about each other' (even though their background information was nil!). He found that this fostered a deep sense of intimacy between strangers. The first two people in this experiment got married six months later! According to Aron, after 20 years of this and other research, the overwhelming predictor of whether or not you will love someone is knowing that that person loves you.

· · · · · · · · · ·

*A successful marriage requires falling in love many times,
always with the same person.*

Mignon McLaughlin

· · · · · · · · · ·

We believe, and research on the brain seems to back this up, that once there is love for a person, that love never really goes away. It can get covered up by layer and layer of resentment and neglect, but it never really disappears. The romantic period and its feelings are in a way a free temporary sample we get, to give us the experience of the power of love. To sustain and enrich it the couple need to put in effort and attend to it, otherwise it will move into dormancy and behave like a recessive gene that needs the right conditions to start working again. Take away the layers and renew loving behaviours, and the romantic circuitry that developed for our initial feelings of love for our partner can open up again and the love will come back as strong as ever – even stronger – because it will be bolstered by a now increased store of love from the attachment circuitry.

• • • • • • • • • •

To get divorced because love has died is like selling your car because it's run out of gas.

Diane Sollee

• • • • • • • • • •

There is, once again, one thing that will make this impossible, at least in the short term, and that is the development of romantic feelings for someone else. In this case, special and more difficult work needs to be done (see the section on affairs) to move that new, or newer, love into recession. This can be done, but it is much, much harder work and will take longer. There is still a very strong cognitive motivator for doing that work, and that is the sobering fact that a very small percentage of extramarital affairs that eventuate in a divorce and then marriage to the new partner work out. In the end, in almost every case, only more pain and confusion is engendered, accompanied by a far more complicated and difficult to manage broken family or families.

Getting help for troubles

In this chapter we have visited some of the larger troubles faced in marriage. Of course, there are many more which could be explored. The very nature of this intimate union seems to guarantee trouble – and at the same time, huge gains in human development unheard of in other arenas. This fact is even more pronounced in the time we are living in. There is a new context developing for human society itself, and since marriage is the foundational unit for society, the potentialities found within the marital union have increased as well as the demands placed on it.

· · · · · · · · · ·

The grass is greener . . . when it's watered.

Anonymous

· · · · · · · · · ·

In the past we learned how to be married primarily through the model of our parents. Now that a new model of couplehood is required, we cannot expect our parents' example to be sufficient. The roles of husband and wife used to be quite rigidly defined, and they were unequal. What is called for now are flexibility and equality. To sum up, we have to turn a corner with respect to marriage, and it is not surprising that our own resources will often prove insufficient in integrating the new rules.

Since the 1960s it has become increasingly evident that couples are having serious difficulties with marriage, and since that time more have been turning to professionals for help. Unfortunately, the best of therapists, with the best of intentions, have almost universally failed to help couples make their marriages work. The vast majority of therapists were trained to work 'one-on-one' and were dismayed with the kind of heated conflicts or manifest deadness that couples brought into their offices. Usually they ended up seeing the partners separately to try to get a handle on the process, but while they were often able to help the individuals, the marriages usually broke up. In brief, therapists were not working with the entity of the relationship, and in fact did not fathom the new phenomenon of marriage. In many cases the most they could do for the relationship was help it end amicably. Therapists were trained specifically not to think of measuring their success according to whether the couple resolved their conflicts and stayed together.

• • • • • • • • • •

Isn't it a bit unnerving that therapists call what they do 'practice'?

Anonymous

• • • • • • • • • •

In this context, it is not surprising that people in troubled marriages turned more often to lawyers than to therapists when the troubles of marriage became too much for them. Yet there were, among the therapeutic community, those who believed in marriage and stayed awake to and concerned about the pain caused by marital breakdown, especially since many had experienced it themselves. A number of these therapists made an honest appraisal of their own failures and started to look at their work in a different way. Independently, a number of them began new approaches to couples therapy, founded on new theoretical constructs. These took time, of course, to develop, and even longer to become known beyond the relatively small circle of couples they worked with. But in the last two or three decades many books have come out describing these new approaches and new theories, and some have become bestsellers, attracting well-deserved attention from a number of media sources.

Similarly, there were a number of educators who, seeing the lack of healthy direction from the psychological community, started to think in new ways about marriage and what could be done about the huge social problems surfacing because of high divorce rates. They developed educational programmes to help couples, and some of these approaches have proved very helpful. Nearly every day new findings from neuropsychological, neurophysiological, anthropological, hormonal and other research shed new light on facts about relationships. Much of this confirms the wisdom that can be gleaned from many of the new approaches to therapy and marriage education. All in all, what we see today is a renaissance in understanding marriage. Therapists around the world are starting to turn the corner, to **believe** in marriage and to get trained in these new approaches.

What does all this mean to couples who want to move their marriage to the higher level of functioning which is increasingly becoming a necessity? First of all, there are a growing number of resources out there and we believe that all couples should become aware of this renaissance in marital understanding and plug into it at some level.

We can discern four entry levels. The first is the level of awareness: this can be developed through reading, attending seminars and talks, or viewing the growing number of video or audio presentations available online. The next level might be attending workshops. Here we move beyond academic understanding into being introduced to new skills and getting some practice with these. The third level is coaching, where a couple gets more direct hands-on help in developing new skills from someone trained in a particular approach. The fourth level is therapy, which goes beyond learning concepts and skills into helping couples make the emotional breakthroughs that may be required to heal the wounds from childhood and make the connections between these and their functioning as a couple. All these levels are best pursued by both the husband and wife together, although, as explored earlier in this chapter, significant success can be achieved by one of them alone in getting the process started. Ultimately, however, it takes two to build a marriage.

· · · · · · · · · ·

*Does your marriage need therapy? If you're like most people, the correct answer may well be yes, but **your** answer is probably no.*

· · · · · · · · · ·

A healthy personality is able to recognize when his or her own personal resources or understanding falls short of addressing a particular problem, and immediately takes steps to get the help needed. This is no less the case with the challenges encountered in marriage. But there is still an idea, held over in many people's minds, that reaching out for help in something so personal as marriage is a weakness, that we should be able to work things out for ourselves.

This sense of privacy concerning our private lives has its wisdom. We should not be reckless about sharing what goes on within our very personal marital sphere with just anyone at any time. However, this kind of independent mindset has some limiting features. If a marriage is thriving, great, but if not, it makes sense to reach out when there is professional help available. Research shows that an average couple waits six years to seek help from the time that trouble starts. This is bad news, because an issue that can be resolved easily with attention and some information becomes deepened and compounded with other issues, making it all the more difficult to resolve. When we need help in other areas of our lives we usually look for it immediately: most people go to doctors, for example, or to other health providers, when they have concerns about their body. Marriage is fundamental to mental health, family health and societal health. Why not get the best of what is out there?

Amazingly, marriages that feel beyond repair or seem to be a hopeless cause can recover and thrive. Nevertheless, there is no need to wait until major ruptures occur before getting help. The new demands for marital functioning should encourage us all to examine and reflect on how we function as a couple, and this should be done with a backdrop of aiming at a high standard, one that almost certainly is far beyond that of our own parents' relationship. With the new and evolving resources becoming more and more available, there is much that can be done to help couples with a yearning to have a stronger, more loving relationship. The nature of this goal is discussed in the final chapter.

· · · · · · · · · ·

Neither you nor your husband should hesitate to continue consulting professional marriage counsellors, individually and together if possible, and also to take advantage of the supportive counselling which can come from wise and mature friends.
Non-Bahá'í counselling can be useful but it is usually necessary to temper it with Bahá'í insight.
On behalf of the Universal House of Justice

· · · · · · · · · ·

10

Marriage Made New

Soon will the present-day order be rolled up,
and a new one spread out in its stead.

Bahá'u'lláh

We stated near the beginning of this book that the coming together of a man and woman in marriage signals the creation of a new entity, an entity that evolves and needs to be kept alive and healthy. In this concluding chapter, we will underline some of the points we have made concerning this entity, make some final practical suggestions for its enrichment and portray some of its transcendent purposes.

It is not marriage that fails; it is people that fail.
All that marriage does is to show people up.

Attributed to Harry Emerson Fosdick

The milieu

We live in a world which, as Marshall McCluhan pointed out several decades ago, has contracted into a global village. More prophetically, Bahá'u'lláh revealed in the 19th century that 'This span of earth is but one homeland and one habitation'. We have yet to learn how to live together in this village, this common habitation.

Our relationships, not just our marital ones, but all our essential ones, are in turmoil. Our relationship to our children, our parents, our friends, our society, the relationship between societies and nations, our political and legal relationships, our economic ties, our relationship to our earth home and to our Creative Source have all shifted massively and humanity is scrambling to find its new ground. Most of us are experiencing these massive shifts as painful and confusing, but the Bahá'í writings, which have anticipated this dislocation in human affairs, make it clear that these changes are necessary and are the birthing pains for the establishment of a new reality, a 'new race of men' in the world. We are making the great shift from our collective adolescence into the coming of age of the human race. These writings also provide the guidance we need to navigate our way through the turbulence.

The Will of God for today, as expounded in the Bahá'í writings, is for us to bring about unity on a global scale. Oneness, according to Bahá'u'lláh, is our primal reality. Through the process of creation, even as it is viewed by science, all things have differentiated in marvellous ways. Humans have differentiated to the most astonishing degree and this process continues in a psychological way for each individual. Thus, oneness is our essence, and the conscious process of achieving unity – or as clarified in the Bahá'í writings, unity in diversity – is our calling. With this being the goal, the relationship between human beings as equals has come to the fore in the Bahá'í teachings.

Humanity has developed through different stages of groupings: families, clans, tribes, villages, cities, nation states and, now, the whole world. At the centre of these expanding concentric circles of unity is the family, and the foundation of the family is the relationship between the wife and husband. Our understanding is that marriage holds within it the seed of the wider unity and is a significant working ground for this ultimate goal. From this perspective we can see how marriage functions not only for the best interests of both partners and their offspring, but that it also serves a higher, more expansive purpose and is a significant aspect of the reshaping of the new world order.

• • • • • • • • • •

Now the new age is here and creation is reborn.
Humanity hath taken on new life.
The autumn hath gone by, and the reviving spring is here.
All things are now made new. . . .
The people, therefore,
must be set completely free from their old patterns of thought,
that all their attention
may be focused upon these new principles,
for these are the light of this time
and the very spirit of this age.

'Abdu'l-Bahá

• • • • • • • • • •

A central theme of this book has been the new reality of marriage in this time. If we fail to realize that the requirements of marriage have expanded and that we need to change our age-old patterns, we will fall into the marital malaise that has seized most couples on the planet. Beyond this, our situation in the world is, in a sense, our malaise in marriage writ large.

In this time of transition marriage can be either a nightmare, or a source of joy and enrichment – the former if we continue our old patterns; the latter insofar as we can awaken to, and move beyond, the unconscious patterns that most of us are still subservient to. The potential for growth and healing within marriage has grown and this institution can now fulfil its highest potential and become an unprecedented source of well-being. We are now in a position to access a new level of consciousness and integrate the new principles which are the very 'spirit of this age'.

This new Revelation, we believe, is the source – consciously or unconsciously, directly or mysteriously – of developments that are propelling us irrevocably towards powerful new realizations. With unity being the Will of God for today, sciences have come into being and made advances which command our attention and interest more and more with each passing decade. In the preceding chapters we have made many references to findings from the social sciences that shed light on the workings of the human mind and how this translates into behaviour. One aspect of this development, as we have mentioned, is the increasing number of references to mindfulness in both the social sciences and medical science. And mindfulness, or wakefulness and a conscious feeling of connectedness to our Creative Source and all that is, can be found at the core of spiritual teaching of all the major religions. The call for wakeful connectedness is a significant link for us and we see it as crucial to the sacred bond of marriage.

How mindful is your marriage?

• • • • • • • • • •

Lay the foundation of your affection in the very centre of your spiritual being, at the very heart of your consciousness, and let it not be shaken by adverse winds.

Attributed to 'Abdu'l-Bahá

• • • • • • • • • •

Our usual state of mind, as negative as this may sound, is unconscious. We are just who we are and experience the world from this taken-for-granted standpoint. A sign of unconscious functioning in marriage is our tendency to think of our reality – our experience and perception – as **the** reality. In this unconscious state we actually remain largely unaware of the characteristics of our own reality simply because we do not step out of it, and therefore lack perspective. Stuck in a taken-for-granted way of being, we remain ignorant of the existence of other realities and therefore deprived of their value to our learning and growth. In this unconscious mode, when we encounter an 'other' who does not fit into our expectation of reality, an alarm is set off which evokes a primal negative response in our being. The 'other' is thus judged without our having any significant knowledge of their reality and experience. The otherness is viewed as pathological, so that rather than try to relate, we attempt to overcome, or 'teach', or escape. In marriage, we inevitably experience otherness in our partner, even though he or she is the one closest and most familiar to us.

· · · · · · · · · ·

A great marriage is not when the 'perfect couple' comes together. It is when an imperfect couple learns to enjoy their differences.

Dave Meurer

· · · · · · · · · ·

The development of mindfulness is a **gradual, unfolding and evolving process.** This process entails ever greater degrees of awakening to the workings of our own inner world, curiosity about, and interest in, the reality of others. Opening to otherness, we come to question long-held assumptions and patterns, assess their utility and purposefully make changes. Thus, with consciousness, intentionality comes to replace reactivity when encountering otherness. Every step in this process, no matter how small or imperfect, is significant and worthy of celebration.

The fascinating side to this is that as each of us becomes more mindful of the other, we become more who we really can be. This, in psychology, is called individuation or differentiation. Being individuated is far from being individualistic and asserting 'this is just who I am'. When we say 'this is just the kind of person I am', we are usually being defensive and what we are defending is mostly our ego. This insistent self has trouble living with otherness, as we have stated earlier, and this is the opposite of being individuated. An individuated person is more awake to what is, more capable of discerning and embracing differences, flexible in responding and open to change. He or she is much less threatened by otherness, more able to recognize and relinquish his or her survival mechanisms, and more capable of intimacy and being in relationship.

• • • • • • • • • •

That is what marriage really means: helping one another to reach the full status of being persons, responsible and autonomous beings who do not run away from life.
Attributed to Paul Tournier

• • • • • • • • • •

Just as the Bahá'í vision of world community is unity in diversity, a healthy marriage is the union of two individuated, differentiated persons. These are people truly capable of loving the uniqueness of each other. Thus, the union of marriage is not ever intended to be enmeshment or unity in conformity, as this would attenuate who we can truly be. Rather, with unity in diversity, we grow together through a true realization of our wider potential and primal oneness. Mindful differentiation always develops through connection, not disconnection.

• • • • • • • • • •

*I used to believe that marriage would diminish me, reduce
my options. That you had to be someone less to live with
someone else when, of course, you have to be someone more.*
Attributed to Candice Bergen

• • • • • • • • • •

As we develop this capacity of mindfulness in marriage, we are
preparing ourselves for meeting the variegated manifestations of
otherness in the world. The challenge for us, as humans, is to gain
conscious recognition of our eternal connection while appreciat-
ing our differences. Building unity, whether in marriage or in the
world at large, requires this.

True love

In the process of having a mindful marriage, how we love also
becomes transformed. We start life as unconscious recipients of
love and most of us start our marital relationship in a similar way.
To various degrees we fall in love. We become love-struck. At this
stage love is a feeling that overtakes and enfolds our being. It is a
gift of God, an exhilarating experience. We have described how
this orientation to love gets challenged during the power struggle stage of marriage. The conflicted feelings of this transitional
period can become a source of misery and separation or, on the
other hand, be used to grow out of habitual patterns into new
heights of recovering our true self. One aspect of our being that
is trying to grow through this period is our capacity to love consciously. Love is trying to mature from a feeling that just happens
to us, into a volitional caring for the other, even in challenging
circumstances.

What love that has matured looks like is the purposeful
movement into the experiential, inner world of our loved
one. We become genuinely interested in the well-being of our

partner. With mindfulness, couples become perpetually curious and actively seek information about each other's inner world, their reality and experience. Since change is the rule of life, and as we all change all the time, we need to keep updated with developments in each other's world, reinforce and encourage each other in our personal and spiritual development.

· · · · · · · · · ·

What else is love but understanding and rejoicing in the fact that another person lives, acts, and experiences otherwise than we do . . . ?

Attributed to Friedrich Nietzsche

· · · · · · · · · ·

A simple way of doing this, informally, is to occasionally ask questions such as: What has been on your mind lately? What are your hopes for the near future? What are your dreams these days? What is your vision for our family? How do you feel about our relationship? How do you feel about your work? What challenges have you been facing lately? How can I better help you on your path? How do you feel about your connection to God? In answering these questions it is helpful to be willing, open, honest and straightforward. In sharing our feelings about the relationship, especially when bringing up shortcomings, it is important to pay attention to the language we use as well. Using 'we' forms rather than 'you' makes it more about the relationship than the other. For example, instead of 'You don't make time for the family', to say 'We still haven't found a way to find more time together.'

· · · · · · · · · ·

Real love is a permanently self-enlarging experience.

Scott Peck

· · · · · · · · · ·

More formally, a couple may decide, at intervals, to create special occasions for discussing their relationship. One practice that we have kept in our own marriage is to spend some time together on our anniversaries and while enjoying a small celebration reflect together on the year that has just passed. We share our views and experience of our relationship, uncover the ways it has deepened and progressed, revisit the challenges we faced and talk more about our dreams for the future.

In a mindful marriage we learn to love more with every passing day, as we get to know more of the other's and our own inner selves. One important element of our spiritual and social development, as enunciated by Bahá'u'lláh, is the act of service. In this Revelation, service to our fellow humans and communities has been raised to the station of worshipping God. In marriage, serving our partner not only helps our spiritual development; it becomes a direct act of love, more especially when we have made the conscious steps to discover what ways serve them best in their journey of life.

In learning to love and serve our partner, rather than acting upon our own assumptions of what love means, it is befitting to learn what love means in their world. In other words, we need to learn our partner's language of love and learn to express ourselves in their language.

Reaching beyond

Our understanding of the Bahá'í teachings is that part of our spiritual development entails reaching out into the world. Gone are the times when even the most sincere and profound secluded contemplative life or monastic existence was acceptable. We are social creatures and there is a need for a couple to reach out directly and to consciously serve and participate in the broader community. Just as couplehood creates occasions for our personal and spiritual awakening, so the world provides unique opportunities to grow further. Beside the positive effects that a family's reaching out will have on society, it is equally important to the development of the marriage and family itself. We, and our marriages, are in need of community, just as we can help in a community's development. One feeds the other.

Getting involved in community-building activities and service projects outside the home gives direction and provides the necessary perspective to our life and internal affairs. The Bahá'ís around the world are involved in community-building and are now moving into the strengthening of neighbourhoods wherever they reside. There is a vast range of service projects that require human resources. There are planned activities for the development of children, programmes to meet the particular needs of adolescents, spiritual enrichment programmes for adults either through creating neighbourhood devotional gatherings or small circles of study, and many other creative ways of enriching our communities. Other than these collective endeavours, Bahá'ís are also involved in visiting each other in their homes, creating bonds of friendship, showing concern for the well-being of their fellow humans and raising the level of conversation to inspire and empower each other's development.

All of these provide great venues to channel some of our inner strengths and capacities as individuals and, as a couple, to better the world around us. Allocating regular time to these and similar activities, putting forth effort and utilizing resources for these purposes, opening our homes and hearts to people of all backgrounds, give a new impetus to our family, both by attracting divine blessings – as promised by Bahá'u'lláh – and by availing our personal and marital life of new dimensions. A shared desire to serve humanity is one of the most powerful ingredients in a healthy marriage and brings fresh energy and orientation to the relationship of a couple.

All along our children are benefiting, either directly from some of the above programmes or through this kind of mingling with a variety of people inside and outside the home. The ground is prepared for them to develop a natural openness and love for other members of the human family. For our children to grow into this kind of activist, humanitarian orientation, we must ourselves model this and accompany them in the process. Thus, we not only open our homes to friends and strangers, we move out into the world, reaching out in ways that help human connection. The alienation that many people feel and the resistance most of us have around doing this kind of work is akin to the estrangement we sometimes encounter in our marital relationship. Thus, learning to work through this in our marriage helps us overcome the psychological resistance many of us feel to reaching out on a community level. Harville Hendrix has written that, as a couple's marriage advances in consciousness they 'begin to turn their energy away from each other toward the woundedness of the world'. Moving out to help the world becomes easier and more natural as we develop a healthy, functioning marriage. Reciprocally, as building a world community is a primary calling for this age, to be truly healthy our marriages must feed this process.

· · · · · · · · · ·

No mortal can conceive the union and harmony which God
has designed for man and wife. Nourish continually the tree
of your union with love and affection, so that it will remain
ever green and verdant throughout all seasons and bring forth
luscious fruits for the healing of the nations.
Attributed to 'Abdu'l-Bahá

· · · · · · · · · ·

One more point about marriage and reaching out: couplehood is strengthened by connecting with other couples, especially couples who are committed and working consciously to develop their relationship. Couplehood not only needs community, it gains strength through a bond with other couples. The institution of marriage is tottering in this time partly because so many of us have, in a sense, walked out on it. Couplehood needs the voice of those who are engaged in doing the work of marriage and will gain benefits from this kind of intercourse. In our encounters with couples in different countries we have realized the lack of this supporting network. We are taking initiatives to create a world wide network of 'committed couples' and hope that couples and communities will take steps to create local support groups everywhere.

• • • • • • • • • •

Spiritual growth is a journey out of the microcosm into an ever greater macrocosm.

Scott Peck

• • • • • • • • • •

Rejuvenating your relationship

To keep the marital relationship healthy and alive we have posited that it is imperative to resolve the issues and differences that will naturally come up. But to keep it vibrant and dynamic we also need to plan fun activities together that refresh us and fill our energy tanks. This means different things to every couple and individual. It is important though to find activities that are pleasant, exciting or refreshing to both. These could be anything from going on short trips together to taking dance lessons, biking, riding or hiking tours, doing sports together, taking art classes, etc. The point is to have some fun time in each other's company. Conscious marriage requires paying attention to these activities that give oxygen to the relationship and nurtures it as well.

Another aspect of a relationship that can contribute to its rejuvenation is the element of surprise and unpredictability. One of the features of romantic love is the ingredient of mystery. During the romantic phase of a relationship we love to surprise each other with little acts of kindness and care, gifts and even sacrifice. During this time, because we have not yet become fully engaged in – or one could say overwhelmed by –the responsibilities of a real married life with all its varied and demanding dimensions, it is easy to pay attention to this and that is partly why it seems to come more naturally. Later in marriage, in order to maintain feelings of joy and love, it is necessary to inject our relationship with these occasional surprise elements. Sending a loving card, a note, a message, a text on the phone to our partner during the day, or surprising them with small acts of kindness or gifts, arranging an activity of our partner's liking or preference, stretching in a direction which our partner likes but is uncharacteristic of us, go a long way to add zest to the marriage. These raise the level of energy in our partner and refresh the relationship.

Generally, sustaining romance, or bringing romance back into a marriage after the romantic phase is past, is part of the work of marriage. One basic way to do this is to remind ourselves of how we behaved when we were first in love with our partner and to revive those same behaviours. We can also re-romanticize our relationship by noticing new things about our partner or even asking them specifically what kind of behaviours really entice them.

These are all acts of love, and because they are done in a conscious manner and often require a stretch from us, mean a lot. This stretch may be into completely new forms of behaviour, or behaviours that we find difficult to make time for or which don't have a place in our routine. In time and with practice these too can become second nature and will be as natural as any other parts of our relationship.

Creating a shared vision

We have outlined the basic foundations to making a marriage rich, fulfilling and growth-promoting, but each couple is starting from a different place, has different propensities and different dreams about where they want to go and what they want to achieve. We could say that each partner has differing ideas about what they want to achieve through the union of matrimony. It is in fact important and helpful for a couple to take time, not only to discuss their dreams for the future in a general way, but to sit down and formulate a shared vision.

• • • • • • • • • •

Those who love deeply never grow old; they may die of old age, but they die young.

Arthur Pinero

• • • • • • • • • •

There are different ways of arriving at this but to provide you with a starting point, we have included a mindful approach in Appendix 3. A few words about this whole process are in order, no matter what approach you choose. We have already said that achieving mindfulness in marriage is an ongoing process which takes time and develops over time. The essence of mindfulness, however, is in the present moment. By being present and awake to our own inner capacities and hopes for the future, as well as those of our partner, we can move toward fulfilling a collective long-term dream which includes each individual's longing and felt calling in life. Having established a shared vision, we can advance towards our goal by breaking the vision down to yearly then monthly goals. If we are very organized we can move into developing weekly 'to do' lists, giving pride of place to the most crucial items. How a family can function is achieved with the steps we take in the **present**, guided by a future vision, which can change as we gain insight and skills in relating and become more tuned to each other and to new possibilities. This contrasts with getting upset with each other or ourselves because we are not there yet, or got temporarily distracted because other things grabbed our attention. This getting at each other or feeling bad about ourselves takes us into our reptilian brain and derails the essence of what we want to achieve, part of which is a peaceful, united and loving process. Frustration over perceived failures when reflecting on our progress or lack of it can always be addressed through using a mindful, empathic mode of consulting such as we have discussed in Chapter 5.

Having clarified all of this, let us share our vision of what a home that has mindful matrimony at its core would be. This may seem idyllic or utopian to some, and we acknowledge that it is definitely not something that is going to occur overnight or, for most couples, over a couple of years. Nevertheless, it is something which can be achieved, and having a picture in one's mind of what is achievable within a family can help infuse your own vision with hope and direction. It is our wish that we can all move, patiently but purposefully, in this direction. So here it is.

The sight and sound of the mindful home

· · · · · · · · · ·

Our wedding was many years ago.
The celebration continues to this day.
Attributed to Gene Perret

· · · · · · · · · ·

What do we envision and perceive in a home where the husband and wife are developing mindfulness? The *sounds* of such a home will be primarily positive sounds, sounds that elevate the soul. Yes, we will hear prayers, and recitation of sacred writings because such a family is awake to its spiritual essence. Sounds of chanting, singing, dancing may all be present in this home because there is life and the couple have learned to celebrate life. Beside this, we will hear encouraging words and an abundance of expressions of appreciation and gratitude for each other and the good that fills their home and their life. We will also hear uplifting conversation, earnest sharing of feelings, different opinions respectfully received, requests kindly worded, discussions on plans and dreams, and sharing of stories. Tone and volume of voice in conversation, especially around sensitive issues, is monitored when feelings tend to intensify. Apologies for shortcomings and lapses are sincerely made and generously received and accepted.

A distinctive sound is that of the laughter that fills the space as well as the heart of the children and adults in this home. There will be the sound of friends, family and guests welcomed warmly, served food and drinks, celebrations, meaningful discussions and heart-to-heart talks around troubles in life. But also, in measured ways, there is the sound of silence, the necessary space for each member to meditate, reflect or relax.

• • • • • • • • • •

A day without laughter is a day wasted.
Nicolas Chamfort

• • • • • • • • • •

What we will *see* is an orderly home, one that looks good and welcoming even if very simple and small. It will have a look of comfort, not just for adults but for the children. It is a haven where the members of the family come to seek respite and rejuvenation, a place where even strangers are made to feel at home.

The children are included in socializing and are sociable and pleasing to the adults. This is not because they have been sternly disciplined, but lovingly guided, within the nurturing matrix of this happy home, to develop virtues such as politeness, obedience, kindness and consideration. Feeling securely attached to their parents and confident in their parents' love for each other, these children blossom more naturally than most, can self-regulate and self-soothe more effectively, and can add to the overall rarified atmosphere of the home. These children are the fruits of the loving union of their mother and father and will carry the influence of this home far beyond its borders and well into the future through succeeding generations.

· · · · · · · · · ·

My home is the home of peace. My home is the home of joy and delight. My home is the home of laughter and exultation. Whosoever enters through the portals of this home, must go out with gladsome heart.

'Abdu'l-Bahá

· · · · · · · · · ·

Layli and Majnun

Let us leave you with a beautiful tale of the mythical lovers Layli and Majnun, as told by Bahá'u'lláh. This tells it all.

There was once a lover who had sighed for long years in separation from his beloved, and wasted in the fire of remoteness. From the rule of love, his heart was empty of patience, and his body weary of his spirit; he reckoned life without her as a mockery, and time consumed him away. How many a day he found no rest in longing for her; how many a night the pain of her kept him from sleep; his body was worn to a sigh, his heart's wound had turned him to a cry of sorrow. He had given a thousand lives for one taste of the cup of her presence, but it availed him not. The doctors knew no cure for him, and companions avoided his company; yea, physicians have no medicine for one sick of love, unless the favour of the beloved one deliver him.

At last, the tree of his longing yielded the fruit of despair,

270

and the fire of his hope fell to ashes. Then one night he could live no more, and he went out of his house and made for the market-place. On a sudden, a watchman followed after him. He broke into a run, with the watchman following; then other watchmen came together, and barred every passage to the weary one. And the wretched one cried from his heart, and ran here and there, and moaned to himself: 'Surely this watchman is 'Izrá'íl, my angel of death, following so fast upon me; or he is a tyrant of men, seeking to harm me.' His feet carried him on, the one bleeding with the arrow of love, and his heart lamented. Then he came to a garden wall, and with untold pain he scaled it, for it proved very high; and forgetting his life, he threw himself down to the garden.

And there he beheld his beloved with a lamp in her hand, searching for a ring she had lost. When the heart-surrendered lover looked on his ravishing love, he drew a great breath and raised up his hands in prayer, crying: 'O God! Give Thou glory to the watchman, and riches and long life. For the watchman was Gabriel, guiding this poor one; or he was Isráfíl, bringing life to this wretched one!'

In this story about lovers we see many of the elements we have been speaking about: the rift in consciousness, the unsettled mind, the trouble which surfaces in the guise of the watchman, the eventual resolution and arrival at the goal. Here is Baha'u'lláh's own explanation:

Indeed, his words were true, for he had found many a secret justice in this seeming tyranny of the watchman, and seen how many a mercy lay hid behind the veil. Out of wrath, the guard had led him who was athirst in love's desert to the sea of his loved one, and lit up the dark night of absence with the light of reunion. He had driven one who was afar, into the garden of nearness, had guided an ailing soul to the heart's physician.

The most telling part of the story is the fact that the trouble, personified by the watchman, led to a spiritual goal, personified by the reunion with Layli. To us, the call here is to internalize the lesson learnt by Majnun and recognize that conflicted situations are there to lead us to greater understanding and greater love. This is embodied in the psychological perspective we have offered in this book: that is, **conflict in marriage is growth trying to happen**. Here is how Bahá'u'lláh puts it:

> Now if the lover could have looked ahead, he would have blessed the watchman at the start, and prayed on his behalf, and he would have seen that tyranny as justice; but since the end was veiled to him, he moaned and made his plaint in the beginning. Yet those who journey in the garden land of knowledge, because they see the end in the beginning, see peace in war and friendliness in anger.

The 'garden land of knowledge' could be **mindfulness** in a situation of conflict. This is the new reflex we are called to develop and this is what this book is all about: a transition to a new reflex where we develop mindfulness in the face of marital trouble. This **new reflex** can then become one of the hard-won lessons of unity which we can pass on – consciously and through the relational model we present and represent – to our children. We also take these new skills into the world: into our immediate communities; into our administrative life; into our workplaces; and into the international arena which is rife with unconscious processes being played out on a large scale. The world as a whole, and the institution of marriage which lies at its core, are in a period of massive transition. Let us, then, commit ourselves to doing this rewarding work of growth in the most crucial of human relationships, the one we have with our helpmeet.

APPENDIXES

APPENDIX 1

Developing the Skills of Sending and Receiving

The discipline of sending

· · · · · · · · · ·

They must then proceed with the utmost devotion, courtesy, dignity, care and moderation to express their views. They must in every matter search out the truth and not insist upon their own opinion, for stubbornness and persistence in one's views will lead ultimately to discord and wrangling and the truth will remain hidden.

'Abdu'l-Bahá

· · · · · · · · · ·

Points to be aware of and avoid as you endeavour to send include:

- in your words, body language, or tone of voice you are subtly or overtly: shaming, manipulating, bullying, blaming, dominating, controlling, criticizing, withholding, belittling your partner (to understand whether or not you are doing this, your partner is probably your best indicator);

- wandering off topic, repeating yourself unnecessarily, analysing, over-intellectualizing, teaching, speaking abstractly;

- saying too much in one go for the other to be able to grasp, or to mirror what you are saying;

- using all-or-nothing phrases like 'you always . . .', 'you never . . .'(your partner has only to think of one exception to what you say and, in his or her mind, will discount the whole phrase);

- tagging on other frustration issues or incidents and going into previous instances in which you were bothered and which you think are related.

The transformation from unconscious to conscious sending:

Unconscious sending	Mindful sending
feels hurt, wants to attack	feels hurt and is curious to explore this
inclined to label, criticize	takes ownership for own feelings
uses sarcasm or shames other	remembers the good in the other
wants to hurt, discredit other	remembers the underlying love

uses 'you language'	uses 'I language' to describe personal feelings
tone of voice becomes accusatory	voice tone carries the energy of primary feeling
desires to make other wrong	desires understanding
lashes out at lapses in partner's listening	gently encourages partner to stay with them

· · · · · · · · · ·

Each of us is responsible for one life only, and that is our own. Each of us is immeasurably far from being 'perfect as our Heavenly Father is perfect': and the task of perfecting our own life and character is one that requires all our attention, our will-power and energy . . . On no subject are the Bahá'í teachings more emphatic that on the necessity to abstain from fault-finding, while being ever eager to discover and root out our own faults and overcome our own failings.

Letter on behalf of Shoghi Effendi

· · · · · · · · · ·

The discipline of receiving

· · · · · · · · · ·

Likewise, when you meet those whose opinions differ from your own, do not turn away your face from them. All are seeking truth, and there are many roads leading thereto. Truth has many aspects, but it remains always and forever one.

'Abdu'l-Bahá

· · · · · · · · · ·

Points to be aware of and avoid as you endeavour to receive what your partner is saying include:

- in your words, body language (including smirks, grimaces, rotating your eyes, etc.), or tone of voice, you are not engaged with their experience but are accessing your own feelings in reaction to their words (to check whether or not you are doing this, your partner is probably the best person to ask);

- you interrupt your partner to 'correct' their version of events;

- you interrupt the sender with your own little comments;

- you have trouble mirroring, or paraphrasing, what your partner says, even when he or she is sending in reasonably small doses;

- you have trouble understanding your partner's hurt feelings;

- your attempts to mirror, validate, and empathize fail to evoke indications in your partner that he or she feels understood.

The transformation from unconscious to conscious receiving:

Unconscious receiving	Mindful receiving
retorts in own mind as sender speaks	engages with what the sender says
internal chatter, not really listening	mirrors in own mind
reactive, lets self get triggered	stays in sender's world
personalizes what is heard	able to stay open to the reality of the other
resists seeing right of sender to be 'other'	able to see and accept the otherness of the other
wants to show sender own pain	engaged with the woundedness of the other
body language is closed	body language is open and accepting
sees other as perpetrator, mean	sees the adult and child in other
is impatient, mind is made up	is patiently curious

APPENDIX 2

An Exercise in Mindful Dialogue

(drawn from a model of Imago dialogue)

This is an exercise to get you started with mindful dialogue and, for this purpose, we suggest doing it in writing first (Step 1). As you get good at this, you can skip the writing stage and move into direct face-to-face dialogue. Doing it in writing helps the sender get clear on what they want to say and how to say it. You can take your time, hone and review what you say in light of the principles of mindful dialogue. Once you are confident that what you have written is a clear, brief, and kindly put expression of your perceptions and inner workings, then you can move on to Step 2, which is delivering what you want to say to your partner face-to-face. It is possible to accomplish the whole process in writing if face-to-face contact is difficult in the beginning. There is an example of this exercise as Jonathon and May might have done it following the instructions below.

Step 1

Identify something that your spouse has done recently that has frustrated you. This doesn't have to be something big. It can be something that happens quite frequently or even something that you have brought up before but not in a mindful manner.

Guidelines for writing:

A.
When you ....
............................(*briefly and concretely describe the action taken or words used by your spouse that frustrated you*) I felt ....
.... (*Here you describe your feeling when your spouse did what you have just described. A feeling is usually one word, sometimes a short phrase. You may write more than one feeling.*)

B.
Feeling this, what I do (or did) was ....
....

(*Identify your reaction in this situation: for example, criticizing your spouse, raising your voice, retreating into yourself, making distance.*)

C.
Instead, what I really yearn for is ....
....

(*Describe concretely the kind of behaviour from your spouse that would really work for you in this situation.*)

Step 2

Tell your spouse: 'I have a frustration I would like to talk about. Is this a good time?' (If your spouse already knows how to respond he or she will say 'Yes', or give a time as soon as possible.)

When the dialogue is ready to begin, start by doing something to calm yourselves down, like taking a few deep breaths, praying, meditating a few minutes, imagining being in a safe, peaceful place. Then share an appreciation with your spouse that has nothing to do with the frustration you are going to bring up. An appreciation can start like this:

Something I appreciate about you is ....
....

Step 3

Sender: You can now proceed to tell your spouse what you have written.

Receiver: Summarize what you have heard and ask 'Am I getting you?'

Sender: If there are important things missing and in want of clarifying, the sender can do this gently.

Step 4

Receiver: Say something like 'I understand you more now,' or 'I can imagine how you felt.' And then, if you would like to share your experience of the situation, say: 'I would like to respond. Are you ready to hear me?'

The roles would then shift and the new receiver gives full attention to the other, following the same structure outlined above.

Step 5

Having now had the chance to visit each other's world and to fully understand each other's point of view, the initial receiver can now offer an amend.

Receiver: 'Something I can do differently to help address your yearning (*from Step 1C*) is ....'

The initial sender then expresses gratitude and offers this:

Sender: 'Something I can do to support you in developing this new behaviour is ....'

If the initial receiver also had a responding frustration that was mirrored by the other, his or her resulting yearning can be responded to using this same, Step 5, process.

Jonathon and May do the mindful dialogue exercise

This is an example of how Jonathon and May might have done this exercise after the rupture following the New Year's Eve party incident described in Chapter 4.

Jonathon: (*having done Step 1, as above, in writing*): I have a frustration to share about the New Year's Eve party. Are you ready to hear me?

May: Yes, I am ready to hear all you have to say about this.

Jonathon: First let me say that I really appreciated that you thought of me when you went shopping for yourself and bought me that shirt. I really like it.

May: So you really appreciated the surprise of the shirt I bought you. You are very welcome for the shirt and thank you for the appreciation. Something I appreciate about you is that you took the initiative to have a dialogue. I know talking about things is not easy for you.

Jonathon: Thank you for understanding this. (*pauses, then continues*) At the party, when you were talking, laughing with, touching and doing things that seemed like flirting to me with that guy, I felt ignored, excluded, humiliated and jealous. I was scared that you were going to leave me, that I was too shy for you and that you want somebody who is more fun than me in your life.

Feeling this, I clammed up and, as it continued, got panicky and insisted that we leave the party.

Instead, what I really yearn for is to be sure that you are with me, feel proud of me as your husband and won't leave me out on a limb when we are out together.

May: (*doing a summary mirror*) I get that, when you saw me chatting away with my friend at the party you felt upset, excluded and humiliated because it seemed like flirting to you. This made you afraid that I liked him more than you and that I might leave you. Am I getting you?

Jonathon: Yes. I felt jealous.

May: You also felt jealous. Instead, what you really want is for me to be proud of being with you and pay attention to you when we go out.

I can understand better now what was going on for you. (*After a pause*) Are you willing to hear what was going on for me?

Jonathon: Yes, I am ready.

May: I hadn't seen any of my friends for a long time and I was really looking forward to having a good time out. When my friend came up and was so friendly and glad to see me I felt really happy and started to feel free again, like before being married. When you slumped back in the chair and became distant I felt upset and abandoned. Feeling this, I decided to just go ahead and have fun on my own anyway. When you insisted on leaving I was really angry.

What I really yearn for, instead, is for you to be more present with others when you are with me, to include yourself and learn to have some fun.

Jonathon (*mirroring May*): You were missing being out with friends and felt glad and free seeing your old friend. When you saw me retreat into myself, you felt abandoned and upset and reacted by trying to have fun on your own anyway. You got really angry that I made us leave the party. And what you really yearn for is for me to be more involved and present with others when we go out. You also want me to learn to have fun. Am I getting you?

May: Yes. And I guess I was behaving a bit out of spite.

Jonathon: I can imagine how much you wanted to have a good time with your friends.

May: Well, I really miss socializing, yes, but I also feel relieved to be talking about this now and feeling understood. One thing I intend to do next time we go out is to stay by your side and include you more in all conversations. I will also make it clear to others in my body language and gestures that you are the most important one to me.

Jonathon: Thank you. That would help me become more involved and present. One thing I intend to do is arrange more outings – at least once a month – and to create more opportunities for us to be with your friends.

May: That sounds wonderful. Thank you. I love being with you.

Jonathon: I love you so much.

Jonathon and May, both feeling very relieved, thankful and a lot closer to each other, fall into a long, loving embrace.

APPENDIX 3

Developing a Couple's Vision

(modelled after the approach used by Harville Hendrix in
Getting the Love You Want)

• • • • • • • • • •

Rivers know this: there is no hurry.
We shall get there some day.

A. A. Milne

• • • • • • • • • •

Here is a process, referred to in Chapter 10, that can be used by a husband and wife to develop a 'Shared Vision' or dream for their marriage. As with other practices recommended in this book, the most essential thing is the process, more than the end product. For this exercise, it is important to find a good block of clear, undisturbed time, and prepare yourselves spiritually so that you can mindfully move forward and not get entangled in differences or frustrations that you may have over what the other puts forward.

Step 1

Individually write down a list of the things that are already working really well in your marriage and your life together and that you value. Every statement in this and other segments of this exercise starts with 'We' and continues with a wording describing how you are as a couple, in the present, written in a positive way. For example, you would write, 'We share most of our meals together as a family,' rather than 'We don't allow the children to watch TV in the living room while we eat.' Strive to think of all aspects of life that involve marriage and family: emotional, spiritual, physical, financial, children, education, careers, place of residence, travel, recreation, extended family, friends, service to the community, giving to charities, etc.

Step 2

Individually write down the things that used to work well in your relationship, for example, when you were in the early romantic stage, but which you no longer do. Even though these are discontinued behaviours from the past, write them as though you were engaging in them in the present. For example, 'We show excitement about seeing each other again after periods of being apart,' rather than 'We used to show excitement about seeing each other after being apart.' Again, think of different aspects of your lives during that earlier period.

Step 3

Individually write down your yearnings, the things you really want but have not achieved, or even started to work on, in your marriage. Allow yourselves to dream here, rather than blocking out certain fantasies or images because they seem too far-fetched or out of reach. Let a kind of stream of consciousness take you along, write down everything you could possibly want from this relationship without censoring, including every aspect of your lives. This includes your physical contact, work life, recreation, material yearnings, home, different places you want to experience or even live in, children's development and education, spiritual goals, community participation, how you resolve conflicts, relations with extended family, health and fitness, and so on. As before, continue to write only positive statements starting with 'We' in the present tense.

Step 4

Individually consolidate your lists. It can help to identify which of the things are most important to you. For example, you might agree to number all items of high importance with a '1', medium importance with a '2', not so important with a '3'.

Step 5

Finally, start to share your list, item by item, with your partner. If, for example, the husband starts, he will read out the first most important item on his list. If the wife has something similar on her list, she reads it out and they then discuss a wording that works best for the two of them. This then becomes the first item on their Shared Vision, which is written down on a separate sheet. If the wife has no such item on her list but agrees that it is an important goal, it still gets written on the Shared Vision list. If, after taking time to understand why this item is important to her husband, the wife does not agree with including it in their shared vision, it is left aside for the moment, without argument.

The wife can then share the first important item on her list. The process will continue in this way until all the items are covered and a comprehensive Shared Vision is achieved. The items that were not agreed to, but which remain important to the partner who proposed them, can be kept on the individual list and reexamined at a later date, perhaps after a month or two when the Shared Vision is reviewed.

Step 6

It is recommended that the Shared Vision be copied in an aesthetically pleasing, or at least neat and legible, way so that each partner has one. It can also be posted in an often viewed place. In subsequent weeks, items on the Shared Vision can be taken one at a time, broken down into behavioural components, and systematically worked on day by day with appreciations for new behaviours reflecting the Vision being shared at the next weekly meeting and a new weekly plan laid out. Not all couples will manage this kind of systematic treatment of the Shared Vision well, but the formulating of a Vision and rereading it at times and returning to it as a couple at intervals is often enough to move a couple's relationship towards it.

Here is an example of a portion of one couple's Shared Vision:

1. We pray together every evening and attend a devotional meeting every week.
2. We show appreciation for each other every day.
3. We resolve conflicts peacefully and have a weekly time for dialogues.
4. We alternate visits with our parents every month.
5. We are debt free except for the house mortgage.
6. We share our bank accounts and make all major spending decisions together.
7. We are open to change.
8. We do some form of exercise or sport together every other day.
9. We get a babysitter and go out on a date at least every two weeks.
10. We feel connected physically and spiritually.

Bibliography

'Abdu'l-Bahá. *Paris Talks: Addresses given by 'Abdu'l-Bahá in Paris 1911–1912*. London: Bahá'í Publishing Trust, 12th ed. 1995.

—.*The Promulgation of Universal Peace: Talks Delivered by 'Abdu'l-Bahá during His Visit to the United States and Canada in 1912*. Comp. Howard MacNutt. Wilmette, IL: Bahá'í Publishing Trust, 2nd ed. 1982.

—.*Selections from the Writings of 'Abdu'l-Bahá*. Comp. Research Department of the Universal House of Justice. Translated by a Committee at the Bahá'í World Centre and by Marzieh Gail. Haifa: Bahá'í World Centre, 1978.

—.*Some Answered Questions*. Collected and translated by Laura Clifford Barney. Wilmette, IL: Bahá'í Publishing Trust, 4th ed. 1981.

Adams, Douglas. *The Hitchhiker's Guide to the Galaxy*. London: Pocket Books, 1979.

Adler, Alfred. *The Individual Psychology of Alfred Adler*. New York: HarperCollins, 1984.

Amen, Daniel G. *The Brain in Love: 12 Lessons to Enhance Your Love Life*. New York: Crown Publishing Group, 2009.

Anderson, Robert Woodruff. *Solitaire & Double Solitaire.* New York: Random House, 1972.

Armstrong, Alison. *Making Sense of Men: A Woman's Guide to a Lifetime of Love, Care and Attention from All Men.* Apache Junction, AZ: Alliance Book Co., 2008.

Aron, Arthur et al. 'The experimental generation of interpersonal closeness: A procedure and some preliminary findings', in *Personality & Social Psychology Bulletin*, 1 April 1997.

Bahá'í Prayers: A Selection of Prayers Revealed by Bahá'u'lláh, the Báb and 'Abdu'l-Bahá. Wilmette, IL: Bahá'í Publishing Trust, 2002.

Bahá'í Marriage and Family Life: Selections from the Writings of the Bahá'í Faith. National Spiritual Assembly of the Bahá'ís of Canada. Wilmette, IL: Bahá'í Publishing Trust, 1983.

Bahá'í Readings: Selections from the Writings of The Báb, Bahá'u'lláh and 'Abdu'l-Bahá for Daily Meditation. National Spiritual Assembly of the Bahá'ís of Canada. Thornhill, Ontario: Bahá'í Canada, 2nd ed. 1985.

Bahá'u'lláh. *Epistle to the Son of the Wolf.* Translated by Shoghi Effendi. Wilmette, IL: Bahá'í Publishing Trust, rev. ed. 1976.

Gleanings from the Writings of Bahá'u'lláh. Translated by Shoghi Effendi. Wilmette, IL: Bahá'í Publishing Trust, 2nd ed. 1976.

—. *The Hidden Words of Bahá'u'lláh.* Translated by Shoghi Effendi. Wilmette, IL: Bahá'í Publishing Trust, 1985.

—. *The Kitáb-i-Aqdas: The Most Holy Book.* Haifa: Bahá'í World Centre, 1992.

—. *Kitáb-i-Iqán: The Book of Certitude.* Translated by Shoghi Effendi. Wilmette, IL: Bahá'í Publishing Trust, 2nd ed. 1983.

—. *The Seven Valleys and the Four Valleys.* Translated by M. Gail and Ali-Kuli Khan. Wilmette, IL: Bahá'í Publishing Trust, 3rd ed. 1986.

—. *Tablets of Bahá'u'lláh Revealed after the Kitáb-i-Aqdas.* Comp. Research Department. Translated by Habib Taherzadeh et al. Wilmette, IL: Bahá'í Publishing Trust, 2nd ed. 1978.

Balyuzi, H. M. *'Abdu'l-Bahá.* Oxford: George Ronald, 1971.

Berger, Peter. *The Social Construction of Reality: A Treatise in the Sociology of Knowledge.* London: Penguin, 1967.

Bible, The New Oxford Annotated. Revised Standard Version. Oxford: Oxford University Press, 1977.

Breakstone, Steve et al. *How to Stop Bullying and Social Aggression: Elementary Grade Lessons and Activities that Teach Empathy, Friendship and Respect.* Thousand Oaks, CA: Corwin Press, 2009.

Burney, Robert. *Codependence: The Dance of Wounded Souls.* Cambria, CA: Joy to You & Me Enterprises, 2011.

Carder, Dave. *Torn Asunder: Recovering from an Extra-marital Affair.* Chicago, IL: Moody Publishers, 1995.

Code, David. *Kids Pick Up On Everything: How Parental Stress Is Toxic To Kids.* CreateSpace (Amazon), 2011.

The Compilation of Compilations, Volumes I and II. Prepared by the Universal House of Justice 1963–1990. Maryborough, Victoria.: Bahá'í Publications Australia, 1991.

Coombs, Robert H. 'Marital status and personal well-being; A literature review', in *Family relations*, vol. 40 (1991), no. 1, pp. 97–102.

Doherty, William J. *Reviving Marriage in America: Strategies for Donors.* Washington, DC: Philanthropy Roundtable, 2006.

Eliot. T. S. *The Cocktail Party*, in T. S. Eliot, *The Complete Poems and Plays.* Orlando, FL: Harcourt, Brace and Co., 1980.

Esslemont, J. *Bahá'u'lláh and the New Era*. Wilmette, IL: Bahá'í Publishing Trust, 5th ed.1987.

Esty, Frances (comp.). *The Garden of the Heart*. New York, Roycrofters, 1930.

Family Life. Comp. Research Department of the Universal House of Justice. Haifa: Bahá'í World Centre, 2008.

Fisher, Helen. *Why We Love: The Nature and Chemistry of Romantic Love*. New York: Henry Holt and Co., 2004.

Friedan, Betty. *The Feminine Mystique*. New York: Norton, 1974.

Glass, Shirley. *Not 'Just Friends': Rebuilding Trust and Recovering Your Sanity after Infidelity*. New York: Free Press, 2003.

Gordon, Thomas. *Parent Effectiveness Training: The Proven Programme for Raising Responsible Children* (1970). New York: Crown Publishing Group, 2000.

Gottman, John M.; Silver, Nan. *The Seven Principles for Making Marriage Work*. New York: Three Rivers, 1999.

Gray, John. *Mars on Fire, Venus on Ice: Hormonal Balance – the Key to Life, Love and Energy*. Austin, TX: Greenleaf, 2010.

Harley, Willard B. *His Needs, Her Needs: Building an Affair-proof Marriage*. Grand Rapids, MI: Revel, 2001.

Hendrix, Harville. *Getting the Love You Want: A Guide for Couples*. New York: Harper and Row, 1988.

Hornby, Helen (ed.) *Lights of Guidance: A Bahá'í Reference File*. New Delhi: Bahá'í Publishing Trust, 1994.

Ives, Howard Colby. *Portals to Freedom*. Oxford: George Ronald, 1943, 1976.

Lasch, Christopher. *The Culture of Narcissism*. London: Abacus, 1980.

Lawrence, D. H. *Letters of D. H. Lawrence*. Cambridge: Cambridge University Press, 1989.

Lee, Sidney (ed.). *The Autobiography of Edward, Lord Herbert of Cherbury*. London: Routledge, rev. ed. 1906.

Love, Patricia; Robinson, Jo. *Hot Monogamy: Essential Steps to More Passionate, Intimate Lovemaking*. New York: Penguin, 1995.

Mclaughlin, Mignon. *The Complete Neurotic's Notebook*. Indianapolis, ID: Castle Books, 1981.

Mead, Margaret. *Male and Female: A Study of the Sexes in a Changing World*. New York: William Morrow & Co., 1949.

Michael, Robert T.; Gagnon, John H.; Laumann, Edward O.; Kolata, Gina. *Sex in America: A Definitive Survey*. New York: Warner, 1995.

Milne, A. A. *Winnie-the-Pooh*. London: Methuen, 1926.

Neustatter, Angela. 'Why marriage is worth the effort', in *The Telegraph*, 17 December 2012.

Nietzsche, Friedrich. *Thus Spoke Zarathustra*. Trans. G. Parkes. Oxford: Oxford World's Classics, 2005.

Peck, M. Scott. *The Different Drum:Community-making and Peace*. New York: Simon and Schuster, 1988.

—. *The Road Less Traveled: A New Psychology of Love, Traditional Values and Spiritual Growth*. New York: Simon and Schuster, 1978.

Pittman, Frank. *Private Lies: Infidelity and the Betrayal of Intimacy*. New York: Norton, 1989.

Real, Terrence. *The New Rules of Marriage: What You Need to Know to Make Love Work*. New York: Ballantine Books, 2007.

Schnarch, David. *Passionate Marriage: Love, Sex and Intimacy in Emotionally Committed Relationships.* New York: Henry Holt and Co., 1997.

Shoghi Effendi. *The Advent of Divine Justice.* Wilmette, IL: Bahá'í Publishing Trust, rev. ed.1984.

—. *The World Order of Bahá'u'lláh: Selected Letters by Shoghi Effendi* (1938). Wilmette, IL: Bahá'í Publishing Trust, 2nd rev. ed. 1974.

Sternberg, Robert J. 'A triangular theory of love', in *Psychological Review*, vol. 93, no. 2 (April 1986), pp. 119–135.

Stoller, Gary. 'Infidelity is in the air for road warriors: Being away from home tempts some to cheet', in *USA Today*, 20 April 2007.

Tagore, Rabindranath. *Sādhanā: The Realisation of Life.* New York: Macmillan, 1916.

Thurber, James; White, E. B. *Is Sex Necessary?Or Why You Feel the Way You Do* (1929). New York: HarperCollins, 2004.

Twain, Mark. *The Diary of Adam and Eve* (1905). New York: Hesperus Press, 2002.

The Universal House of Justice. *Messages from the Universal House of Justice 1968–1973.* Wilmette, IL: Bahá'í Publishing Trust, 1976.

Updike, John. *Marry Me: A Romance.* New York: Knopf, 1976.

Waite, Linda et al. *Does Divorce Make People Happy?* National Survey of Families and Households (NSFH), University of Florida, 2002.

D.W. Winnicott. *Playing and Reality.* Harmondsworth: Penguin, 1971.

References

NOTE FROM THE PUBLISHER: The Internet is both a blessing and a curse for authors and editors: a blessing in that it provides an almost inexhaustible source of quotations; a curse in that practically none of them are referenced and so it is difficult to know whether the person who is supposed to be the source of the quotation actually said or wrote it at all. Every effort has been made to find reliable sources for the quotations in this book; the phrase 'attributed to' is intended as a warning that we have failed to do so. The quotations concerned are all on the Internet in myriad websites and often quoted differently. Eagle-eyed and knowledgeable readers may find entertainment in letting the publisher know of any authentic sources for the 'attributed' quotations here.

Page

12   'In every marriage more than a week old . . .': Robert Anderson, *Solitaire & Double Solitaire*, p. 39.

13   'In the opinion of the world . . .': attributed to Anne-Sophie Swetchine (1782–1857), Catholic mystical writer and '*femme de lettres*'.

15   'O Son of Man! . . .': Bahá'u'lláh, Hidden Words, Arabic no. 4.

16   'We're all citizens of the womb . . .': from 'Work Your Way Out', Ani Difranco (b. 1970), American singer–songwriter.

18   'A baby is God's opinion that the world should go on': Carl Sandburg, *Remembrance Rock* (1948), p. 7.

18   'O Son of Bounty! Out of the wastes of nothingness . . .': Bahá'u'lláh, Hidden Words, Persian no. 29.

19   'The precursor of the mirror is the mother's face': D.W. Winnicott, *Playing and Reality*, p. 138.

21   'The desolation and terror . . .': Francis Thompson (1859–1907), English poet, from a late notebook.

21   'Self has really two meanings . . .': Letter on behalf of Shoghi Effendi to an individual, 10 December 1947, in Hornby (ed.), *Lights of Guidance*, no.386, p. 113.

22   'Life is just a chance to grow a soul': Arthur Powell Davies (1902–1957), Unitarian minister.

24   'You don't really understand . . .': attributed to William T. Thammeus, columnist, *The Kansas City Star*.

25   'One of the most obvious results . . .': Georges Courteline (1858–1929), French dramatist and novelist, in *La Philosophie de Georges Courteline*.

25   'Most of us become parents . . .': Mignon McLaughlin (1913–1988), American journalist, in *The Complete Neurotic's Notebook*.

26   'Don't worry that children never listen to you . . .': Robert Fulghum (b. 1937), American author and Unitarian minister. See www. robertfulghum.com.

27   'The walls we build around us . . .': Jim Rohn (1930–2009), American entrepreneur and author.

28   'Your children vividly remember . . .': Mignon McLaughlin, *The Complete Neurotic's Notebook*.

29   'As any action or posture long continued . . .': Dr Samuel

Johnson (1709–1784), in *The Rambler*, no. 173 (12 November 1751).

30   'The life history of the individual . . .': Ruth Benedict (1887–1934), American anthropologist.

30   'Feelings are not supposed to be logical . . .': attributed to David Borenstein, American journalist and author on social entrepreneurship.

31   'Did you ever stop to think . . .': A. A. Milne (1882–1956), English author of *Winnie-the-Pooh*.

32   'Our own physical body possesses a wisdom . . .': attributed to Henry Miller (1891–1980), American writer and painter.

33   'When it comes to getting things done . . .': attributed to Colleen C. Barrett (b. 1944), American businesswoman, past President of Southwest Airlines.

33   'Kids: they dance before . . .': William Stafford (1914–1993), American poet and pacifist.

34   'Adolescence is a new birth . . .': G. Stanley Hall (1844–1924), American psychologist and educator, author of *Adolescence* (1904).

35   'Don't hold your parents up to contempt . . .': attributed to Evelyn Waugh (1903–1966), English writer.

37   'Relationships are all there is . . .': attributed to Margaret J. Wheatley, American writer and management consultant.

38   'When a girl marries . . .': attributed to Helen Rowland (1875–1950), American writer and humourist.

38   'My advice to you . . .': attributed to Socrates (c. BC 469–AD 399), Athenian philosopher.

39   'Everything that rises must converge': Pierre Teilhard de Chardin, 'The New Spirit', in *The Future of Man* (1942).

40 'People see you as an object . . .': Candice Bergen (b. 1946), American actor.

41 'God's wisdom hath decreed . . .': 'Abdu'l-Bahá, in *Family Life*, p. 4.

42 'Marriage is an alliance . . .': attributed to George Bernard Shaw (1856–1950), Irish playwright.

44 'On an unconscious level . . .': Harville Hendrix, *Getting the Love You Want*, p. 51.

50 'religion . . . the essential connection . . .': 'Abdu'l-Bahá, *Some Answered Questions*, no. 40, p. 158.

53 'any romance that does not end in marriage fails': John Updike, *Marry Me*, p. 85.

53 'It would be impossible . . .': attributed to Fran Lebowitz (b. 1951), American humourist.

56 'Marriage, n. . . .': Ambrose Bierce, *The Devil's Dictionary.*

58 'I grew up to have my father's looks . . .': attributed to Jules Feiffer (b. 1929), American cartoonist.

60 'How strange that we should . . .': Scott Peck, *A Different Drum*, p. 69.

60 'the evil spirit, Satan . . .': 'Abdu'l-Bahá, *The Promulgation of Universal Peace*, pp. 294–5.

67 'The world in the past . . .': 'Abdu'l-Bahá, quoted in Esslemont, *Bahá'u'lláh and the New Era*, p. 149.

68 'Almost no one is foolish enough . . .': Sydney J. Harris (1917–1986), American journalist.

68 'a new race of men . . .': Shoghi Effendi, *The Advent of Divine Justice*, p. 16.

68   'generation of the half-light': Shoghi Effendi, *The World Order of Bahá'u'lláh*, p. 168.

69   'After all these years . . .': Mark Twain (1835–1910), 'Adam's Diary', in *The Diary of Adam and Eve.*

69   'Marriage is our last, best chance to grow up': attributed to Joseph Barth (1746–1818), Maltese and Austrian opthalmologist.

70   'fortress for well-being and salvation': Bahá'u'lláh, in *Bahá'í Prayers*, p. 118.

72   'The current of the world has its boundaries . . .': Rabindranath Tagore (1861–1941), 'The Problem of Evil', in *Sādhanā: The Realisation of Life* (1916).

74   'I draw circles . . .': Friedrich Nietzsche (1844–1900), German philosopher, in *Thus Spoke Zarathustra.*

79   'It's a slippery slope, Carrie . . .': *Sex and the City*, American TV series (1998–2004), created by Darren Star from the original book by Candace Bushnell.

82   'Let there be no secrets . . .': attributed to 'Abdu'l-Bahá by Ahmad Sohrab, unauthenticated.

89   'One of my greatest lessons . . .': Bob Burg, business guru, 'One of the secrets for a great marriage', at www. smartmarriages.com.

97   'He hath let loose the two seas . . .': Qur'án 56:62, quoted in a prayer for marriage revealed by 'Abdu'l-Bahá, in *Bahá'í Prayers*, p. 119.

98   'For every one of you . . .': Bahá'u'lláh, *Gleanings*, no. CXXIII, para. 3, p. 261.

99   'the home is an institution that Bahá'u'lláh has come to strengthen and not to weaken': Letter on behalf of Shoghi Effendi to an individual, 14 May 1929, in *Family Life*, p. 16.

99   'every aspect of a person's life . . .': Letter from the Universal House of Justice to the European Bahá'í Youth Council, 7 December 1992.

100   'You can never be happily married to another until . . .': attributed to Jerry McCant.

101   'you must ever press forward . . .': 'Abdu'l-Bahá, *Paris Talks*, no. 29, p. 89.

101   See, for example, Gottmann and Silver, *The Seven Principles for Making Marriage Work*.

104   'above all else it is the prince of virtues': Bahá'u'lláh, Lawḥ-i-Dunyá, in *Tablets*, p. 88.

104   'the tongue is for mentioning what is good . . .': Bahá'u'lláh, Kitáb-i-'Ahd (Book of the Covenant), in *Tablets*, pp. 219–20.

106   'Say: No man can attain his true station . . .': Bahá'u'lláh, in *Compilation of Compilations*, vol. 1, no. 167.

107   'The Lord, peerless is He, hath made woman and man . . .': 'Abdu'l-Bahá, *Selections*, no. 92, p. 122.

109   'In all things it is necessary to consult . . .': Bahá'u'lláh, in *Compilation of Compilations*, vol. 1, no. 170.

110   'Consultation bestoweth greater awareness . . .': Bahá'u'lláh, in *Compilation of Compilations*, vol. 1, no. 168.

110   'The first condition is absolute love and harmony . . .': 'Abdu'l-Bahá, *Selections*, nos. 45, 44, p. 87.

111   'Family consultation employing full and frank discussion . . .': Letter from the Universal House of Justice to an individual, 1 August 1978, in *Compilation of Compilations*, vol. II, no. 2160.

113   'It is incumbent upon all the peoples of the world to reconcile their differences': Bahá'u'lláh, *Gleanings*, no. IV, para. 1, p. 6.

114 'Peace is not the absence of conflict . . . ': Dorothy Thompson (1893–1961), American journalist and broadcaster.

115 'Gather ye together . . .': Bahá'u'lláh, *Gleanings*, no. CXL, p. 217.

116 'My calamity is My providence . . .': Bahá'u'lláh, Hidden Words, Arabic no. 51.

118 'Say: all things are of God': Bahá'u'lláh, Kitáb-i-'Ahd, (Book of the Covenant), in *Tablets*, p. 222.

119 'and if a man has ten bad qualities . . .': attributed to 'Abdu'l-Bahá, in Esslemont, *Bahá'u'lláh and the New Era*, p. 83.

120 'Every one of the friends should highly praise the other . . .': 'Abdu'l-Bahá, in *Compilation of Compilations*, vol.I, no.181.

123 'If the fire of self overcome you . . .': Bahá'u'lláh, Hidden Words, Persian no. 66.

124 'in this glorious dispensation we should not belittle anyone . . .': 'Abdu'l-Bahá, *Selections*, no. 15, p. 30.

125 'Help him to see and recognize the truth . . .': Bahá'u'lláh, *Gleanings*, no. V, para. 3, p. 8.

126 'The first duty of love is to listen': Paul Tillich (1886–1965), German-American theologian and philosopher.

126 '. . . we must be willing to clear away . . .': 'Abdu'l-Bahá, *Paris Talks*, no. 41, p. 140.

126 'To the questioner He responded first with silence . . .': Howard Colby Ives, *Portals to Freedom*, pp. 194–5.

128 'The fact that we imagine ourselves to be right . . .': 'Abdu'l-Bahá, *Paris Talks*, no. 41, p. 140.

128 'Do not allow difference of opinion . . .': 'Abdu'l-Bahá, ibid. no. 15, p. 46.

130 'Nothing is too much trouble when one loves . . .': 'Abdu'l-Bahá, quoted by Howard Colby Ives, *Portals to Freedom*, p. 52.

131 'No man shall attain the shores . . .': Bahá'u'lláh *Kitáb-i-Íqán*, para. 1, p. 3.

132 'And if he meeteth with injustice . . .': Bahá'u'lláh, *Seven Valleys*, p. 13.

133 'In order to find truth, we must give up our prejudices . . .': 'Abdu'l-Bahá, *Paris Talks*, no. 41, pp. 139–40.

134 Thomas Gordon, from *Parent Effectiveness Training*.

136 'There is no place for you to flee to in this day': Bahá'u'lláh, *Epistle to the Son of the Wolf*, p. 52.

137 'the union must be a true relationship . . .': 'Abdu'l-Bahá, *Selections*, no. 84, p. 117.

139 'Marriage, like a submarine . . .': Frank Pittman (1935–2012), American psychiatrist.

140 'Murder is born of love . . .': attributed to Octave Mirbeau (1848–1917), French novelist.

141 'Getting divorced just because . . .': attributed to Zsa Zsa Gabor (b. 1917), Hungarian-born American actor.

141 'Each divorce is the death of a small civilization': attributed to Pat Conroy (b. 1945), American writer.

142 'The place of the father in the modern suburban family . . .': attributed to Bertrand Russell (1872–1970), English philosopher and logician.

144 'The people we loved the most . . .': Robert Burney, *Codependence: The Dance of Wounded Souls*.

145 'No matter how free divorce . . .': Margaret Mead (1901–1978), in *Male and Female*, p. 188.

145 'It is necessary but insufficient . . .': Frank Pittman (1935–2012), American psychiatrist.

146 'Passion is the quickest to develop . . .': Robert Sternberg, in 'A triangular theory of love'.

147 'At the gate of the garden . . .': attributed to 'Abdu'l-Bahá, Inez Cook's pilgrim notes, in Esty, *The Garden of the Heart*, dedication.

148 'Do men think when they say "We believe" . . .': Qur'án 16: 124.

148 'If men or women contemplate an escape . . .': Alfred Adler (1870–1937) Austrian psychologist, founder of the school of individual psychology.

148 'Lay the foundation of your affection . . .': attributed to 'Abdu'l-Bahá by Ahmad Sohrab, unauthenticated.

151 'marriage must be a union of the body and of the spirit . . .': 'Abdu'l-Bahá, *Selections*, no. 84, p. 117.

152 'How many a man hath secluded himself . . .': Baha'u'lláh, Kitáb-i-Aqdas, para. 36, p. 31.

153 'The sexual embrace . . .': attributed to Marcus Aurelius (AD 121–180), Roman Emperor.

154 'His sexual attitudes are permissive . . .': Christopher Lasch, *The Culture of Narcissism*, p. xvi.

155 'For all our "sexual liberation" . . .: David Schnarch, *Passionate Marriage*, p. 99.

158 'Your feelings have a bigger impact . . .': David Schnarch, ibid. p. 83.

159 'It takes a long time . . .': David Schnarch, ibid. p. 37.

160 'Love is a choice you make from moment to moment': attributed to Barbara De Angelis (b. 1949), American author.

162 'While the urge to eat . . .': James Thurber and E.B. White, *Is Sex Necessary?*

162 'Women need a reason to have sex. Men just need a place': attributed to Billy Crystal (b. 1948), American actor, writer and film director.

164 'You know that look women get . . .': attributed to Steve Martin.(b. 1945), American actor.

164 'Among men, sex sometimes results in intimacy . . .': attributed to Barbara Cartland (1901–2000), English romantic novelist.

166 'I'm too shy to express my sexual needs . . .': attributed to Garry Shandling (b. 1949), American comedian.

167 'The proper use of the sex instinct . . .': Letter on behalf of Shoghi Effendi to an individual, 5 September 1938, in Hornby (ed.), *Lights of Guidance*, no.1156, p. 344.

168 'The art of love . . . ': Albert Ellis (1913–2007), American psychologist.

168 'intimacy is nature's latest "experiment" . . .': David Schnarch, *Passionate Marriage*, p. 38.

170 'there is an amnesic effect . . .': Daniel G. Amen, *The Brain in Love*, pp. 65–6.

172 'A fellow ought to save a few of the long evenings . . .': Kin (Frank McKinney) Hubbard (1868–1930), American cartoonist and humourist.

175 'The world in the past has been ruled by force . . .': 'Abdu'l-Bahá, quoted in. Esslemont, *Bahá'u'lláh and the New Era*, p. 149.

176 'At present in spheres of human activity . . .': 'Abdu'l-Bahá, *The Promulgation of Universal Peace*, pp. 136–7.

177 'I refuse to believe that trading recipes is silly . . .': Barbara Grizzuti Harrison (1934–2002), American essayist.

179 'The source of all life and knowledge . . .': D. H. Lawrence, letter to Arthur McLeod, 2 June 1914, in *Letters of D. H. Lawrence*, p. 181.

181 'He is half of a blessed man . . .': William Shakespeare, *King John*, Act II, scene ii.

182 'And each man stands . . . .': Elizabeth Barrett Browning (1806–1861), *Napoleon III in Italy*, verse 8.

183 'Behind every successful man is a surprised woman': Maryon Pearson (1901–1989), Canadian wit, wife of Lester Pearson, Canada's 14th Prime Minister.

183 'We must ever praise each other': 'Abdu'l-Bahá, *The Promulgation of Universal Peace*, p. 410.

183 'One must talk . . .': attributed to Marguerite Duras (1914–1996), French writer.

184 'Given the cultural barriers . . .': Barbara Ehrenreich (b. 1941), American writer and political activist.

184 'It is not what we learn in conversation . . .': Agnes Repplier (1855–1950), American essayist.

185 'Don't have sex man . . .': Steve Martin, American actor.

186 'The difficulty with this conversation . . .': Douglas Adams (1952–2001), English writer, author of *The Hitchhiker's Guide to the Galaxy*.

186 'One has to grow up with good talk . . .': attributed to Helen Hayes (1900–1993), American actor.

188 'Women have served all these centuries . . .': Virginia Woolf (1882–1941), *A Room of One's Own*.

189 'The world has never yet seen a truly great and virtuous nation . . .': Elizabeth Cady Stanton (1815–1902), keynote address at Seneca Falls, 1848.

189 'Men will often admit other women are oppressed . . .': Sheila Rowbotham (b. 1943), English writer and activist.

193 'My wife has a slight impediment in her speech . . .': attributed to Jimmy Durante (1895–1980), American comedian and singer.

194 'Some of us are becoming the men we wanted to marry': Gloria Steinem (b. 1934), 'Leaps of Consciousness', speech at 3rd Annual Conference on Women and power, Omega Institute, 2004.

196 'No woman is required to build the world by destroying herself': attributed to Rabbi Sofer (Moses Schreiber) (1794–1839), German/Hungarian Jewish leader, author of *Chasam Sofer*.

196 'Instead of getting hard ourselves and trying to compete . . .': attributed to Joan Baez (b. 1941), American singer–songwriter.

197 'Respect a man, he will do the more': attributed to James Howell (?) (1594–1666), Welsh writer.

198 'Men weren't really the enemy . . .': Betty Friedan (1921–2006), *The Feminine Mystique*.

198 'The world of humanity has two wings . . .': Attributed to 'Abdu'l-Bahá, quoted in Balyuzi, *'Abdu'l-Bahá*, p. 476.

199 'Love is the will to extend oneself . . .': Scott Peck (1936–2005), *The Road Less Traveled*.

201 'The troubles of this world pass . . .': Letter on behalf of Shoghi Effendi to an individual, 5 August 1949, in Hornby (ed.), *Lights of Guidance*, no. 1014, p. 297.

202 'Because the superior man . . .': attributed to Lao Tzu. Chinese philosopher, 6th century BC.

203 'The success tactic of babyhood . . .': Harville Hendrix, *Getting the Love You Want*, p. 79.

204 'I first learnt the concepts of non-violence . . .': attributed to Mahatma (Mohandhas K.) Gandhi (1869–1948), leader of Indian nationalism.

205 'I found one day in school a boy . . .': attributed to Bertrand Russell, cited in Breakstone et al., *How to Stop Bullying*.

205 'Jealousy consumeth the body . . .': Bahá'u'lláh, Tablet to a Physician, quoted in Esslemont, *Bahá'u'lláh and the New Era*, p. 108.

208 'You ask how to deal with anger . . .': Letter on behalf of the Universal House of Justice to an individual, 17 July 1979, *Compilation of Compilations*, vol. II, no. 2339, p. 455.

209 'They must then proceed . . .': 'Abdu'l-Bahá, *Selections*, no. 45, p. 88.

210 'Guilt is anger directed at ourselves . . .': Peter McWilliams (1949–2000), American author.

211 'He that cannot forgive others . . .': in Lee (ed.), *The Autobiography of Edward, Lord Herbert of Cherbury*, p. 34.

211 'To forgive is to set a prisoner free . . .': Lewis B. Smedes (1921–2002), *Forgive and Forget*.

212 'Anger makes you smaller . . .': attributed to Cherie Carter-Scott (b. 1949), American author and life coach.

212 'Maybe our trouble is . . .': John Updike, *Marry Me*, p. 50.

214 'I'm tempted to go to all the buildings . . .': Shirley Glass, *Not 'Just Friends'*.

216 'Infidelity flows from a belief . . .': Frank Pittman (1935–2012), American psychiatrist.

216 '. . . when you're cheating on her . . .': Phil McGraw (b. 1950), American TV personality ('Dr Phil') and psychologist.

217 'Men's affairs in particular . . .': Shirley Glass, *Not 'Just Friends'*.

218 'For men, the strongest predictor . . .': Shirley Glass, ibid.

218 'Adult children of parental affairs are at particular risk . . .': Dave Carder, *Torn Asunder.*

219 'Those who flee temptation . . .: Lane Olinghouse, American writer.

220 'Secrecy is the protection . . .': Dave Carder, quoted in Stoller, 'Infidelity is in the air for road warriors – Being away from home tempts some to cheat', *USA Today*, 20 April 2007.

224 'If addiction is judged by . . .': attributed to Rob Stampfli (1914–2002), Swiss scientist.

225 'She goes from one addiction to another . . .': attributed to Ellen Burstyn (b. 1932), American actor.

227 'Whether you married the right or wrong person . . .': Hilary Hinton ('Zig') Ziglar (1926–2012), American author and motivational speaker.

229 'Hell is oneself; Hell is alone . . .': T.S. Eliot, The Cocktail Party, Act I, scene iii.

229 'O Son of Being! How couldst thou forget . . .': Bahá'u'lláh, Hidden Words, Arabic no. 26.

232 'Delight not yourselves in the things of the world . . .': Bahá'u'lláh, *Gleanings*, LXVI, para. 6, p. 127.

233 'I have enough money to last me the rest of my life . . .': attributed to Jackie Mason (b. 1931), American comedian and actor.

233 'I'm living so far beyond my income . . .': attributed to e.e. cummings (1895–1962), American poet.

234 'Together make mention of noble aspirations and heavenly concepts': Words attributed to 'Abdu'l-Bahá by Ahmad Sohrab, unauthenticated.

234 'Should a man wish to adorn himself . . .': Bahá'u'lláh, *Gleanings*, CXXVIII, para. 4, p. 276.

235 'Whatsoever deterreth you . . .': ibid.

235 'My problem lies in reconciling . . .': attributed to Errol Flynn (1909–1952), Australian-American actor.

237 'The most important thing a father can do for his children . . .': attributed to Rev. Theodore Martin Hesburgh (b. 1917), President Emeritus of University of Notre Dame.

237 'Truly, the Lord loveth union and harmony . . .': Bahá'u'lláh, Kitáb-i-Aqdas, para. 70, p. 44.

238 'When there are kids involved . . .': attributed to Carl Whitaker (1912–1995), American psychiatrist and family therapist.

241 'Nearly every major social problem . . .': William J. Doherty, *Reviving Marriage in America*.

242 'Instead of getting married again . . .': attributed to Groucho Marx (1890–1977), American comedian and film star.

244 'Happy marriages begin . . .': attributed to Thomas Mullen (b. 1974), American novelist.

245 'What counts in making a happy marriage . . .': attributed to Leo Tolstoy (1828–1910), Russian writer, in Neustatter, 'Why marriage is worth the effort'.

246 'Love never dies a natural death . . .': attributed to Anaïs Nin (1903–1977), French-Cuban writer.

247 'A successful marriage requires falling in love many times . . .': Mignon McLaughlin, *The Complete Neurotic's Notebook*.

248 'To get divorced because love has died . . .': Diane Sollee, founder and director of SmartMarriages; see www.smartmarriages.com.

253   'Neither you nor your husband should hesitate . . .': Letter on behalf of the Universal House of Justice to an individual, 17 July 1979, *The Compilation of Compilations*, vol II, no. 2339, p. 454.

254   'Soon will the present-day order be rolled up . . .': Bahá'u'lláh, *Gleanings*, IV, para. 2, p. 7.

254   'It is not marriage that fails . . .': attributed to Harry Emerson Fosdick (1878–1969), American liberal preacher.

255   'This span of earth is but one homeland . . .': Bahá'u'lláh, Kalimát-i-Firdawsyyih (Words of Paradise), in *Tablets*, p. 67.

256   'Now the new age is here . . .': 'Abdu'l-Bahá, *Selections*, no. 205. pp. 252–3.

257   'Lay the foundation of your affection . . .': attributed to 'Abdu'l-Bahá by Ahmad Sohrab, unauthenticated.

258   'A great marriage . . .': Dave Meurer, American humourist.

259   'That is what marriage really means . . .': attributed to Paul Tournier (1896–1986), Swiss physician.

260   'I used to believe that marriage would diminish me . . .': attributed to Candice Bergen (b. 1946), American actor.

261   'What else is love . . .': attributed to Friedrich Nietzsche (1844–1900), German philosopher.

261   'Real love is a permanently self-enlarging experience': Scott Peck, *The Road Less Traveled*.

264   'begin to turn their energy away from each other . . .': Harville Hendrix, *Getting the Love You Want*, p. 257.

264   'No mortal can conceive the union and harmony . . .': attributed to 'Abdu'l-Bahá by Ahmad Sohrab, unauthenticated.

265   'Spiritual growth is a journey . . .': Scott Peck, *The Road Less Traveled*.

267   'Those who love deeply never grow old . . .': Arthur Pinero (1855–1934), English actor and dramatist.

268   'Our wedding was many years ago . . .': attributed to Gene Perret, American comedy writer.

269   'A day without laughter is a day wasted': Nicolas Chamfort (1741–1794), French writer and wit.

270   'My home is the home of peace . . .': 'Abdu'l-Bahá, *Compilation of Compilations*, vol. I, no. 859, p. 397.

270   'There was once a lover . . .': Bahá'u'lláh, *Seven Valleys*, p. 13.

273   'They must then proceed . . .': 'Abdu'l-Bahá, *Selections*, no. 45, p. 88.

275   'Each of us is responsible for one life only . . .': Letter on behalf of Shoghi Effendi to an individual, 12 May 1925, in Hornby (ed.), *Lights of Guidance*, no. 312, p. 92.

275   'Likewise, when you meet . . .': 'Abdu'l-Bahá, *Paris Talks*, no.15, pp. 45–6.

285   'Rivers know this . . .': A. A. Milne, *Winnie-the-Pooh*.